D0721923

Praise for *The Secret to GE's Success*

"Once again, Bill Rothschild's incisive analysis captures the 'pearls' of decisions and wisdom that underpin General Electric, one of the century's enduring success stories. As the book so clearly points out, the leadership in talent, technology, and financial structuring has adapted to changing global markets and environments. I am a GE alumna, and I still adhere to the tenets so well documented in the book."

Mylle Mangum
Chairman and CEO
IBT Enterprises

"In his fifth book, Bill Rothschild has synthesized the key elements of success in a simple word 'Latin' and has illustrated how GE has adapted those elements over its history to become one of the most successful companies in the world. He has created a book that is as consuming as a novel by using the GE story, and, at the same time, a hands-on workbook to evaluate yourself and your business. The 'takeaways' are rich, and, for me, the key is the absolute commitment to the identification and investment in its leadership. GE is an example for us all in that there are not many companies today that do not have at least one ex-GE leader or that have not adapted some form of their leadership evaluation process to fit their needs."

Rich Spriggle
Vice President-Human Resources
Dana Corporation

"If you ever wondered why GE has been one of the most successful companies in the world for the past 125 years, Bill Rothchild's *The Secret to GE's Success* will answer your questions. Rothschild's in-depth analysis of GE's values, practices, and policies reveals the foundations of how the company has been able, decade after decade, to adapt and respond to a constantly changing environment; deal with crisis; create unique value for customers; maintain competitive advantage; recruit and develop in-depth executive and management talent not only for its own needs but also for the 'export' market of companies in need of talented leadership; and provide a superior return for investors.

"This book is a must read for the student, teacher, manager, executive, and anyone who is interested in how an organization can not only survive but thrive in a world of constant change, challenge, opportunity, and threat. It is a lucid, penetrating, clear, well-written page turner."

Warren J. Keegan
Distinguished Professor of Marketing and International Business
Lubin School of Business, Pace University

THE SECRET TO GE's SUCCESS

William E. Rothschild

McGraw-Hill

New York Chicago San Francisco Lisbon London Madrid Mexico City Milan New Delhi San Juan Seoul Singapore Sydney Toronto

The McGraw-Hill Companies

1 2 3 4 5 6 7 8 9 0 FGR/FGR 0 9 8 7 6

ISBN-13: 978-0-07-147593-8
ISBN-10: 0-07-147593-1

McGraw-Hill books are available at special quantity discounts to use as premiums and sales promotions, or for use in corporate training programs. For more information, please write to the Director of Special Sales, Professional Publishing, McGraw-Hill, Two Penn Plaza, New York, NY 10121-2298. Or contact your local bookstore.

Library of Congress Cataloging-in-Publication Data
Rothschild, William E.
The secret to GE's success / by William E. Rothschild.
p. cm.
ISBN 0-07-147593-1 (hardcover : alk. paper) 1. General Electric Company—History. 2. General Electric Company—Management. 3. Electric industries—United States—Management—Case studies. I. Title.
HD9697.A3U558 2006
338.7'62130973—dc22 2006028762

This book is dedicated to the "secrets of my personal success"...

My loving friend and partner . . . my wife, Alma

My four great children, their spouses, and my grandchildren:
Rob and Linda—Rob, Tim, Sabrina, and Naomi
Steve and Jayne—Lili and Aimee
Karen and Scott—Jack, Katie, and Will
Bill and Lisa—and their twin girls,
Adison and Jaydin

Contents

INTRODUCTION

The Five Ingredients of GE's 126-Year Success

THIS BOOK is intended to acquaint you with the leaders and adaptable strategies that have enabled this 126-year-old institution to become a managerial, technological, and financial leader—and as a result, to boast of having one of the most valued stocks in the world.

This book will teach you how and when to:

- Create a succession system that identifies the right leader for the right time.
- Recognize when even seemingly successful strategies need to be adapted and changed. Forget the old adage "If it ain't broke, don't fix it!"
- Develop a farm system to create a deep, skilled, and loyal managerial and professional bench.
- Take a stand against social, political, and economic policies that can prevent your company from controlling its own destiny.

- Establish, adapt, and use systems—in finance, strategic planning, and human resource management—that lend stability to the organization and help it make progress toward its overall goals.

In short, this book moves beyond folklore and platitudes and clearly describes and explains why GE has been one of the best-led companies over its century and a quarter of operations and why it is likely to *continue* to be a leader.

Over the past two decades, there have been dozens of books written about the magic of General Electric, especially during the Welch years. Many of these books, unfortunately, have ignored or downplayed the company's previous 100 years of significant achievements and occasional failures. But this is a mistake. We can learn a great deal from this company's long history and see how its present and recent successes have grown naturally out of the contributions of generations who have built this unique corporation into one of the world's most venerable brands.

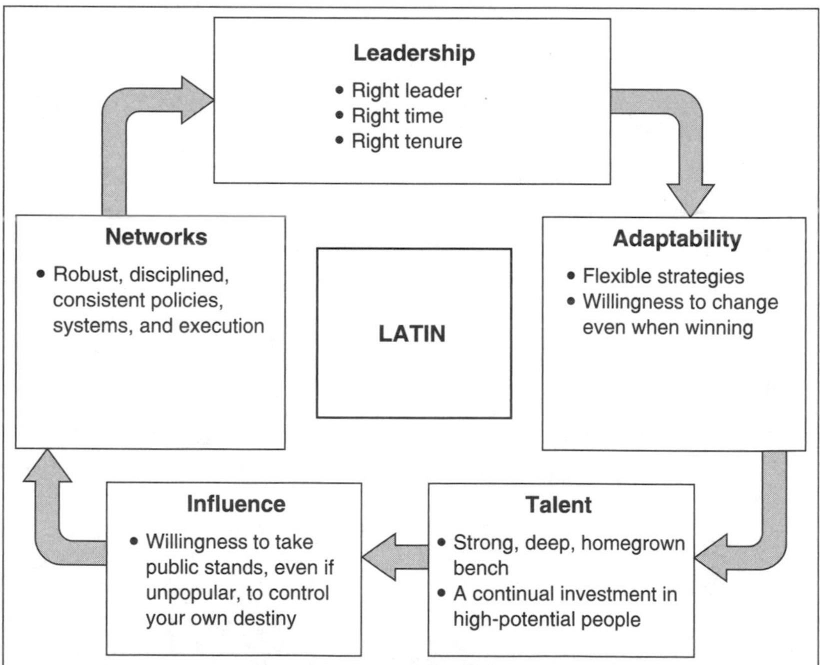

Exhibit I-1 The five key ingredients that have combined to make GE successful: leadership, adaptability, talent, influence, networks.

General Electric, the oldest company tracked by the Dow Jones Industrial Average, continues to grow and prosper, even as its peers have either been driven out of business or are presently operating as mere shells of their former selves. This book identifies and explains the five key reasons for GE's success over its near-126-year existence.

Exhibit I-1 summarizes some of the key elements included in each of these five success factors. This type of exhibit will be used often throughout the book to show what was unique about the company in each of the key stages in its development.

The book will demonstrate that even though GE was strong in each of these areas, it was the *integration* of all five, over a sustained period of time, that made the company different. It is this difference that has contributed to GE's unique 126-year winning streak.

LATIN

General Electric's success can be summarized by the acronym LATIN, which stands for these five success factors:

- Leadership
- Adaptability
- Talent
- Influence
- Networks

SUCCESS FACTOR 1: LEADERSHIP

Over the years, GE has been able to select leaders who have been willing to share both power and rewards. All of its 10 leaders, each with an average tenure of 12.6 years, have had very different personalities, skills, and abilities, which have meshed with the unique needs of the company at the time. In fact, since its inception, GE has had a shared-leadership team approach. It has actively and systematically sought out the insights and recommendations of its management team members. The value of this approach may sound obvious—but many companies fail to use it.

Further, when GE's leaders have retired, they have left the company and stepped down from its board of directors—thereby allowing their respective successors to lead the company without any interference. Again, this may sound like Management 101—but history provides countless examples of clouded successions in which successors have been overshadowed by their predecessors, which has prevented them from putting their own stamp on the company and *leading*. GE has consistently been out front on this important management practice.

SUCCESS FACTOR 2: ADAPTABILITY

GE's management has anticipated and responded successfully to major market shifts. Drawing on its inherent strengths and resources, the company moved from being a leading electrical systems and products company to being a highly diversified, multi-industry global corporation.

When its ability to grow profitably and meet investor expectations was challenged, it adopted its current "strategic portfolio" management and decision-making approach, which has enabled the company to pursue the most attractive opportunities open to it and to discard those that didn't fit.

The book will discuss and assess how the current leader, Jeff Immelt, is following the same tradition of systematic change in the company's focus and portfolio.

SUCCESS FACTOR 3: TALENT

General Electric has had a very simple, consistent philosophy about people and talent. The company has recognized from its inception that people are a valuable resource and asset rather than an entry on the expense side of the ledger. Its leaders have consistently invested in a continuing effort to develop the skills of talented people on a career-long basis in all of the key business functions.

This has given GE a very strong and deep bench, which has provided the company the great luxury of having the right talent at the right time in sufficient depth. In the early 1930s, this philosophy was expanded to include management. In the 1950s, GE institutionalized the concept of "professional management"—an approach that had both strengths and weaknesses but certainly served the company well in important ways.

But GE went well beyond simple training in its approach to talent. It also developed the ability and willingness to adopt what I call a "human-resources-portfolio" approach that evaluated all of the company's key professionals and managers and focused on only those who made the cut. In short, one of the real keys to GE's success has been selectivity in all aspects of the business, including its human resources.

GE's leaders also have demonstrated that they cared about their employees and other key stakeholders and were willing to share the wealth while providing programs and benefits to help its key constituents in good times and bad. This unique and consistent concern about people is truly a unique part of GE's success and is one that will be discussed in great depth throughout the book.

SUCCESS FACTOR 4: INFLUENCE

The fourth success factor is influencing key stakeholders. All organizations have multiple stakeholder groups, including investors, stockholders, management, employees, customers, suppliers, governments, unions, and communities. Each of these groups has power and can impact the organization's ability to execute its strategies. Some stakeholder groups are stronger than others. Some are supportive of the company's leadership; others are adversarial.

Over its long history, GE has acknowledged the power of stakeholders and has ranked some of them higher or lower, depending on the specific circumstances of the time and place. Investors, stockholders, customers, and employees have been consistently high on the corporate priority list, and GE's leaders have been consistent in trying to ensure that their interests have been satisfied.

But GE's leaders have taken different stands with other stakeholder groups. During the joint tenure of Gerard Swope and Owen Young, for example, in the early decades of the twentieth century, GE was a strong ally with Big Government and Big Labor. But during the Ralph Cordiner era and subsequent decades in the twentieth century, these groups were considered adversaries, and the company took steps to minimize or even negate their power.

GE's long experience underscores not only the critical importance of recognizing the different expectations and needs of key stakeholder organizations, but also being selective in how they are addressed. The company has learned—sometimes the hard way—that you can't be all things to all people and succeed. Sometimes you have to take a stand and meet the expectations of those stakeholders who appear to be most important to your company's current health and future prospects even if that means that you will frustrate (and possibly energize) other groups. In short, I believe that GE has demonstrated that it is okay to be politically incorrect at times.

SUCCESS FACTOR 5: NETWORKS

From its inception, GE has pursued highly conservative, disciplined financial policies that have earned the company a AAA credit rating. It has implemented those policies through an integrated set of management systems, which I will refer to as "networks." These networks have been remarkably robust and disciplined. They have enabled the company—which has grown increasingly complex over the years—to consistently meet its promises and its key stakeholder expectations. These networks will be discussed through each stage of the company's history.

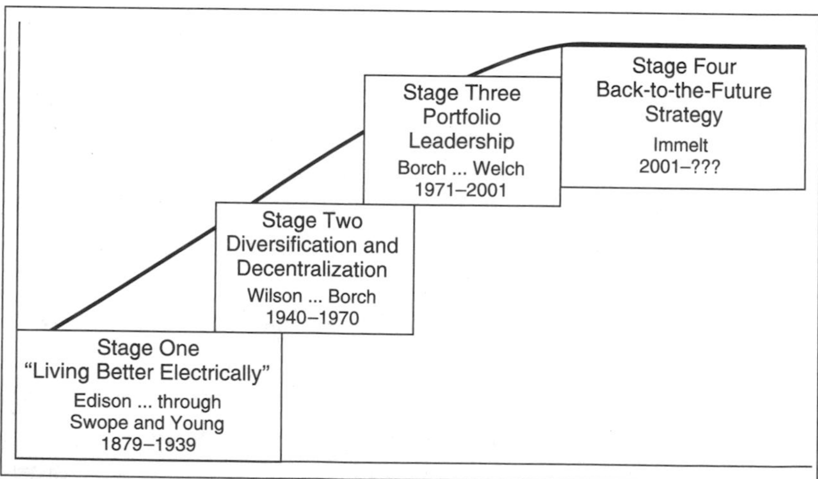

Exhibit I-2 The four stages of GE's 126-year history from the beginning to the present.

THE FOUR STAGES OF GE'S STRATEGIC HISTORY

This book covers GE's successes and failures over its four major stages (see Exhibit I-2). I will describe the five success factors in each stage and provide an objective assessment of what was done in each realm—both positive and negative.

Stage One: "Living Better Electrically"

During this period, GE developed and led the electrical industry with a series of unique strategies and an unusual willingness to recruit a diverse group of talented professionals and managers. The company also demonstrated a surprising willingness to take stands on major socioeconomic and political issues, even if those stands were not necessarily popular.

This period begins in the late 1870s with the original Edison General Electric Company, founded and led by Thomas Alva Edison. The book describes Edison's "failed strategies" and explains how the company's key investors—under the leadership of Henry Villard and J. P. Morgan—took control and merged the company with Thomson-Houston to form the General Electric Company.

The next phase in this first stage was led by Charles Coffin and Edwin Rice. They were able to grow the company and at the same time defend and enhance its strong technological portfolio.

Swope and Young were the successors to Coffin and Rice, and they were able to jumpstart what was called the "Benign Cycle": a system whereby GE used its consumer and industrial application innovations to stimulate demand for electrical generation, transmission, and distribution systems. It was an economic engine of astonishing power.

GE became dominant—in fact, the world leader—in every phase of the entire electrical cycle. Meanwhile, Swope and Young joined with their key competitor, Westinghouse, to form a new venture, RCA, in an effort to break into (and ultimately, control) the infant broadcasting industry. This was the same strategy that they had successfully used in the electrical industry; in this case, as it turned out, Swope and Young were outmaneuvered by the legendary David Sarnoff, and they therefore lost control of this very attractive new venture.

Beginning with Coffin, but later pushed by Swope and Young, GE instituted very powerful human resource systems that permitted the company to develop a "strong, loyal, and trained" bench of professionals and leaders. Both Swope and Young made major contributions to solving the social, political, and economic issues facing the United States in the Great Depression. These included being architects of Social Security and the National Recovery Administration, as well as inviting the Congress of Industrial Organizations (CIO), which today is the Congress of Industrial Unions, to organize and represent GE employees. This provided GE with labor peace from the mid-1930s to the late 1940s, while other major companies were afflicted with violent and bloody labor strikes.

Stage Two: Diversification and Decentralization

Using its unique technological prowess, its money, and its deep managerial strengths, GE moved from being a "pure" electrical company to a highly complex and diversified company, and it instituted unique management systems and human resource programs to make it work.

World War II transformed GE from a single-industry giant to a highly diversified, complex organization. Although this stage started with the war, it continued through the quarter century following the end of the global conflict. Throughout this period, GE was able to build on its inherent strengths to create many successful businesses. The focus was on internal development, rather than acquisitions or mergers, and GE was single-minded in its pursuit of organic growth.

Beginning in the early 1950s, GE's leader, Ralph Cordiner, decided that if the company was to remain a successful, diversified company, it would need to train managers who could manage any business, regardless of its industry or size. He therefore instituted a very innovative professional management training program that came to underpin both the company's diversity and—arguably—its success. Cordiner strongly believed that both organized labor and Big Government were major threats to the company's ability to control its own destiny, so he instituted a very aggressive and adversarial antilabor and anti–Big Government program called "Boulwarism." Cordiner hired a declining actor named Ronald Reagan to serve as the company's corporate spokesman. As many commentators have observed, this corporate relationship was the watershed event in Reagan's conversion from liberal to conservative, and it eventually contributed to his election as president.

Cordiner's record was marred—and his successes obscured—by the price-fixing scandal known as the "Great Electrical Conspiracy." I call this event "GE's Watergate," and I think the analogy is apt. The unraveling of the industrywide scandal, involving GE and 28 other manufacturers, forced a change in GE's succession plan and slowed the growth of the company. To GE's credit, rather than just trying to "fix what was broken"—that is, define the problem narrowly—the company made major changes in how it operated, and it embarked on a risky business development approach. The key lesson? Although a partial solution was appealing, it probably wouldn't have been sufficient.

Fred Borch took over from Cordiner. His major challenge, he soon realized, was that the company's revenues had hit a $5 billion plateau and wouldn't move. In response, he initiated a "Growth Council" to identify major growth opportunities that (1) related to GE's strengths and (2) were growing faster than the GNP. As an outgrowth of the council's work, GE elected to simultaneously pursue nine major new growth areas.

These included four product-oriented ventures (nuclear, computers, plastics, and aircraft engines) and five service opportunities (entertainment, community development, education, financial and personal services, and medical services). At the same time, many of the business units embarked on major global growth initiatives.

In retrospect, we can see that these multiple initiatives—new products, new services, new venues—collectively represented a "bridge too far" for GE. The company clearly had begun to believe its own press clippings about its abilities: that it could "be all things to all people" and that a "GE manager could manage anything." But the propaganda turned out to be wrong, and the company's overreaching had serious negative impacts on its bottom line. This was called the period of "profitless growth," and it was the major reason why the company embarked on its next stage of development.

Stage Three: Portfolio Leadership

This was the period when GE demonstrated the willingness to continually challenge its business portfolio and force itself to (1) focus on specific markets and industries that were best suited to it and (2) discard those that presented a bad strategic and financial fit. In this stage, GE changed its core business from technology to financial services, and it used the resulting financial clout to enhance all of its major businesses.

The failure of five of his nine new ventures compelled Borch to rethink the company's strategies and portfolio mix. He instituted a strategic-thinking and decision-making process that forced all of the company's business units to systematically and critically assess their portfolios. For the first time in the company's history, pruning and restructuring existing businesses became possible—even laudable. GE disposed of many "losers," and it aggressively redeployed its resources into more attractive businesses.

Reginald Jones, a finance-oriented executive who was appointed to succeed Borch, was even more demanding in terms of financial performance. He forced the company's leaders to continually evaluate its portfolio and—based on that evaluation—allocate resources to those businesses that were most attractive and profitable and dump those that weren't.

Jones made one of the most expensive acquisitions in U.S. history—Utah International, in 1976—in an effort to push GE into the international mining sector. But the acquisition failed to meet the company's expectations, and ultimately it was divested by Jack Welch. During his final five years at the helm, Jones focused on succession planning, a process leading to the appointment of Welch as his successor.

The Welch era is probably one of the most publicized and promoted periods in any company's history. There have been literally hundreds of books, articles, and case studies written about how Welch was able to turn an old, tired, bureaucratic company into a dynamic and entrepreneurial organization. Welch reigned for 20 years: a remarkable feat in itself. He took major steps to restructure the company, initially concentrating on pruning and exiting businesses. This earned him the unflattering nickname of "Neutron Jack"—which he loathed—since it was said he killed the people and preserved the buildings.

Under Welch's leadership, GE became the most highly capitalized company in the world. It successfully transitioned from being a product-oriented company to being an integrated service organization, with the largest share of its revenues generated by financial services.

This book will put Welch and his 20-year tenure in a historical perspective. It will show how he continued to build on the foundations and strengths of the organization he inherited while also emphasizing the new contributions he made to the strategic leadership and systems of the company.

The key lesson of this period is that all organizations must be willing to challenge the status quo—both good and bad—and make the appropriate changes. Remarkably, GE was willing to make these kinds of far-reaching changes while it still had options, and it didn't wait until it was too late. This is a major difference between GE and other companies: Most organizations refuse to change when things are going well. They wait so long that by the time drastic change affects them, they go into a reactive mode that usually involves massive, gut-wrenching maneuvers.

Another lesson is that it is critical for a company's leaders to understand why they believe that one sector is more attractive (or less attractive) than another. It's important for companies to see that these kinds of judgments include both quantitative and qualitative elements. In other words, there are judgments that lie *behind* the numbers, and those judgments have to be surfaced and understood.

Stage Four: Immelt's "Back-to-the-Future" Strategy

This is the current period of GE's evolution, and the book offers a preliminary assessment of how its current CEO is refocusing the company while trying to grow it bigger and bigger.

This stage begins with the selection of Jeff Immelt to succeed Jack Welch. I titled this stage "Back to the Future" because I believe that Jeff is trying to build on the successes of the pre-Welch era while continuing to build on Welch's financially based strategies. An alternative title could be "What Do You Do When You Succeed a Legend?"

Immelt took over a company that had become inextricably identified with Welch himself. It seemed unlikely that the company's financial performance could continue indefinitely; therefore, a correction—perhaps a major one—was overdue. But Immelt's timing was terrible: Three days after he took office, the country and the world were changed forever by the horrific terrorist attacks of 9/11.

I will examine and evaluate what Immelt has done to date and how it compares with both Welch and the 100 years before Immelt took over. I will highlight some of the similarities and differences with past successful and unsuccessful strategies and policies. Since it is impossible to predict how successful Immelt will be, the book will focus on placing his moves in a historical perspective. I will use my personal experiences as a basis to identify the positives and potential pitfalls of some of his strategic and tactical moves.

Making Use of the Success Factors

The final chapter highlights GE's specific, actionable success factors to enable you to determine what might work for you.

Although I strongly believe that we can learn from the past and adapt some of these lessons to fit our own situations, it is important to continually ask "So what?" What does this really mean, and is it relevant to me? Where it is appropriate, I will highlight some of these "so what's" in a section entitled "Takeaways" and ask that you take some time to think about what you have read and determine its relevance to you. It is vital to recognize that just because something worked in the past for GE, it may not work in the future for you.

The last chapter, entitled "Success Factors," summarizes what I believe to be the most useful lessons to be derived from GE's experience—and therefore, from this book. These include the following:

- Avoid cookie-cutter succession planning.
- Create and meet realistic expectations.
- Share power and rewards—avoid being greedy!
- Let your successor take over and lead without interference from you when you retire.
- Avoid trying to be all things to all people—take your shots selectively.
- Know what you like and be willing to exit and prune even your core businesses.
- Admit your mistakes and move on.
- Build your own farm system for key positions.
- Seek out the insights and recommendations of your team, but remember that the buck stops with you.
- Take public stands when needed to control your own destiny.
- Build strong financial, strategic, operational, and human resource systems, but be willing to periodically adapt and modify them if required—without succumbing to fads, of course.

What follows are the trials, triumphs, and lessons of GE, starting with a remarkable individual named Thomas Alva Edison.

"Living Better Electrically"

GE's First Stage, 1879 to 1939
Edison–Swope/Young

HIGHLIGHTS

- *Selecting the wrong technology.* In 1879 Edison formed Edison General Electric to provide direct current (DC) systems to supply electricity. Unfortunately, alternating current was preferred by the marketplace, and Edison was ultimately forced to give up control of the company.
- *A perfect marriage.* Investors, led by Henry Villard and J. P. Morgan, took over the company and merged it with Thomson-Houston to form the General Electric Company in 1893.
- *Crisis management.* The Panic of 1893, which almost forced GE into bankruptcy, led to the creation of GE's highly regarded conservative accounting and financial systems, which focused on return on investment and having positive cash flows.
- *Patents.* Coffin and Rice (1893 to 1922) led the company and developed a strong patent portfolio that permitted the company to be a U.S. electrical industry leader and form major alliances and partnerships worldwide.

- *"Benign Cycle."* Swope and Young (1922 to 1939) stimulated electrical demand by providing a complete line of innovative and high-quality consumer and industrial goods, which required the electric utilities to continue to invest in new and expanded generation, transmission, and distribution networks.
- *RCA.* GE and Westinghouse created RCA, but they were forced to divest their ownership and were denied the opportunity to use their strong technological and patent positions in the emerging broadcasting and communications industries.
- *Strong and deep bench.* Throughout this period, all of the GE leaders established human resource systems and practices to attract, train, develop, and retain a strong talent base.
- *Social activists.* Swope and Young took an active part in helping both GE and other American workers to survive the Great Depression, and they were major contributors to several key Roosevelt policies, including the National Recovery Act (called the "Swope Plan"), Social Security, and the Young Plan.
- *Sought help and shared wealth.* GE created a unique independent management and professional society, called the "Elfuns," to permit key employees to provide counsel and guidance to the senior management and to help these individuals enhance their personal security and wealth via one of the first mutual funds.
- *Voluntary unionization.* Rather than be forced to accept unionization, Swope and Young invited the CIO's United Electrical Union (UE) to organize the company. This led to decades of labor peace at a time of highly violent strikes in other major industries.

CHAPTER

Selecting the Wrong Technology

BEFORE DESCRIBING each stage of General Electric's history, I will summarize some of the highlights of that period and relate them to the five key success factors that I've already identified (and captured in the acronym LATIN).

The first stage was led by the legendary Thomas Alva Edison. Edison was an entrepreneurial, disciplined risk taker whose primary objective was to solve major problems—and, in the process, create new markets and industries. Like most entrepreneurs, he fell in love with his own solutions. In some cases—including his approach to electrical power generation and distribution—he was unable to see that the technology he had selected was not the best in the eyes of the potential customers and the public in general. He used a variety of techniques, including scare tactics, to try to bring the public around to his point of view, but ultimately he failed and lost control of his company.

Since Edison was not sufficiently flexible, investor Henry Villard was brought in to save the company. He was able to put together a very effective merger with the Thomson-Houston company, enabling the new General Electric Company to offer both alternating current (AC) and direct current (DC) systems, while also improving the company's market position in the emerging power traction market and preserving its illumination dominance.

Edison's major contribution was to instill in the company a highly disciplined, systematic approach to research and development; this has been a continuing strength of GE over its 126-year history.

Edison and Villard defended the company's strong lighting patent position with a combination of innovations and aggressive legal actions. Backward integration, financing the new electrical industry, and creating a strong brand were other key elements of the strategy.

The Edison/Villard team provided a strong foundation for the new company and enabled it to become a market leader (see Exhibit 1-1).

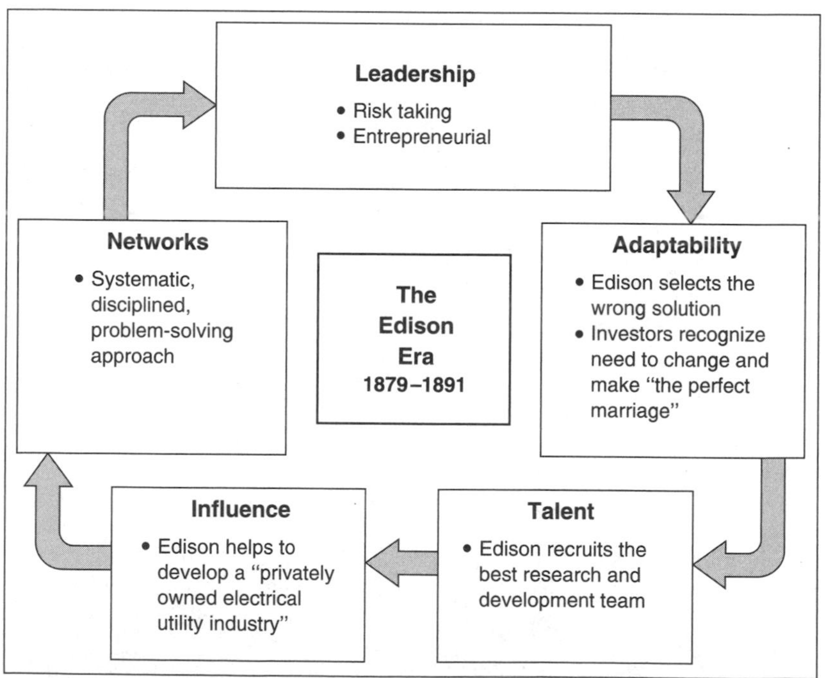

Exhibit 1-1 LATIN and the Edison era.

EDISON'S STRATEGIES

- Focus on real problems and systematically try to solve them.
- Patent and copyright everything.
- Control the key elements of the value chain.
- Finance and develop privately owned utilities.
- License and form alliances.
- Brand the Edison name.
- Aggressively sell and defend technological solutions even if they are not the best solutions.

A PROBLEM SOLVER

Thomas Alva Edison was a unique combination of inventor, entrepreneur, and businessman. He held patents on key components of the telegraph, telephone, and motion-picture projection system, as well as the incandescent lamp.

He established dozens of companies to capitalize on these patents, including companies that commercialized the phonograph, movies, and electric storage batteries. Each was incorporated separately, although all used (and reinforced) the Edison brand. "Edison believed that the real profit in innovation was made not in selling patent rights but in making and selling innovations."[1]

In 1879, Edison founded the Edison General Electric Company to develop a complete integrated electrical DC system, which would provide illumination to displace the gas lamp in residential, commercial, industrial, and street-lighting applications.

"THERE ARE NO RULES"

Edison was intent on solving problems, but he wasn't discouraged when things didn't go according to plan. He was adept at reworking his plans to take advantage of changed circumstances. "Just because something doesn't do what you planned it to do doesn't mean it's useless," he once said. "Hell, there are no rules here—we're trying to accomplish something."[2]

To help "accomplish something," Edison established unique laboratories in Menlo Park and West Orange, New Jersey. He developed a highly disciplined approach to inventing, innovating, and improving marginally on the products of others. For example, he required all employees to document both their successes *and* their failures and to evaluate what made the difference. He not only worked on new ideas and products but he also evaluated other inventors' ideas and products, again to learn from their successes and failures. In some cases, he improved on the ideas of others, resolving problems that caused the original product or concept to fail.

AGGRESSIVELY DEFENDING AND EXTENDING PATENTS

Edison's disciplined research, development, and problem-solving approach resulted in a remarkable 1,093 patents in a wide variety of areas. Edison pursued patents even when his claim on a particular innovation was dubious. As a result, more than 500 of his patent applications were rejected. For Edison, this was simply a cost of doing business.

In addition, Edison aggressively defended his patents. He litigated readily if he believed that his patents were being violated. In some cases, he even litigated when they were not being infringed upon because he recognized that litigation was costly and he had deeper pockets than most of his competitors. Small-scale inventors didn't have the financial resources to sustain long and costly legal actions, so they often gave ground in the face of Edison's legal actions.

CONTROLLING HIS OWN DESTINY

Edison used a combination of alliances, partnerships, and equity positions in the key components and systems that were required to produce his DC electrical generation and lighting networks. Through this kind of vertical integration, he retained control of his destiny (see Exhibit 1-2).

Edison founded the Edison Machine Works, for example, to manufacture the dynamos and large motors required for a lighting system. Edison Shafting Manufacturing Company provided the belts, pulleys, and rotating bars used in the shafting gear assemblies. Edison Electric Tube Company manufactured the underground conductors. Generators were built by the Edison Electric Illuminating Company.

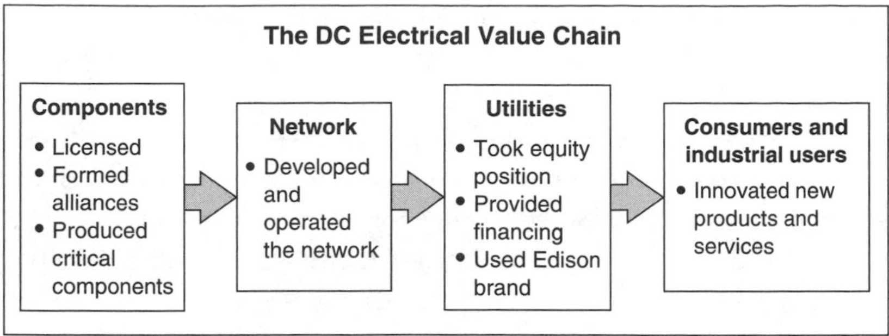

Exhibit 1-2 Edison influenced and controlled all of the key elements of the value chain.

At first these companies were independent entities, but they were later merged into the Edison General Electric Company by Henry Villard. Edison initially licensed Bergmann & Company to manufacture electric lamp fixtures, sockets, and other products that used electricity. Later, this company was acquired and merged into the Edison General Electric.

The final link in the chain was to provide construction services to help build the networks. Edison established the Thomas A. Edison Central Station Construction Department to do this job.

BUILDING DEMAND

Edison's strategy was clear and simple: Build the network. Then develop products that would use the system. Use these tactics to force the network providers to build bigger, better, and more sophisticated electrical systems, all of which the Edison GE Company would provide.

This strategy became known as the "Benign Cycle," and it will be discussed in greater detail in Chapters 2 and 3. It was the same strategy used by Standard Oil and other commodity industries, and variations on it are still used today by companies such as Intel and other electronics companies.

FINANCING CUSTOMERS

Edison realized that the new electric utilities were not able to get the funding required to purchase his systems. He decided, therefore, that he would take an equity position in his customers. This practice added risk to his company, but it was necessary to get the systems installed.

Edison elected not to own and operate his own utilities but rather to just invest in them and have them as loyal customers. This was a different strategy than that adopted by telephone pioneer Alexander Graham Bell, who elected to own and operate the entire system from product to service delivery. Edison's strategy also has modern-day equivalents. In Chapter 9, I'll describe how financing customers became a key element in Jack Welch's successful strategies of the 1980s and 1990s.

LICENSING RATHER THAN OWNING

Edison recognized the need to have a presence in major European and Latin American markets—both for offensive and defensive reasons.

On the offensive side, he wanted to increase the odds that his DC technologies and patents would become the international standard. Defensively he wanted to keep the foreign manufacturers busy protecting their home markets and not exporting to the United States. Rather than own his own affiliates, he licensed other companies in key countries. The Global Edison: Allies and Licensees is a listing of his licensees and the dates he created the alliances.

THE GLOBAL EDISON: ALLIES AND LICENSEES

European

- Companie Continentale Edison, 1882
- Deutsche Edison Gesellschaft, 1883
- Edison and Swan United Electric Light Company, Ltd., 1882
- Edison Electric Light Company of Europe, Ltd., 1880
- Societa Generale Italiana Di Elettricita Sistema Edison, 1883
- Societa D'appareillage Electrique, 1882
- Societe Electrique Edison, 1882
- Societe Industrielle et Commerciale Edison, 1882
- Edison Spanish and Colonial Electric Light Company, 1882

Latin America

- Argentine Edison Light Company, 1883
- Compania Electrica De Edison, 1885
- Edison Electric Light Company of Cuba and Porto Rico, 1881
- Edison Electric Light Company of Havana, 1881

THE EDISON BRAND

It was common at this time for companies to be named after their founders. Edison was a strong proponent of this strategy. He used his name in all of the companies he led, as well as in the electric utilities he sold to. It is interesting to note that even today there are utilities, such as Consolidated Edison and Commonwealth Edison, that were tied to but not owned by Edison and that nevertheless used his name to differentiate their offerings. (However, Edison was disappointed that the company he helped to create was not named after him.)

Other companies such as Westinghouse and Siemens used their founders' names for the companies they owned but not for their customers. In contrast, Edison made the Edison brand a key part of his overall differentiation strategy. From the beginning and continuing into the present, branding is still a major part of GE's successful strategy. We will see later that though the Edison name was dropped from the GE logo, even today GE strongly protects and uses the General Electric name and the GE monogram, although it is no longer just an electrical company.

PRIVATE RATHER THAN GOVERNMENT-OWNED ELECTRIC UTILITIES

Early in Edison's business career he learned how difficult it was to make money by selling to the government. He found that governmental organizations were too bureaucratic, took a long time to make decisions, and often didn't have the financial resources to make a purchase; thus they were unattractive.

Building on his strengths and strong lighting patents, Edison focused on private companies to provide illumination and power traction products, systems, and services. His primary emphasis was on the illumination markets, while his competitors concentrated more on motors and drive systems for industrial uses. He was a strong proponent of having private electrical utilities rather than government-owned institutions. This has continued to be a major GE policy and will be discussed in more detail in Chapter 5.

SELLING THROUGH INTERMEDIARIES RATHER THAN DIRECTLY TO CONSUMERS

It is also interesting to note that Edison elected not to sell directly to consumers but instead to have the electric utilities sell the electrical products to the consumers. Even as recently as the mid-1930s, consumers purchased their lightbulbs and electric appliances from electric utilities. In some cases, lightbulbs were free. This was similar to the Bell systems' control over all of the telephones used by consumers. The distribution and retailing of electrical and illumination products changed in the 1920s, but it was not until the 1970s that consumers could purchase and hook up their own phones.

LOOKING FOR A BETTER WAY

Edison recognized that there was a need for public and home lighting that was safe, easy to use, and efficient. "Ye Olde Lamp Lighter" was required to individually light and extinguish the gas lamps. So Edison created a system that would illuminate and extinguish by just hitting a switch in the central plant. This was a great competitive advantage over the gas industry, and you might say that Edison's vision was to "pass gas."

Edison's new-market development strategy was not unique—all of the peer companies, such as Westinghouse and Thomson-Houston, followed the same strategy. But Edison had a competitive advantage in his more disciplined approach. He was strategic in his research and development, and he was willing to carefully analyze his competitors' products and concepts in depth. Further, he required that failures be carefully recorded and evaluated so that he could learn from both what worked and what didn't work. In many cases, he even was able to solve his problems and use the solutions to improve the quality and performance of his innovations.

Edison's disciplined approach to research and development and his aggressive patent filings became a consistent practice in GE and led to GE's development of a very strong patent portfolio. This contributed to the company's market leadership. Up to the 1970s, GE continued Edison's integration systems strategy and offered the customer a complete solution and not just products. Later, the company's Benign Cycle strategy accelerated the development of new, innovative consumer, industrial, and commercial products to stimulate demand and require the utilities to continually expand and upgrade their networks.

COMPETITIVE STRATEGY

Edison had not only to convince the public to use electricity instead of gas for illumination but he also had to compete against other technologies that were designed to do the same thing. Unfortunately, he didn't select the customers' preferred solution, and so he had to defend a losing technology.

LOOKING FOR MORE THAN ONE SOLUTION

Assume that there is more than one way to solve a problem. If you select the second-best solution, you must do something to discredit the other approach. Let's look at one such situation in-depth in which GE bet on the wrong solution and then had to scramble to make the best of it.

As noted above, there are two principal ways of generating and transmitting electricity: direct current and alternating current. Edison selected the DC approach, while others—primarily George Westinghouse and Thomson-Houston—selected AC.

AC required that the voltage be reduced, transmitted, and distributed to local users by a central electricity-generating plant, while DC technology was generated and transmitted locally. The AC approach was centralized, while DC was decentralized.

A FORMIDABLE COMPETITOR

George Westinghouse was Edison's major American competitor. Westinghouse first achieved recognition for his invention of air brakes for railroad cars. This breakthrough came in Schenectady, New York, where Westinghouse's father had a factory and George attended Union College.[3] George became interested in electricity, and he studied the Edison DC approach. He concluded that DC was too inefficient to be scaled up because doing so meant large currents and serious power losses. Westinghouse decided to investigate the alternating current technology, which had already been tested and used in Europe.

Westinghouse imported a number of Gaulard-Gibbs transformers and a Siemens AC generator to begin his experiments, and he moved his company to Pittsburgh. Assisted by William Stanley, the developer of the transformer, Westinghouse built and installed the first multiple-voltage AC power system in Great Barrington, Massachusetts. The system was driven by a hydropower generator, and it produced 500 AC volts, which was stepped up to 3,000 volts for transmission and then stepped down to 100 volts to power electric lights. He formed the Westinghouse Electric & Manufacturing Company in 1889.[4] Westinghouse achieved immediate success, installing 30 AC lighting systems within a year.

The system was limited both by the lack of an effective metering system and a workable AC motor. In 1888, Westinghouse and his engineer Oliver Shallenger developed the much-needed power meter. He then licensed the AC motor patents of Nikola Tesla, who had worked for Edison but who had left because of his interest in AC (rather than DC) technology.

THE WAR OF THE CURRENTS

Since it appeared that Westinghouse had come up with an approach to powering lamps that at least some customers preferred, Henry Villard and other GE investors scrambled to find ways to discredit AC technology. They settled on a series of promotional campaigns that focused on the relative safety of the two technologies.

AC depended on first stepping up voltages and then stepping them back down through the use of transformers. Seizing upon this, Edison, who didn't mind stretching a point to make one, claimed that high-voltage systems were unnecessarily hazardous. Westinghouse pointed out, correctly, that the advantages of AC vastly outweighed the disadvantages—and that in any case, the risks of high voltage could be contained. He replied that the risks could be managed and were outweighed by the benefits.[5]

Meanwhile, Edison tried to persuade state legislatures to limit allowable power-transmission voltages to 800 volts, which was a move that effectively would have killed AC. This effort failed, but the crafty and determined Edison succeeded on other fronts.

In the spring of 1888 the New York Legislature passed a law establishing electrocution as the state's official method of execution. Seeing an opportunity in the new law, Edison went to work trying to affect the conclusion of the state commission that had been appointed to decide whether to power the "electric chair" with AC or DC current.

The Edison research facility hired two researchers—Harold Brown and his assistant, Dr. Fred Peterson—who set out to prove that AC was best suited for electrocution. In other words, Edison wanted to prove that the competition was better suited for dealing death. Apparently, not much was made of the fact that Peterson was the head of the very same state commission charged with deciding between AC and DC—a decision that he helped make while on the payroll of the Edison Company.

WESTINGHOUSED!

Perhaps not surprisingly, the commission chose AC as the preferred current for executing prisoners, and on January 1, 1889, the world's first electrical execution law went into full effect. Westinghouse, understandably upset at Edison's tactics, protested the decision, and he refused to sell any AC generators directly to prison authorities. Edison then obligingly provided the state with the necessary AC generators. It was a brilliant, if somewhat underhanded, coup. For years afterward, people referred to inmates who died in electric chairs as having been "Westinghoused."

WESTINGHOUSE'S AC TECHNOLOGY PREVAILS

But Westinghouse knew that he had science on his side. He continued to pursue AC technology, and he scored highly visible successes—for example, his company built the huge generators needed to harness the energy of Niagara Falls in 1895. Westinghouse reinforced his company's technological edge by acquiring the exclusive American rights to manufacture the advanced Parsons steam turbine in America. By most measures, therefore, George Westinghouse was a formidable competitor to Edison, often beating the more celebrated inventor at his own game. Had Westinghouse not lost control of his company during the Panic of 1907, the outcome of the Westinghouse/GE wars might have been very different.

The failure of Edison and Villard to counter the Westinghouse success forced a major change in the company strategy and ultimately forced Edison to leave the company. Edison's departure moved the company into its next stage of development.

IF YOU CAN'T BEAT THEM, JOIN OR ACQUIRE THEM

When it became painfully obvious to the Edison investors that publicity and financing were not able to compensate for betting on the wrong technology, Henry Villard and his investment banker, J. P. Morgan, accepted reality and sought to merge the company with a strong AC player.

A PERFECT MARRIAGE

As noted above, Henry Villard, a major investor, was selected to lead the company and to find a way for the company to get access to AC technology. Villard had started his career as a journalist, married the daughter of antislavery crusader William Lloyd Garrison, and made his money by investing in the development of the U.S. railroad system.

Villard sought a merger partner that would enable Edison GE to offer both AC and DC systems as a way of strengthening its position in the power traction segment. He was highly successful in this effort, finding the right partner in the Lynn, Massachusetts–based firm of Thomson-Houston.

Thomson-Houston had been founded by Elihu Thomson, who held over 700 patents in his name. Among his inventions were the transmission of alternating current by transformers, the three-coil dynamo, improvements in arc lighting, the induction motor, the development of the electric meter, and improvements in the design of X-rays.

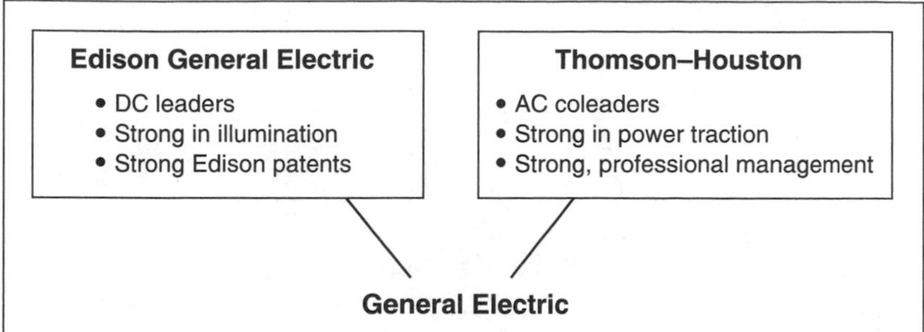

Exhibit 1-3 The synergies created by the merger of Thomson-Houston and Edison GE to form the new General Electric Company.

The two companies were highly complementary (see Exhibit 1-3). Edison had a strong lighting and DC patent portfolio and in fact was the American leader in DC technology. Thomson-Houston was second in the AC segment, behind Westinghouse. Edison GE had a strong position in the illumination market, and Thomson in the power traction market.

This combination enabled the new General Electric Company to become the electrical systems and products leader in both major technologies and application segments. The merger strengthened the new company's technological and market positions and—even more important—gave GE the benefit of a strong leadership team. Charles Coffin, who came over from Thomson-Houston, turned out to be a major contributor to GE's successful growth in the early 1900s.

TAKEAWAYS

One of the things I learned in my career was to continually ask this key question: *So what?* History is almost always interesting, but its *usefulness* isn't always obvious. At the end of most of the chapters in this book, therefore, I'm going to recommend that you sit back, reflect, and ask yourself this key question:

How do these principles and strategies apply to my organization?

In other words, what can I learn from the long-ago (and not so long ago) experience of GE?

Leadership

Edison, although not without his flaws, can be seen as an excellent example of an entrepreneurial risk taker. He was focused on what he believed was the best solution, and he was not easily deterred from his chosen path.

Edison was what I call a "missionary leader," and he was clearly suited to the challenge of leading a new business. But Edison's example also illustrates the limitations of this type of leader when the game changes and it turns out that the company has bet on the wrong horse. Fortunately for GE's long-term health, the company's investors recognized Edison's limitations, and they were willing to move on to another leader and a new strategy.

- *Recommendation.* Take a look at where your business is in its life cycle and determine whether the current leader—even if that leader is you—is the right leader for the future. If not, then it is critical to start now to identify potential successors. Most important, make sure that you avoid the trap of the carbon copy and that you find or cultivate leaders who are suited to the needs of the future.

Adaptability

Edison focused on *solving problems to make a profit*. This is (or should be!) the focus of all business enterprises. Let's examine the elements of his strategy and see how you can use them.

Disciplined evaluations and research. Edison was willing to evaluate other people's ideas and concepts—even when the concepts had failed—to determine if there was a way to make them viable. Contrary to the historical myth, he didn't invent the lightbulb, but he improved on others' ideas, and—with help of highly skilled people—he solved the challenge of providing a durable source of illumination. He thereby developed a highly successful product and business. Significantly, he documented everything—even his failures. A century later, American business executives would be marveling at the "Japanese" concept of documenting engineering and design failures. Edison did it first.

- *Recommendation.* If you are developing new products or services, follow Edison's disciplined and systematic approach and be willing to rethink your own failures and the failures of others. (At the very least, you won't make the same mistake twice!)

Protect patents and copyright everything. Edison was an aggressive patent filer. Remember that he had over 500 rejections along with over 1,000 approved patents. You must be willing to defend your patents, and you must not allow others to capitalize on your own investments in innovation. This is particularly true today when there are so many people—indeed, even whole nations—who are willing to steal your ideas and use them without acknowledging your ownership or paying you for the right to use those ideas. The pirating of music, films, and software is a powerful example of such theft in today's global economy.

- *Recommendation.* Protect your intellectual properties. Aggressively defend any violations, or even potential violations, before it is too late.

Make your technology the industry standard. Edison recognized the need to dominate the market and control all of the vital parts of the system. He did this via equity ownership, licensing, partnerships, and helping to finance his customers. It is vital that you gain a major share of a new market, especially if there are other substitutes or competing technologies.

- *Recommendation.* Do whatever it takes to legally gain and maintain the dominant share of a new emerging market. Of course, this begins with making sure that your technology is at least good enough—if not truly superior—and that it is constantly being improved. It generally also requires the creation of strong alliances and a willingness to share opportunity with others. The contrasting histories of Microsoft and Apple make these points in contemporary terms.

Help your customers succeed. Edison took an equity position in many of his electric utility customers, and he provided them with all the help they needed to be successful. He permitted them to build on his own name, thereby lending them credibility and—at the same time—

reinforcing his "brand." Making your customer a profitable, long-term winner is usually vital in new industries.

- *Recommendation.* Work with your customers to be successful and provide them with the resources needed to win. This may require providing managerial, marketing, and strategic services at little or no cost. Financing may be needed, although you shouldn't use your own money unless it is absolutely necessary. We will discuss this further in Chapter 3.

If you guess wrong, fix the problem. Edison picked the wrong technology, and he was unwilling to accept this reality. Instead, he tried to use safety as an issue to suppress the competition, but he failed. He waited too long to accept reality, and as a result he lost his company.

- *Recommendation.* Though this is a difficult step to take, it is critical that you recognize that your solution may not be the best one. If you are wrong, admit your mistake and try to obtain the rights to use the preferred approach. Once an industry standard has emerged and an installed base is in place, there's rarely any point in arguing with that standard.

CHAPTER

Becoming the Leader

THE SECOND KEY to building a healthy organization requires growing the business. In many cases, this is achieved by growing market share. This requires the ability to balance short-term survival expectations and long-term growth expectations. GE's first leaders were able to do both, and over its first three decades, the company strengthened its hold on the market and became one of the leaders of the emerging worldwide electrical industry.

As noted in Chapter 1, the merger of Thomson-Houston and Edison General Electric did more than enable the new company to offer both AC and DC technologies and become a strong player in both the illumination and power traction segments. In addition, it provided the company with a unique, highly skilled CEO: Charles Coffin.

Unlike most executives of his day, Coffin was ahead of his time—he was a strong proponent of consultative and participative management. He was able to grow the company by attracting very talented scientists and continuing the disciplined, systematic research and development instituted by Edison and Houston. Additional deals permitted the company to protect and enhance its strong patent portfolio. This included creating, in conjunction with Westinghouse, the Board of Patent Control and solidifying the company's legal participation in cartels and industry associations.

It was during this period that GE instituted its strong, transparent, and disciplined accounting and financial systems, which would become its hallmark. This enabled the firm to improve several key metrics, such as return on investment (ROI) and cash flow.

This was also the time when the company initiated and invested heavily in its womb-to-tomb selection, training, and development programs. In short, this was the period that provided GE with the firm foundation upon which its management systems and innovation would be built. So let's probe deeper into the strategies, tactics, and policies of the Coffin era (see Exhibit 2-1).

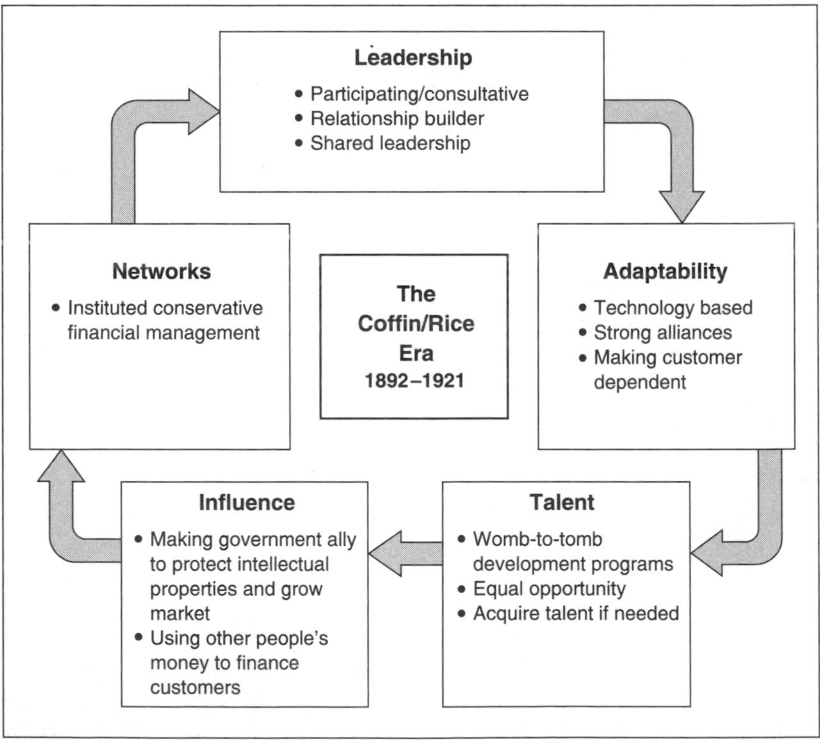
Leadership
• Participating/consultative
• Relationship builder
• Shared leadership
Networks
• Instituted conservative financial management
The Coffin/Rice Era 1892–1921
Adaptability
• Technology based
• Strong alliances
• Making customer dependent
Influence
• Making government ally to protect intellectual properties and grow market
• Using other people's money to finance customers
Talent
• Womb-to-tomb development programs
• Equal opportunity
• Acquire talent if needed

Exhibit 2-1 LATIN and the Coffin/Rice era.

A MANAGEMENT PIONEER

Edison provided a good foundation for the new company, and Villard was able to find a strong, compatible merger partner. But it was critical that the new company be carefully managed. This was the second stage of the company's electrical growth period, and in Charles Coffin GE was fortunate to have the right leader at the right time. This would emerge as yet another key to GE's long-term success.

THE RIGHT LEADER FOR THE RIGHT TIME

Acquisitions and mergers require leaders who are able to integrate diverse cultures and technologies. Coffin's consultative and participative style of leadership was ideal for achieving this result. He was highly successful in developing long-term relationships with all key stakeholders and in dealing with financial crises.

Coffin became president and CEO in 1892. Coffin's associates, according to one historian, described him as "a gracious gentleman and delightful companion. He never ordered one of them to do anything, preferring to rely on his powers of suggestion. In his turn, he graciously sought and welcomed suggestions from those around him—and then decisively made up his own mind on key questions."[1] Significantly, Coffin always referred to his employees as "associates" rather than as subordinates. His consultative leadership style presented a sharp contrast to most of the business leaders of the day, who tended to be autocratic to a greater or lesser extent.

Coffin built strong relationships with all of his key stakeholder groups. Customers and competitors knew him as both the outstanding statesman and the outstanding salesman of the electrical manufacturing industry. He took a personal interest in major negotiations, often drawing up business proposals in his own hand for important customers.[2]

At tense meetings, he knew both how to relieve the pressure with an appropriate anecdote and also how to push for closure. He built strong relationships with both employees and vendors. He understood when to change a product's features to get customers to buy something new—

and he also knew *what* to change. Under his watchful eye, new products were introduced in all of the major consumer areas. Coffin effectively combined internal developments and selective acquisitions to provide a continuing stream of new products.

ONE OF THE FIRST CRISIS MANAGERS

Coffin's greatest test came in his first year as president with the Panic of 1893. This was a major financial collapse and panic that threatened GE's very existence. The company was highly leveraged because Edison and Villard had taken equity positions in companies owned by their key customers. This put the company in a cash flow bind, and—when the stock market crashed—almost forced the company into bankruptcy.

This was when Coffin first demonstrated his strong negotiating skills, cutting a critical deal with J. P. Morgan. Morgan agreed to advance the needed money as payment for GE-held utility stocks. This saved the company and "made possible its rapid recovery and growth during the remainder of Coffin's tenure."[3]

Coffin and GE's financial strategies and policies were profoundly influenced by this traumatic event, and the philosophy that was born at that time still guides the company today.

CONSERVATIVE FINANCIAL MANAGEMENT PRACTICES

The company's close call with bankruptcy made Coffin and his team recognize that they must avoid taking the risks inherent in funding their major customers. The company instituted a strong, transparent financial and accounting system that used ROI and cash flow as its two primary measures.

One of the results of this new strategy was the establishment of the "J. P. Morgan connection." GE and Morgan became strong allies, and the Morgan organization was given a seat on the GE board of directors. It also became a major GE financial partner. The Morgan connection lasted until the early 1980s, when GE began increasing its emphasis on financial services.

Coffin's ability to recognize and respond to change is one of the major reasons that General Electric still exists and has been as successful as it has been. Most important, the company was able to move from being the *owner* of utilities to being primarily the major *supplier* of utilities.

GE's conservative accounting and its keen focus on cash flow enhanced its reputation among the Wall Street and investment banking sets. GE became a safe haven for individual investors, providing growth and stability even in the troubled early 1900s. It is still one of the most widely owned stocks in the world, and its broad ownership base is not accidental. Having many owners, most of them small, has enabled the company's management to avoid being dominated by any one group of external investors (and thereby keep control of the firm). For example, even though Morgan was an investor in and a financier of GE, he and his company were never the dominant shareholders.

DEFENDING AND ENHANCING A STRONG TECHNOLOGY BASE

A technology-based strategy requires that a company continue to invest in product and systems development and then institute a strong legal strategy to protect and enhance its patent portfolio. Coffin and his team were successful in doing both.

Coffin recognized that it was critical to have a continuing stream of innovative products and also to enhance the company's strong patent portfolio. To achieve these ends, he created a world-renowned research and development center staffed with highly skilled people. Their job was to develop new and improved electrical systems—including generation, transmission, and distribution products—as well as illumination products.

Overall, Coffin was able to develop and implement a highly integrated strategy. He grew GE's revenues and earnings, and he positioned the company to lead in all of its chosen market segments. Let's review each of these strategies in more depth.

USING TECHNOLOGY AND PATENTS TO GAIN THE COMPETITIVE ADVANTAGE

A Strong Research and Development Center and Program

Edison was one of the first professional R&D leaders who systematically provided a steady and consistent stream of new, innovative products. However, Elihu Thomson was also a prolific inventor and held over 700 patents, many of which were central to the development of the electric industry.

Research and development made up a key element of General Electric's strategy from its inception until the beginning of the 1970s. (It appears that Jeff Immelt, the current CEO, is working to reestablish GE as a technology-based company. This will be discussed further in Chapter 14.)

Coffin recognized the need to continue this important activity to ensure that the company remain a technological innovator and leader. In 1900, Coffin hired Willis R. Whitney, an MIT chemist, as the first director of the GE Research Laboratory. Initially this group consisted of three people working in a barn beside the Erie Canal in Schenectady, New York.

The team quickly grew as research contributed to the development of many new products. Early additions to the staff included chemist Irvin Langmuir, the first U.S. industrial scientist to win the Nobel Prize. It is interesting to note that even though GE was a leading electrical company, most of its great scientists were chemists, and this led to many chemical and materials innovations, which led in turn to the development of several GE-engineered materials businesses.

During the first half of the twentieth century, the laboratory developed patents that enabled the company to maintain and enhance the Edison patents. These included ductile tungsten filament and "gas-filled" lamps. In addition, it developed the modern X-ray tube; the modern process of making silicones; Calrod heating elements (used in electric stoves); and the magnetron tube, which is the basis of the microwave oven.

IF YOU CAN'T HIRE, ACQUIRE THE COMPANY

Coffin recognized that people were the heart and soul of any successful business, and so he was willing to take extraordinary steps to get the people he wanted. The recruitment of Charles Steinmetz is a perfect example.

Thomas Edison had recognized Steinmetz's genius, and he made him an offer to join Edison General Electric Company. Steinmetz was not interested and wanted to stay with his current employer. In 1893, Coffin tried again, but Steinmetz declined again, so Coffin decided that the only way to get Steinmetz was to buy the company owned by Steinmetz's employer, Rudolph Eickemeyer. This move gave GE access to the Steinmetz patents and systems and made Steinmetz an employee of the new GE. (This strategy is still very common. Quite often the reason that large companies such as Microsoft and GE purchase start-ups is to acquire the people and their intellectual properties.)

In 1894, Steinmetz was transferred to Schenectady GE and assigned to the new calculating department. He worked on many highly complex projects, including the building of the generators at Niagara Falls. He retired in 1903 to become a professor at Union College, but he remained a company consultant.

One humorous incident happened when Steinmetz was a consultant. He was asked to help diagnose a problem with a major customer's turbine generator—a problem that no one had been able to solve. Steinmetz went to the site, examined the problem, and drew a line with chalk on the turbine to show where the rotor was out of alignment. He then submitted a bill to the company for $10,000. GE and the customer were shocked at the charge and demanded a detailed invoice. Steinmetz complied with an invoice that stated, "Cost of chalk, one dollar; cost of knowing where to place the chalk line on the turbine, $9,999.00." The invoice speaks to both Steinmetz's genius and his maverick nature.

Aggressively Protecting Intellectual Property

Edison was obsessed with protecting all of his innovations, so he aggressively and systematically patented everything he worked on. Since the new GE was now in the alternating current business, there were many legal contests between GE, Westinghouse, and others. These disputes not only inhibited new product development but they also emerged as a large financial burden on the companies affected. Even the federal government became concerned, and it sought a solution that would enable companies to gain cleaner patents and reduce the number of lawsuits.

The Board of Patent Control

With federal government permission, General Electric and Westinghouse established and operated the Board of Patent Control from 1896 to 1911. This organization had two key objectives:

1. *Defend GE and Westinghouse patents.* When an inventor filed for an electrical-related patent, the filing was immediately sent to the Board of Patent Control to determine if the application was in violation of GE and Westinghouse patents. If the patent filing was viewed as a violation, the board would take immediate legal action to stop the new patent from being approved.
2. *Acquire new patents.* If the application was *not* a violation, either the GE or Westinghouse representative could try to acquire the patent. If the inventor refused to sell the patent, the board members sometimes decided to litigate and tie up the patent in the courts. In most cases, the small inventor lacked the funds to fight in court, so he or she would often sell the rights at a nominal price.

Though this appears to be an abuse of power by today's standards, it was legal and supported by Washington.

PATENTS AND LEGAL MUSCLE REMAIN VITAL TO GE'S STRATEGY

Though institutions such as the Board of Patent Control no longer exist, most successful organizations aggressively defend their patents in court, and they still count on the fact that smaller companies will be unable to finance the legal costs involved in patent disputes.

Legally maneuvering to aggressively defend patents and copyrights continues to be a major aspect of GE's corporate strategies. GE has always maintained a strong legal department, and the company has used these talents not only to defend itself but also to enhance its intellectual properties. This is a key element to GE's continued success. In fact, in 2005, GE's legal department was one of the 10 largest "law firms" in the United States, with more than 1,100 lawyers on staff.

USING LICENSES TO MAINTAIN COMPETITIVE POSITIONS

GE's Edison patents and supporting technology were so strong that independent lamp makers had a very hard time competing. In 1901, several smaller producers joined to form the National Electric Lamp Association (NELA).

Rather than fight this organization, GE supported it and licensed its members to use the strong GE lighting patents to produce their products—provided that they follow specific rules about how they branded, sold, and priced their products.

- *Mazda brands.* At this time, all electric lightbulbs sold in the United States were branded Mazda, "the goddess of light." There were three Mazda brands:
  - Edison Mazda, used exclusively by GE
  - Westinghouse Mazda, used exclusively by Westinghouse
  - National Mazda, used by the other 30 NELA members[4]
- *Types of licensees.* In addition, as part of the licensing agreement, General Electric established two types of licensing agreements, which they cleverly called "Class A" and "Class B."
  - *Class A licenses.* Westinghouse was the only Class A licensee, since it also had a strong patent portfolio that was used by NELA. Westinghouse was permitted to develop its own sales strategy and to price the bulbs and export them without GE's permission.
  - *Class B licenses.* There were 30 companies in this category, which included Sunbeam. Under the Class B licensing terms, GE determined the prices that the companies would use to sell their lamps, allocated the number of units they could produce, and prohibited them from exporting their lamps offshore. Because of GE's strong lighting patents, the company was able to ensure that the lamp was "value priced" and not permitted to become a commodity.

Organizations such as the NELA were legal and quite common at this time. Again, the U.S. government supported the formation of these types of organizations to protect its emerging industries and their technological positions. Similar cartels were prevalent in Europe, put in place by European nations to protect their own indigenous technology companies.

And, as with any technology company, the major underpinning of such support was a strong patent position, which GE had and continued to develop via its investment in R&D and its leadership of the Board of Patent Control. These types of agreements allowed smaller companies to remain in the market and to benefit from the pricing and control of supply. It was considered to be a win-win situation for all of the parties, but obviously it was anticompetitive, and it kept electric lamp prices high.

It is tempting to condemn such arrangements, which would not be tolerated today. But one of the lessons of business history is that it's important to judge businesses and their leaders by *the standards of their day* rather than by our own. By that standard, GE was a skilled and powerful competitor playing by the rules.

HOW TO COME OUT AHEAD EVEN WHEN YOU LOSE

In 1911, as a result of a major antitrust investigation, both the Board of Patent Control and the National Electric Lamp Association were dissolved.

During the investigation, General Electric was found to control more than 75 percent of the NELA members. Rather than fighting the verdict, GE requested—and was granted—permission to acquire selective members of the NELA organization and integrate them into GE as subsidiaries. The result was that GE and Westinghouse became the dominant players in the electric lamp market.[5]

Foreign producers such as Siemens, Philips (a GE licensee), and General Electric Company of the United Kingdom were not major players in the U.S. lamp market until the 1970s, when the game changed and the pricing and supply control of the key American leaders was taken away by the discontinuance of what was called "agency pricing," as will be explained further in Chapter 5.

FINANCING THE CUSTOMER

Embryonic capital-intensive industries, including electric utilities, require continuing access to low-cost capital. GE elected to establish third-party financing for these new companies rather than investing in them directly. GE formed and used the Electric Bond and Share Company (EBASCO) to provide financing and strategic help to the new fledging utilities, and in return it exercised significant influence over their customers' decisions and strategies.

USING OTHER PEOPLE'S MONEY TO FINANCE CUSTOMERS

GE management recognized that electric utilities required a steady stream of low-cost capital to invest in growing their systems and purchasing innovative products and services. Edison decided to invest directly in these utilities, but the Panic of 1893 made the new GE recognize that it could not afford to assume this risk on its own.

"In 1905," according to one account, "GE formed the Electric Bond and Share [Company] (EBASCO) to finance electric utilities. The group subsequently became one of the three dominant U.S. gas and electricity utility holding companies."[6]

EBASCO did more than just get money for the utilities. It enabled utilities to convince state regulators to set their rates (and by extension, their profits) based on a percentage of their investments. This meant that the more that the utilities invested in equipment and systems, the more they made. There were several positive results of this action. One was that the electric utilities were highly attractive to investors because their earnings were highly stable and predictable. This also made their stocks very attractive to small investors, including the fabled "widows and orphans" who needed secure income from their investments.

Meanwhile, since the utilities were encouraged to continue to invest and upgrade their systems, this rate-setting structure was also highly attractive to the electric equipment companies such as GE. GE was able to sell new equipment to utilities that were continually investing in new innovative, reliable, and efficient products and systems. This in turn, made the United States' electrical systems the best in the world—a claim that, unfortunately, can't be made today.

Clearly, EBASCO was a win-win for everyone. Further, EBASCO created a strong holding company that controlled companies all over the nation, including some in Pennsylvania, Texas, Idaho, Montana, and Florida. GE was a major owner of EBASCO until it distributed its EBASCO shares to its stockholders in 1924.[7]

Through its stake in EBASCO, therefore, GE maintained an ownership stake in utilities, and it thereby influenced how they were managed. For obvious reasons, GE favored private, stockholder-owned electric utilities, and it was an outspoken opponent of government-supported efforts such as the Tennessee Valley Authority (TVA). In Chapter 5, we will discuss how the TVA was involved in what was called the "Great Electrical Conspiracy."

MAKING CUSTOMERS HIGHLY DEPENDENT

New companies need help in a variety of activities, ranging from selecting their equipment to managing and developing their people. GE made the electric utilities highly dependent by providing long-range capacity planning, developing their professionals, and providing a steady stream of more efficient and innovative products and systems.

PROVIDING A CONTINUOUS STREAM OF INNOVATIVE AND/OR MORE EFFICIENT PRODUCTS AND SYSTEMS

GE provided a continuous stream of new and innovative products that made electricity more efficient, safer, and cheaper. GE worked with the utilities to plan their capacity additions, and it recommended that they have at least an excess capacity of 17 percent to ensure that they could always stay ahead of their customers' growth. Once again, of course, this enabled GE and the other electrical systems companies to keep their plants operating at optimum levels.

TRAINING THE CUSTOMERS' MANAGERS AND PROFESSIONALS

Many electric utility executives, engineers, and professionals were graduates of GE's test and management programs. Since GE kept only a percentage of the trainees, the company encouraged those who didn't make the GE team to work for the electric utilities. This cultivated strong bonds between "GE alumni" and the company.

These mutually beneficial relationships between manufacturers and their customers were very common and were practiced in all major industries. It was the personality and skills of Coffin and his team, however, that made GE's even more successful.

WOMB TO TOMB

Coffin recognized the need to hire the best people and keep them loyal. He instituted several major training programs that still exist today, and he hired qualified people regardless of their race, religion, or politics.

BUILDING A STRONG AND DEEP BENCH

From its inception to the present, GE has had a strong farm system organization. The company has always believed in the concept of recruiting young, retaining the best, and building from within.

Coffin and his management team recognized early that it was very important to recruit talented individuals early in their careers and then provide the training and work assignments to enhance their skills and company loyalty.

In 1901, GE established apprentice programs in Schenectady, Lynn, Bridgeport, and Fort Wayne, which were the major manufacturing locations. A combination of work assignments and evening classes were developed in four areas: machinist, draftsman, blacksmith, and moulder. Upon completion of a course, the graduates were awarded a "certificate of apprenticeship." This program was one of the key programs in the company until the 1950s. There were ties to local universities so that the apprentices also could work on getting engineering and technical degrees.

Coffin knew that the company needed competent, GE-trained and GE-loyal engineering staff, so he created the Engineering Test Program. This program was an entry-level program for all engineering recruits. The trainees were assigned to specific "testing" operations in the product departments, as well as the General Engineering Laboratory. Some were sent to the Corporate Research and Development Center.

Coffin also recognized the need to hire talented nontechnical college graduates, so he established the Business Training Course (BTC). The college recruits were given a variety of financial assignments, and they were required to take very intensive accounting and financial courses two nights a week. The trainees had to take weekend exams, and they were given grades as though they were in college.

Grades and work appraisals were used to determine who would be promoted. The best graduates were assigned to the Auditing Staff, enabling them to learn about the various company operations and enhance their ability to lead in these businesses. Graduates of the Auditing Staff became the financial linchpins, and often the general managers, of the company's business units.

This is the program that I joined in 1955. I was a Fordham University Russian language and area studies major, and I had never had an accounting course in my life. I soon found that I was not alone. More than half the BTC enrollees were liberal arts majors. GE believed it was the trainee's *ability*, rather than his or her undergraduate major, that mattered.

All of the GE training programs had six common characteristics:

1. *The programs recruited from the best technical high schools, colleges, and universities.* The apprentices were recruited from the best high schools; the engineering and BTC program candidates came from the best colleges and universities. The recruiters' focus was on the candidates' ability to learn, not just on their experience. This candidate selection process resulted in programs being filled with excellent and committed students. It also resulted in strong relationships between GE and the best high schools, colleges, and universities.

2. *The GE training programs focused on the GE Way of doing things.* Even if you were a skilled engineer or accountant, you often had to forget what you had learned in school and relearn the GE Way. Some of the trainees found this difficult, so it was often easier for GE to hire those with less education in an area and train them than it was for GE to convert those who already believed they knew how to do it. (My lack of previous accounting knowledge made it easier for me to learn the GE Way, in contrast to those participants who already had accounting degrees and had to "unlearn" what they already knew and then relearn the GE Way.)
3. *The program trainers assigned challenging work.* All of the programs used work assignments that were designed to help the participants practice what they were taught. GE was able to develop such challenging teaching materials because the program administrators assigned a "mentor" and "counselor" to each student to help him or her learn and adapt.
4. *The programs included tests and work appraisals.* The BTC, for instance, had Saturday morning examinations at the end of each course, and these three- to four-hour exams were as rigorous as any college or university exam. Numeric grades were given and posted for all to see, just as they would have been in college. (I was amazed at having to take exams and get grades. I was equally amazed at how competitive the program was.)
5. *Up or out.* Throughout its history one of GE's strengths has been its willingness to focus on the best and "prune" those not making the grade. So too did the company let go of those students in its training programs who couldn't get the grades GE was looking for. The company used a combination of exams and work assignment appraisals to determine whether a trainee would (a) continue in the program, (b) be asked to leave the program but be allowed to stay with the company, or (c) be asked to leave the company outright.
6. *GE gave certificates, not advanced degrees.* Though the GE training programs were intensive and demanding, the graduates received only a GE certificate and not an advanced degree. This was done to ensure that the graduates stayed with GE and were less marketable on the open market. This policy has been changed in recent years and will be discussed further in Chapter 14.

A PIONEER IN EQUAL OPPORTUNITY EMPLOYMENT

Coffin and his management team focused on talent regardless of race, religion, or national origin. There are several noteworthy illustrations of the company's willingness to hire minorities. As one example, we have already mentioned how GE purchased Rudolph Eickemeyer's company as a way to get Charles Steinmetz, who was Jewish and suffered from physical handicaps.

Another noteworthy example is that of Lewis Howard Latimer, the self-educated son of a black slave. Latimer was awarded his first patent in 1874, and he aided Alexander Graham Bell in his patent filings. In 1884, Latimer became a drafter-engineer for the newly formed Edison Electric Light Company, and six years later he became a drafter and patent expert in the company's legal department. He later joined the Board of Patent Control as the chief drafter and full-time patent consultant.[8]

SHARED LEADERSHIP IS BORN

Many companies are led by highly autocratic, dominant individuals who stifle creativity and the insights and inputs of others. In contrast, since early in its history, GE has had a "shared-leadership approach." It began with Coffin, when he hired Edwin Rice to succeed him.

When Coffin decided to step down as CEO, he selected his close associate Edwin W. Rice, Jr., to succeed him. Rice had the opportunity to go to college but instead decided to create Thomson-Houston—with Elihu Thomson—to develop an entire range of electrical equipment, from generators to meters. Rice's own inventions included a voltage regulator used on Thomson-Houston dynamos. But his real talents lay in manufacturing management. At the age of 22, he became Thomson-Houston's Lynn, Massachusetts, factory manager.

With the formation of General Electric in 1892, Rice got a chance to exercise his administrative talents on a larger stage. He became GE's first technical director, and in 1896 he was appointed vice president of manufacturing and engineering. In this post, he recognized the need to supplement the empirical techniques of the Edison/Thomson era with modern science and mathematics. He was impressed with Steinmetz's genius. With Rice's strong backing, Steinmetz rose to the post of consulting engineer.

Rice—reserved and judicial in temperament—succeeded Charles Coffin as president of GE in 1913. Shortly after his appointment, however, Coffin became concerned about Rice's limitations as a business executive, so he decided to develop a new shared-leadership approach for the company. Under this arrangement, Coffin continued as chairman of the board, focusing on long-term planning and maintaining the strong relationships he had built over the years with customers, regulators, and other external stakeholders.

Shared leadership subsequently emerged as one of the hallmarks of GE. Both Coffin and Rice were highly respected, both inside and outside the company. Although their personalities and talents were very different, they both had strong leadership skills. Having the benefit of a *pair* of strong leaders reduced the chances of GE's falling victim to the whims of an individual or becoming "captured" by a single dominant point of view. Contrast this with the experience of the Ford Motor Company. Henry Ford's single-mindedness was an asset in the founding years of that company, but over the years, his authoritarian streak and his rigidity almost destroyed the company.

As I studied GE leaders and management, it became clear that GE has embraced a shared-leadership approach more or less continuously since the combination of Coffin and Rice. The company has divided responsibilities for internal and external leadership across two (or more) strong-minded individuals, and for nearly a century it has derived great benefit from that approach.

Coffin and Rice moved the company from its infancy into its adolescence. They built an enduring foundation of products, relationships, philosophy, and people.

In 1922—as we will see in the next chapter—they turned over the company to a remarkable team, which proceeded to transform the company into the leader of the electrical industry worldwide.

TAKEAWAYS

Let's look again at the material in this chapter through the LATIN lens—leadership, adaptability, talent, influence, and networks—and ask the all-important question: So what?

Leadership

Coffin was a participative and consultative leader who was willing to share his leadership and authority. This was vital to getting the newly merged company fully integrated.

- What is your leadership style? Is it the most appropriate style for your organization's current situation?
- Do you share power and seek out the opinions and insights of others both inside and outside the organization?

Adaptability

GE readily changed its approaches—even its core strategies—when it became clear they were no longer viable. For instance, it established EBASCO to finance utilities when it was clear that it could no longer afford the risk of providing the financing itself. It acquired the members of NELA when the government required that the organization be dissolved. It strengthened its own legal organization when the Board of Patent Control was declared illegal.

- Are you willing to change your way of doing business, or do you defend a strategy of dubious long-term viability?
- Are you willing to form alliances and—when it makes sense—share both risks and rewards?

Talent

GE was willing to recruit the best people, even when that required taking extraordinary steps (such as purchasing an entire company to get one genius). GE's leaders looked past superficial issues such as skin color, religion, or physical appearance. The company established programs to recruit the best people, thereby ensuring that it had the skills onboard to execute its strategies.

- Do you hire the best, regardless of personal characteristics (for example, race, religion, appearance, or political beliefs) that don't bear on business issues?
- Are you willing to invest in the development of your employees?

Influence

GE proactively influenced government policies concerning patents and licenses, and it used alliances to gain and maintain strong market positions. But the company also proactively tested these relationships in the courts, and it was prepared to regroup when an existing approach proved unsustainable.

- Do you influence federal, state, and local governments to enhance and sustain your competitive position? Do you have an alternative strategy in place for the day when external circumstances (for example, an adverse court ruling) make an existing approach no longer viable?

Networks

GE installed strong accounting and financial systems and then used them to operate the company in a disciplined way. The company established a strong research and development program and then protected its intellectual properties aggressively.

- Do you have strong and transparent accounting and financial systems?
- Have you created mechanisms for producing a continuing flow of innovative products and services?
- Are your patents and copyrights protected globally? Do you aggressively defend them?

CHAPTER

Seeking Advice and Sharing the Wealth

FOR GE, the period from 1922 to 1939 is best captured by the opening line of Charles Dickens's *A Tale of Two Cities*: "It was the best of times, it was the worst of times."

The first seven years were clearly the best of times, as growth and prosperity spread worldwide. The consumer class was born. People in the developed world were able to earn enough not only to survive but also to build homes, acquire automobiles, purchase radios, and even invest in companies. Many discovered the phenomenon of Wall Street—a wealth-generation machine formerly restricted to the already rich few—and they began speculating heavily. It was, in the words of one commentator of the day, an "entrepreneurial riot."

Because many European economies had been devastated by the sustained carnage of World War I, American companies often found they had a new competitive advantage on the world stage. Though antitrust laws were passed to limit the power of monopolies, there were still strong, international cartels that influenced, even dominated, many industries, including the electrical markets.

But then came the Great Depression: the worst of times. This was a period of massive layoffs, bankruptcies, bread lines and soup kitchens, and increasing violence and social unrest. Many of those investors who had been swept up in the Wall Street euphoria of the 1920s lost everything and found themselves destitute.

Among other things, this led to an increasing concern about mitigating the impact of poverty and protecting workers' rights, in part by providing social security, pensions, unemployment benefits, and life and disability insurance. Governments became more aggressive in their regulation of business and passed laws that enhanced the power of unions while decreasing the influence of corporations.

Toward the end of the 1930s, the specter of global conflagration arose again. In Europe, a resurgent Germany first threatened and then invaded its neighbors. Eventually, Great Britain stood alone against Hitler's forces. President Franklin D. Roosevelt scrambled to find a way to aid the United Kingdom without antagonizing America's powerful isolationists. He eventually came up with the so-called Lend-Lease program, which—as it turned out—not only served as England's lifeline but greatly enhanced the manufacturing clout of the United States.

For all of these reasons, and more, this was a period that called for business leaders—corporate executives who were able to take full advantage of the overheated growth of the Roaring Twenties and subsequently deal with economic collapse. These business leaders had to enable their companies to survive and also to withstand the pressures of government controls and the increasing power of unions.

GE was blessed with such leadership. The team of Gerard Swope and Owen D. Young was skilled at making hay while the sun shone—but they also kept the company profitable in the Depression years, even though gross revenues dropped by a staggering 75 percent (see Exhibit 3-1).

GE asked its workers to shoulder some of the burden. In some of the business units, for example, employees worked only four days a week to help avoid layoffs. But the company also did its share. It instituted innovative pension, insurance, and unemployment policies to help employees, and—not incidentally—hold on to its best people. And management *listened*.

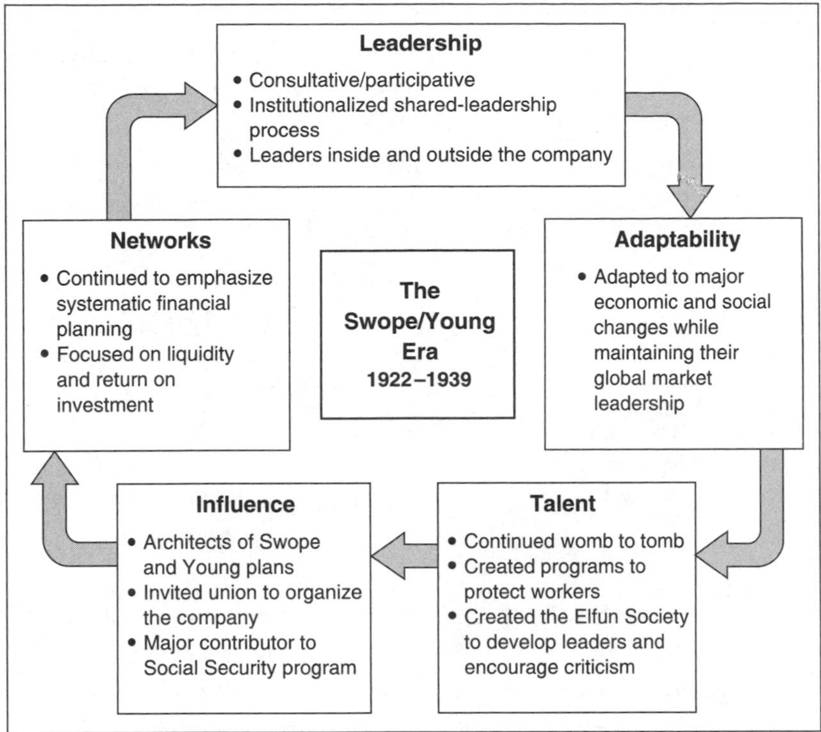
Leadership
• Consultative/participative
• Institutionalized shared-leadership process
• Leaders inside and outside the company
Networks
• Continued to emphasize systematic financial planning
• Focused on liquidity and return on investment
The Swope/Young Era 1922–1939
Adaptability
• Adapted to major economic and social changes while maintaining their global market leadership
Influence
• Architects of Swope and Young plans
• Invited union to organize the company
• Major contributor to Social Security program
Talent
• Continued womb to tomb
• Created programs to protect workers
• Created the Elfun Society to develop leaders and encourage criticism

Exhibit 3-1 LATIN and the Swope/Young era.

Swope and Young sought out the opinions and recommendations of their management ranks by creating a unique management association, the Elfun Society. They even invited a union to organize GE so that the company could avoid the violence and strikes that were becoming endemic in the automobile, coal, and transportation industries.

Both of GE's leaders made significant contributions to government policies. Young, for example, helped draft the post–World War I German reparations policy, which informally became known as the "Young Plan." For his part, Swope developed cornerstones of President Roosevelt's New Deal, including the National Recovery Act and the Social Security Administration.

THE NEW GE LEADERSHIP TEAM

In 1922, Coffin and Rice retired and appointed another leadership team to take over the company. The team consisted of Gerard Swope as president and Owen D. Young as chairman. Once again, there was a clear division of labor: GE's president would serve as the chief executive and operating officer of the company, and its chairman would focus on external affairs and longer-term strategies.

Gerard Swope was an 1895 graduate of MIT, with a bachelor of science in electrical engineering. Upon graduation, he joined Western Electric, held numerous management positions, and became an expert in international business. Charles Coffin hired Swope in 1919 to lead his newly formed International General Electric Company (IGE), which was the foreign sales and export arm of the company until the mid-1960s. In 1922, Coffin appointed Swope the president of the parent company.

Swope was far from the typical corporate leader. Among other things, he was Jewish, an avowed Zionist, and a socialist. A GE associate once summarized his career and his personality as follows:

> **Probably no man in his generation has been more ardently devoted to his country and its interests and more willing to devote his great energies and abilities unsparingly to this work than Gerard Swope. These qualities have manifested themselves in everything with which he has come into contact. And in all his activities, whether as business executive or economic leader, his thinking is of a fundamental and analytic quality undoubtedly influenced by his engineering training.[1]**

Owen D. Young was the other member of this unique leadership team. After graduating from Boston University Law School, he joined a major law firm. His success in winning several cases against GE led Coffin to offer him a job as GE's chief counsel and vice president in charge of policy.

Young was a talented conciliator and mediator. His ability to achieve agreement among people of widely diverging views came into full play in 1919, when—at the request of the government—he created the Radio Corporation of America to combat threatened foreign control of America's struggling radio industry. He served as RCA's board chairman until 1929. Because of his work with the Dawes Committee, which focused on the difficult issue of German reparations, *Time* magazine named him its 1929 "Man of the Year."

During their 17-year tenure, these two remarkable leaders were able to grow GE, defend it against foreign competitors, initiate a major new venture (RCA), and mitigate the misery and perils of the Great Depression.

WE WELCOME YOUR CRITICISM

Swope and Young were consultative leaders, who actively sought out and used the advice of their management. The creation in 1928 of the Elfun Society, an independent management association, serves as a remarkable illustration. In effect, the Swope/Young team set up a mechanism whereby managers and professionals could challenge the company's policies and strategies without fear of retribution—and indeed, with the expectation that their criticisms would be heard and valued.

The Elfun Society had five objectives:

1. To *provide a forum for GE managers* through which the managers could give their insights, critiques, and recommendations to the Swope/Young team
2. To enable GE managers and professionals to *create personal wealth* by investing in other companies via one of the first mutual funds
3. To *recognize the company leaders*
4. To provide an opportunity for managers and professionals to *develop their leadership skills*
5. To *create a fraternal spirit* that would cut across all of the businesses

GE'S NOVEL SOCIETY

Gerard Swope explained his concept of this novel society in a remarkable statement, which—although long—deserves to be included and read in its entirety:

> We have in the whole General Electric Company 75,000 people of whom approximately 900 (1.2% of the total) are participating in the investment in the Electrical Funds. In this group,

which represents the brains and the leadership of the Company, not only along executive but research and engineering lines, is the hope for the future.

I have thought it would be fine to organize this group more effectively than we have in the past, not as a part of the General Electric organization, but bringing the members of this group into a Society which would be their own, which would be separate and independent of the Company, and where we can have an open forum for discussion, where any question may be asked and will bring somebody to his feet to answer it.

We would like to have this body just as critical, just as radical as they feel the circumstances demand. If we could fill this body of executives and leading men with the spirit of adventure to try even unheard of things, the Company would either make progress or go broke, and the older of us would try our best to keep it from going broke.

Maybe you will think it is a curious thing for the man who happens to be President of the great organization, the General Electric Company, to be asking for such an open forum, where critical and radical thoughts may be expressed. I do not think that big organization is asleep, but I am sure that it is not awake to the great opportunity of doing even greater and better things than we have in the past. If we go forward with this *spirit of adventure*, we are sure to have better chances of accomplishing something.

And this is the basis on which I ask you to consider organizing this group into an informal society, which will be separate and distinct from the organization of the General Electric Company; to adopt a simple name, a simple constitution and by-laws, and choose officers who will represent you and to whom you can send whatever suggestions you wish, and put yourself and your vitality into it. And in the future, the President of this organization will preside at these informal meetings, which, as I said before, should be kept separate and apart from any regularly organized activity of the Company.[2]

The society adopted the name "Elfun," which was a contraction of the words *electrical funds*. Within a year of its founding, 12 geographically oriented chapters were established, with 841 members. They adopted, as Elfun's slogan, the Latin phrase "*Semper Paratus*"—"Always Ready" and like a fraternity even had their own emblem, which members proudly displayed on their suits and ties (see Exhibit 3-2).[3]

Thus was set the original philosophy that guided Elfun throughout its first two decades. Forum meetings, spirited debate, and an Elfun suggestion activity were some of the techniques used to prompt self-scrutiny to the benefit of GE.

Meanwhile, in conjunction with the Elfuns, Swope created one of the world's first mutual funds: the Elfun Funds. This fund invested in a portfolio of companies and enabled its owners to create personal wealth. Remarkably, the Elfun Funds focused on finding suitable investments *other than GE stock*. Swope did not want his managers to have all their eggs in one basket—even the GE basket—so he set up mechanisms for individual portfolio diversification. These funds still exist today and are part of the GE Fund family.

Exhibit 3-2 The symbol the Elfuns adopted to show how the members met under the elms. (*Source*: www.elfun.org/history.)

CIO: PLEASE ORGANIZE OUR COMPANY

Swope and Young didn't ask for the opinions of just their management; they also sought advice and counsel from labor unions.

Of course, this was not unprecedented in GE's history. In 1918, Coffin had established Works Councils to get worker input and to help management understand the employees' perspectives. These councils continued in operation until 1928, when the Wagner Act—also known as the National Recovery Act (NRA)—was enacted.

The NRA was interpreted by the courts to mean that organizations such as the Works Councils were equivalent to "company unions" and were therefore unconstitutional. It is ironic that the NRA turned out to be the cause of the decline and fall of the Works Councils since—as will be described later in this chapter—Swope was one of the architects of that landmark piece of legislation.

In 1930, Swope approached the American Federation of Labor (AFL) and asked it to form a union within GE so that he could continue to have the benefit of workers' insights and recommendations. This was consistent with Swope's own socialistic leanings, and it certainly represented his judgment about what would be best for the company. But the AFL considered itself a craft union rather than an industrial union, and it therefore refused to organize the company.

When the Congress of Industrial Unions (CIO) was formed to represent industrial workers, Swope soon asked it to organize GE. The CIO's leaders accepted, and they formed the United Electrical Union (UE) to organize and represent General Electric's hourly employees.

By all accounts, the union was delighted with what it found at GE. "The contract and conditions of GE workers," the UE noted, "were comparable to, and in some ways better than, those in other major industries such as auto, steel and rubber, and others."[4]

Swope and Young's attitudes and actions toward organized labor were highly unusual for the time. Most of the major companies resisted—even violently fought—the unionization of their workers. There were bloody riots in the automobile, coal, and steel industries, and union organizers were beaten and killed.

The electrical industry did not escape this strife: Emerson Electric in St. Louis suffered through the longest sit-down strike in U.S. history up to that point. But Swope and Young completely sidestepped this type of bitter conflict. In fact, there were no strikes at all at GE until 1947, after the Swope/Young team was gone and a new team had adopted a very different philosophy toward unions and workers.

To encourage all employees to provide recommendations on how the company could improve its operations and products, GE introduced one of the first formal suggestion systems. A management committee evaluated these suggestions, and if they were adopted, the employees were awarded a percentage of the savings.

On a personal note, while a member of the Employee Relations Program in the distribution transformer department in Pittsfield, Massachusetts, I was responsible for administrating the suggestion system at that facility. At that time, all suggestions had to be submitted in written form. I thought that it would be useful to incorporate new technology into the submission process, so I set up a tape recorder, encased it in a large "golden ear," and encouraged employees to record their ideas.

This approach succeeded in stimulating more suggestions, but—I have to admit—it also elicited some anonymous comments that were not printable, let alone "implementable." From this experience, I learned firsthand of the wisdom of Swope and Young: Employees *did* have many good ideas, and—given the right encouragement and incentives—they *could* help make GE's operations more efficient, productive, and cost-effective.

PROTECT THE EMPLOYEES

Swope and Young continued to build a strong farm system that encouraged employees and managers to make a lifetime commitment to the company. GE emerged ever more clearly as a womb-to-tomb organization. The entry-level training programs that were initiated by Coffin were expanded and institutionalized, and the Elfun meetings at Association Island served as an early forerunner of more formal types of executive education.

But the GE leadership team went beyond just providing a career path and developing its employees' skills. It introduced a number of unique programs to protect the employees and help them prepare for the future. For example, health and life insurance programs were introduced to ensure that the employees' widows and children were protected if the employee was injured, got sick, or died. This program was unique at this time.

SHARING THE DEPRESSION BURDEN

In 1929, the stock market collapsed, and the world suffered the greatest economic depression in modern times. As noted, GE's revenues dropped more than 75 percent during this period. In comparison to many of their peers, who instituted sweeping layoffs—and in many cases put skilled and loyal employees out on the street—Swope and Young were both more compassionate and more pragmatic. They recognized that if they wanted to keep talented people, they would have to take steps to minimize the Depression's impact on them.

Three key programs were introduced:

1. *Unemployment benefits.* GE provided loans and relief to those workers the company could not continue to employ.
2. *Guaranteed work program.* GE's electric lamp business allowed workers to share the pain. Instead of just laying off 20 percent of the workforce, it instituted a program that allowed employees to reduce their work hours from five days a week to four. Because each worker took a 20 percent reduction in pay, the program permitted GE to keep everyone employed.
3. *Profit sharing in the 1930s.* Another important innovation of the Swope/Young era was the introduction, in 1930, of a profit-sharing plan. This was unique in several ways. First, it was offered at a time when many companies were having trouble simply surviving. Second, it was offered to all employees, regardless of their position in the company. Again, this plan was consistent with the socialistic philosophies held by Swope and supported by Young.

THE GE PENSION TRUST

Coffin initiated GE's first pension program in 1912. This was a noncontributory form of pension. These types of pension programs were very popular with the workers because they didn't have to make personal contributions, so they appeared to be a free benefit. The limitation of this type of pension, of course, was that it was completely dependent on the health of the company. If the company went bankrupt or was liquidated, the pension disappeared with the company, leaving the workers with no pension at all.

Swope and Young recognized this limitation, so—in 1923—they established a unique pension trust that protected the worker from this problem. This defined-benefit program required that both the employees and the company make contributions, and its capacity as a trust meant that it was protected by law and that workers could collect from the trust even if the company were no longer in business.

The creation of a trust was highly innovative for the time, and it has helped GE avoid many of the problems that most U.S. companies—including giants such as IBM and GM—have experienced in the recent past. The trust required that the money be used exclusively for pensions, and it also required that the company fund it annually. But if the trust could earn enough to fund itself GE had no obligation to contribute during that year.

GE PENSION TRUST IS A WIN-WIN EVEN TODAY

GE's approach to funding pensions has had positive results both for the employees and the company. The employees know that they will have a pension regardless of the company's performance, and the company is not saddled with obligations it may not be able to fulfill. It is worth noting that many companies today are being negatively impacted by their pension contributions, and some have even gone into bankruptcy to get out from under their pension obligations.

Unlike other companies that had outsiders manage their pensions, General Electric has managed its own pension funds. Based on information provided by the company in its annual reports and the Web site of the GE Workers United, it is clear that GE has done a great job managing these pension funds and has met its pension requirements while generating a significant amount of earnings for the company.

Let's review some of the facts about the GE pension program today:

- As of December 2005, GE provided its guaranteed pensions to 628,000 active employees, vested former employees, and retirees, and it had grown the trust assets to more than $50 billion.[5]

- The company has not had to contribute any money to the trust since 1987 and doesn't plan to contribute any funds to the plan in 2006. In fact, the pension funds have contributed more than $13 billion in earnings to the company since 1990.[6]

SHARING THE WEALTH IS A KEY TO GE'S SUCCESS

Unquestionably, the Swope/Young era employee-protection plans have become a major contributor to GE's overall success. The company has continued to create and implement programs before they became commonplace—and in many cases, before they were demanded. Even though Swope was a socialist and provided these programs because it was consistent with his personal philosophies, his successors have continued and have even improved on the benefits and pension programs.

I am not in a position to judge Swope and Young's successors' motivations. It seems clear, however, that they have believed that it is vital to reward and protect employees, key professionals, and managers, and they have taken steps to foster employee loyalty and commitment to the company.

HEALTH AND HAPPINESS

Swope and Young did more that just provide for the economic and work health of all of their employees. The major plant locations had clinics to care for the workers if they desired to use them. They also maintained recreational, baseball, football, basketball facilities and teams, golf clubs, and dining clubs for the employees at all levels to help them keep fit and to provide entertainment. This was notably different from the policies of other companies, which tended to restrict these perks to their senior executives.

Again on a personal note: In 1955, I was assigned to study the utilization and cost effectiveness of the Schenectady recreational facilities. I concluded that many of the facilities were no longer needed because (1) there were equivalent community facilities by that time, and (2) GE employees clearly preferred these community facilities and activities and didn't use the GE offerings. As a result, many of these facilities were closed, and the GE funds were turned over to their community equivalents such as the YMCA and YWCA.

INFLUENCING PUBLIC PROGRAMS

Swope became one of the architects of the National Recovery Act, the National Labor Relations Board, and Social Security.

SWOPE'S CONTRIBUTION TO THE NEW DEAL

Gerard Swope strongly believed that U.S. companies should be permitted to participate in associations to enhance industry growth and profitability. That was the capitalist and oligarch in Swope. At the same time, he equally believed that workers needed to be protected with insurance, unemployment benefits, and pensions.

His brother, Herbert Bayard Swope, a Pulitzer Prize–winning editor of the *New York World*, was a close friend of Bernard Baruch, and President Roosevelt used his talents as an unofficial envoy during the New Deal period.

Because of his reputation, skills, and brother's connections, Gerard Swope played a significant role in the Roosevelt New Deal programs and policies. His two most noteworthy contributions were the National Recovery Act (originally called the "Swope Plan") and the creation of Social Security. Both of these contributions were highly consistent with what Swope had done in General Electric to grow the company, stabilize the electrical industry, and protect the workers.

THE SWOPE PLAN: LEGALIZED CARTELS TO PROTECT BUSINESS AND EMPLOYEES

On May 22, 1933, at a U.S. Senate Finance Hearing, Senator Thomas P. Gore condemned the Swope Plan as follows:

> **I think this plan is as revolutionary as anything that happened in this country in 1776 or in France in 1789 or in Italy under Mussolini or in Russia under Stalin.[7]**

At the time, others concluded that:

> **Although the New Deal and its most significant component, the National Recovery Administration (NRA), are generally presented as the progeny of FDR's brain trust, as we have seen the essential principles had been worked out in detail long before FDR and his associates came to power. The FDR group did little more than put the stamp of academic approval to an already prepared plan.**
>
> **The Roosevelt NRA was in its details a plan presented by Gerard Swope (1872–1957), long-time president of General Electric Company. This Swope Plan was in turn comparable to a German plan worked out in World War I by his opposite number Walter Rathenau, head of German General Electric (Allgemeine Elektizitäts Gesellschaft) in Germany, where it was known as the Rathenau Plan. In sum, the Swope Plan was a transparent device to lay the groundwork for the corporate state by defusing potential labor opposition with a massive welfare carrot. The Swope Plan and Bernard Baruch's earlier and similar proposal became the Roosevelt National Recovery Act."[8]**

Harsh language, perhaps, but not totally inaccurate. The Swope Plan *was* radical, at least by the standards of the day. Here are some of the highlights of the plan:

1. *Industrial trade associations* were created, and all companies that employed more than 50 workers were required to join the appropriate trade association within three years. These associations worked like the cartels, effectively allocating market share, fixing prices, and requiring all members to follow their rulings.
2. *The Federal Trade Commission* was deputized to oversee the associations and industries and to ensure that they operated both legally and fairly.
3. *Workers* were given life and disability insurance, pensions, unemployment benefits, and workers' compensation.

Again, these were sweeping changes, but there was nothing in the Swope Plan that should have surprised people who knew about (1) Gerard Swope's socialistic political leanings and (2) what he and Young had done to grow GE and protect the company's workers. Simply put, he advocated the sharing of the wealth, and—under extremely trying circumstances—thereby created a win-win solution for all the key stakeholders.

GUARANTEED PENSIONS FOR ALL AMERICAN WORKERS

The Swope Plan proposed to Roosevelt that the entire country install a "GE type pension trust plan" that would ensure that the workers were able to not only survive but also enjoy the fruits of their labor in retirement. Swope was a major contributor to the Social Security Act of 1935, which created the following:

1. An old-age pension system funded by contributions from workers and employers
2. A system of unemployment insurance funded by employers alone
3. Several programs of social welfare supported by ordinary public funds for such particularly needy groups as single mothers with children in the home, the elderly poor, and the disabled[9]

In short, it provided the foundation for the modern welfare state, about which people have had strong opinions ever since. But again, Swope's participation in the creation of the Social Security system should not have come as a surprise. He was simply applying what he learned at GE to a similar problem on the national stage. Unfortunately, for a variety of reasons, the Social Security program has not proven as financially healthy as the GE pension plan, and it therefore is less likely to provide the level of benefits that some people have been counting on for their retirements.

BEING POLITICALLY INCORRECT IS OKAY

Part of the uniqueness of Swope's contributions was his willingness to take a public stance on a major and controversial public-policy issue such as Social Security. But he was not alone in this kind of courage. His partner, Owen D. Young, behaved similarly when he agreed to help figure out whether and how Germany would pay reparations to the victorious Allies after World War I.

Though a Democrat, Young took on this knotty problem for Herbert Hoover's Republican administration. His contribution lay in designing a program that would allow Germany to pay its war-related debts and still survive the crushing impact of the Depression. A successor to the Dawes Plan, it became known as the "Young Plan."

There were numerous critics of the Young Plan, and some believed that it helped Hitler gain power by contributing to Germany's economic and political destablization. Nevertheless, in 1929 Young was named *Time* magazine's "Man of the Year" for his contribution to this major international effort. He also was considered to be a potential candidate for the presidency of the United States, but he declined this honor.

He continued serving the public even after his retirement from GE. In 1946, for example, New York governor Thomas E. Dewey called upon him to head the state commission that laid the groundwork for the state university system in New York—a contribution that would benefit many generations of young people.

STEINMETZ: ANOTHER SOCIALIST LEADER

Both Swope and Young, therefore, were willing to provide public service and contribute to major socioeconomic and political issues, even at the risk of having their reputations impugned and attacked. I should point out that this willingness was not just limited to the senior management. Another key GE leader who demonstrated a willingness to help solve social problems was Charles Proteus Steinmetz.

In Chapter 2, I described how Coffin was so impressed with the genius of Steinmetz that he acquired the company that Steinmetz was working for so that he could get him to join General Electric. But Steinmetz was more than a great scientist; he was also highly active in local social and socialist causes. He served as president of the Schenectady Common Council, and he also served six years on the Schenectady Board of Education, four of them as its president. In Schenectady at that time, some students were able to attend school only half a day due to lack of classroom space. Steinmetz pushed successfully to get more schools built in the city, resolving the space crisis and extending the school day for many students.[10]

TAKEAWAYS
Leadership

Coffin was a consultative and participative leader, and his successors Swope and Young took this commitment to a higher level by creating ways for managers and employees to contribute to the company's strategies and policies. Their invitation to the CIO to organize the company without conflict was another unique contribution to participative and consultative leadership.

- *Recommendation.* Determine what you can do to increase the participation and contribution of all key employees at all levels. Consider the idea of an independent association to enable employees and others to provide insights without the threat of being considered untrustworthy or uncooperative.

Sharing the wealth. Swope and Young and their successors have been willing to share the profits of the company among all key stakeholders and not just maximize the returns for a few.

- *Recommendation.* Ask how willing you are to share the wealth fairly. Unfortunately, many executives today are willing to lay off people, close plants, and even harvest their companies for personal gain. Where do your personal needs stop, and when does the greater good start to get considered?

Talent and rewards. Swope and Young ensured that their human resource programs went beyond training; they included benefits, pensions, and other reward systems to enable the employees to grow and prosper and to look forward to their retirements with confidence. However, it must be emphasized that Swope and Young required that employees contribute to their pensions and benefits and not get a free lunch.

- *Recommendation.* Review your total human resource strategy and be sure that it includes the type of benefits and perks that will attract and retain key people. It is not enough to just train and develop people; you must include a concern for key benefits. At this time, the kinds of health and pension programs that Swope and Young installed are being challenged and even eliminated at many companies. But this can be a major mistake, since it may signal a lack of interest in the "full needs" of people.

Influencing key stakeholders. Clearly, Swope and Young went beyond their corporate duties, narrowly defined, when they helped resolve major economic, societal, and political problems. They led during one of the most turbulent times in our nation's history, and—despite personal attacks—they were consistently willing to help.

- *Recommendation.* Ask how willing you are to help, even if—as a result—you come under scrutiny, heat, and even attack. How willing are you to take a stand and make a contribution?

CHAPTER

Staying No. 1

NOW LET'S look a little more closely at the growth strategies that GE embraced in the 1920s and 1930s, which continued the company's evolution to being one of the world's most powerful and successful organizations.

When Swope and Young took over, the electrical industry was still in its early growth stages. They recognized that GE needed to help stimulate electrical demand so that the electric utilities would continue to grow and purchase new systems and upgrade their existing systems. Coffin had already started on this path, but it was Swope and Young who enhanced and perfected this process of stimulating electrical demand, known as the "Benign Cycle."

SWOPE AND YOUNG GROWTH STRATEGIES

- Benign Cycle strategy
- Retailer franchising

- Controlling retail prices: consignment selling
- Financing the retailer and consumer: GE Credit
- Aggressive advertising and promotion
- Relationship selling
- RCA venture: using core competencies to diversify
- Using equity and licenses to protect domestic markets

In order to stimulate consumer and industrial demand, GE combined selective acquisitions and internal developments to produce an array of new electrical consumer, industrial, and commercial products.

In addition, the leadership team created strategies and programs to enable it to control structures and pricing at both the wholesale and retail levels so that electrical products would not degenerate into commodities.

On the world scene, the team led organizations to maintain their strong patents and inhibit foreign competitors from taking market share. Using the company's telecommunications skills, GE ventured with Westinghouse to form RCA. The leadership team's strategies contributed to GE's growth in the 1920s and enabled the company to withstand revenue losses during the Great Depression.

Let's examine each of these strategies in more detail.

THE BENIGN CYCLE STRATEGY: STIMULATING ELECTRICAL DEMAND

Exhibit 4-1 is a diagram of the concept underlying the Benign Cycle strategy. In simple terms, it means that GE's key objective was to provide a continuing array of new electrically powered products, devices, and systems for all of its key market segments. These new products would increase the need for more electricity to be generated, transmitted, and distributed by the electric utilities. Utilities would have to purchase bigger and improved systems to expand their networks.

GE would benefit from not only selling these new products but also from selling its electric utility systems, products, and services. This is a very typical strategy for any network-based business, but GE helped pioneer the model and refined it to an extraordinary degree.

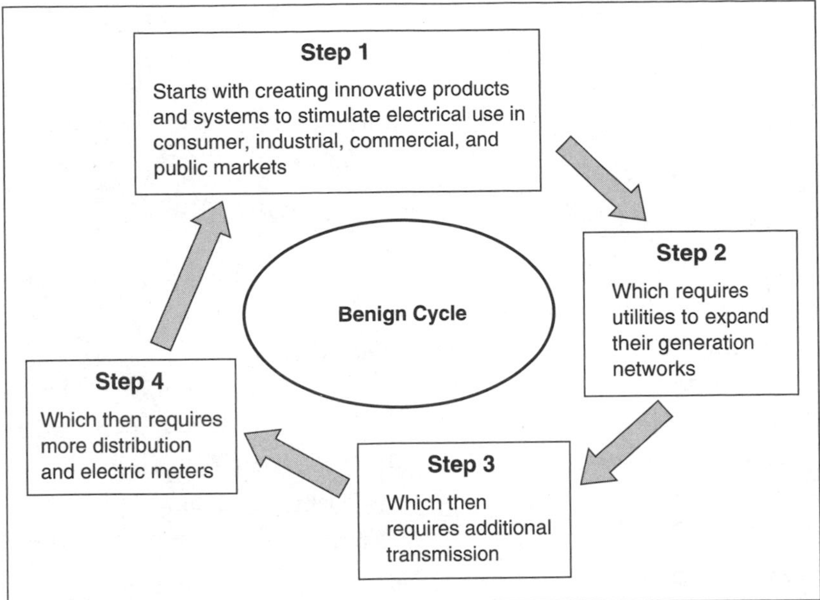
Step 1
Starts with creating innovative products and systems to stimulate electrical use in consumer, industrial, commercial, and public markets
Step 2
Which requires utilities to expand their generation networks
Step 3
Which then requires additional transmission
Step 4
Which then requires more distribution and electric meters
Benign Cycle

Exhibit 4-1 GE created innovative consumer and industrial products to stimulate electrical demand, which meant that utilities had to continuously add to and upgrade their generation, transmission, and distribution systems.

"LIVING BETTER ELECTRICALLY": THE CONSUMER PRODUCTS STRATEGY

Through a combination of internal developments, acquisitions, and cross-licensing, GE provided a new and rich array of products. These new offerings enabled consumers to cook and refrigerate their foods, wash and dry their clothes, vacuum their homes, and keep cool in the summer heat.

In 1919, Coffin had acquired Hotpoint, the developer of the electric stove. GE's R&D group improved the quality, safety, and effectiveness of the electric stove with the development of the Calrod heating units. Hurley Manufacturing Company, producer of the Thor line of electric washers and driers, was acquired and integrated into the new home appliance business. In 1927, GE added the innovative "monitor top" refrigerator to its line. Electric fans were introduced, enabling the consumer to cool off in the summer heat. Premier Vacuum Company, one of the innovators of the electric vacuum cleaner, came into the fold.

The cumulative message from all these innovations was clear: The consumer should enjoy life and "live better electrically." The GE monogram became synonymous with quality and innovation; it also became one of the most prized brands worldwide.

RETAILER FRANCHISING

Swope recognized that it was important to have quality retailers and distributors to sell these innovative products. Rather than setting up a network of GE-owned-and-operated stores, therefore, he created a retail franchise system.

Individual merchants were carefully selected to represent GE and to sell the GE product lines. Significantly, these retailers were granted an exclusive territory. They also were given business, accounting, and sales training, and they were supported by a strong advertising and sales promotion program.

CONTROLLING LAMP PRICES WITH AGENCY AGREEMENTS

In order to reduce the capital and cash needs of these independent businesses, GE instituted consignment selling and the agency system, similar to the approach it used in its electric lamp franchises.

Again, the strategy was straightforward: GE maintained ownership of the products from their manufacture to sale; the dealers and distributors never really owned the products that the consumer purchased. This permitted GE to set and enforce pricing at the retail level. The dealers had to follow the GE pricing guidelines, and they could discount the products only when there were company-authorized sales. As part of the GE franchise agreements, retailers could sell GE products only to consumers and not to other distributors or retailers. This prevented them from dumping excess stock and thereby eroding prices.

This was common practice at the time, and it is still used today in the automobile industry, where franchised outlets are controlled by the automakers.

Retailers were trained to provide after-sales repair and maintenance services and to be the exclusive provider of GE factory-authorized parts. The parts and service business was a very high margin revenue source because the parts were priced high and only authorized dealers could order and install them.

CONTROLLING RETAIL PRICES WITH CONSIGNMENT SELLING

Agency agreements were highly attractive for the dealers and distributors because it meant that they didn't have to use their own cash or credit to purchase the products. It also prevented discounting and price margin erosion. This pricing strategy was used by GE into the mid-1950s, and it was stopped when the fair-trade rules were declared illegal constraints of trade.

THE BIRTH OF GENERAL ELECTRIC CREDIT

GE also recognized that it was important to provide financing to its franchised dealers, which would enable them to purchase inventory and devise their own floor plans. Floor planning allowed the retailers to display and demonstrate the products so that consumers could see for themselves the value and unique features of the GE line.

In 1932, in order to offer these financial services to retailers and to provide consumer credit and financing, Swope formed the General Electric Credit Company (GECC). The GECC was a key element of the consumer strategy. It later became General Electric Capital Corporation, and it emerged as a major element in the Jones and Welch financial services strategies.

Becoming a GE-franchised dealer was very attractive, and franchises were difficult to get. This created a very loyal and strong retail structure. The arrangement lasted until the late 1950s, when the advent of discounters and (as noted above) the outlawing of fair-trade rules changed the relationships and economic value of authorized retail dealerships. (This will be discussed further in Chapter 6.)

AGGRESSIVE PUSH-AND-PULL ADVERTISING

Swope and his team recognized that another key element to creating consumer demand and increasing market size and growth was national and local advertising. Using the power of the GE monogram, GE developed very extensive consumer advertising and promotion. It combined getting the consumer into the GE retail store with training the retailer's sales force to *get the order*.

GE trained the sales force, and it also provided displays and promotional on-floor materials to improve the quality and effectiveness of those materials.

GENERAL ELECTRIC SUPPLY COMPANY: A WHOLESALER WHEN NEEDED

Wholesale distribution was another key element to this strategy. Like the retail marketplace, GE preferred to use independent distributors and wholesalers rather than having a company-owned wholesale network. Swope recognized, however, that this was not always possible.

Often, there were no qualified wholesalers in a region, especially in new regions. In other cases, the independents turned out to be not sufficiently skilled. In 1929, therefore, GE established the GE Supply Company. GE Supply handled a complete line of GE consumer, lighting, industrial, and commercial products, focusing primarily in areas where GE's distribution was weak or nonexistent. In some situations, it acquired existing wholesalers who were not able to compete or whose owners had retired or died and there was no one to continue the franchises. Note that Jeff Immelt decided to sell GE Supply to a French electrical supply company in 2006 so that the company could focus on higher-return business segments. Even though the new company would sell GE products, GE products represented only a small piece of the overall revenues.

RELATIONSHIP SELLING

Relationship selling has long been an integral part of GE's success. Coffin created strong relationships with the managers of electric utilities. Swope did the same in the consumer retail and distribution segments.

Like Coffin, Swope developed long-term partnerships with the retailers and provided them with the services they needed to succeed. In turn, the retailers were expected to build strong relationships in their communities, selling on value, innovation, and service rather than on price. The GE brand supported the retailers' ability to build consumer confidence in the company.

It is interesting to note that GE has never been a true "consumer company" in the sense that it has always relied on intermediaries to deal with the consumer. In fact, GE has treated the consumer business more like an industrial business, and it has prospered by establishing a network of selected intermediaries rather than by trying to sell directly to consumers.

USING STRENGTHS TO DIVERSIFY

Today, it is called "building on core competencies." In simple terms, growing your business often means (1) figuring out where you have a competitive advantage and (2) building on it.

Beginning with Swope, the company took several of its unique abilities and used them to create new ventures. One was in the broadcasting arena and the other in materials.

EARLY DIVERSIFICATION MOVES

Radio and Television

- 1922: Entered the radio broadcasting business with WGY in Schenectady, which broadcast the first U.S. radio drama (*The Wolf*)
- 1928: Began broadcasting television programs, including the first show ever to be on TV (*The Queen's Messenger*)
- 1940: Expanded broadcasting by relaying TV broadcasts from New York City and by starting FM broadcasting

Materials Innovations

- 1940: Started the silicones business by inventing new silicone chemistry[1]

Overall, the Swope/Young consumer strategy was a master stroke, and it made the GE brand and product line the best in the industry. True, the strategy followed the same logic as Coffin's, but it extended into a new key market that not only was a business of its own but also served as a means to sell more power equipment to the utilities. This strategy continued to work even through the Depression, and it changed only under the pressures of World War II.

GE AND WESTINGHOUSE CREATE RCA

In 1906, Ernst Alexanderson—a Swedish immigrant and GE engineer—developed the alternator that permitted voice transmission to become a reality, which became the keystone of the radio industry.

In 1915, Guglielmo Marconi, whose American Marconi Company had already purchased one of the Alexanderson alternators for broadcast purposes, agreed to pay $4 million for several more alternators. Under this contract, GE began installing a huge 200-kilowatt machine coincident with the United States' entry into World War I. Completed in 1918, the 200-kilowatt alternator broadcast news of the armistice across the Atlantic. The timing of these events—although entirely coincidental—convinced many in the government that radio was more than merely a communications tool; it was a vital national interest.

Franklin Delano Roosevelt, the assistant secretary of the Navy during World War I, did not want control of this technology to pass into foreign hands. Bowing to pressure from Roosevelt and others in government, GE subsequently refused to sell American Marconi any additional alternators. It was a devastating blow, since Marconi was convinced that the Alexanderson alternator was the only means by which he could span the globe with wireless communication. Marconi asked David Sarnoff, a young Russian émigré and technical genius, to evaluate the situation, and Sarnoff reached the same conclusion.

In 1919, Coffin proposed that American Marconi merge with GE. The proposal was accepted, and Radio Corporation of America was formed, co-owned by GE and Westinghouse. (GE owned 60 percent of the new company; Westinghouse owned the remaining 40 percent.) RCA was given access to the American patents of General Electric, AT&T, Westinghouse, United Fruit, and the U.S. Navy. RCA then purchased British Marconi's controlling interest in American Marconi.

David Sarnoff was appointed RCA's general manager, and Owen Young its chairman. Young, of course, continued to be GE's chairman. Because the newly created RCA had no manufacturing operations of its own, all RCA products were to be manufactured by GE and Westinghouse.

In 1922, AT&T established a radio station in New York (WEAF) and formed the Broadcasting Corporation of America, which it sold to RCA in 1926. RCA then established the National Broadcasting Company (NBC). RCA owned 50 percent of these shares, while GE had 30 percent and Westinghouse the remaining 20 percent.

In January 1928, the ever-innovative Ernst Alexanderson transmitted a video image three inches square from his lab to his home in Schenectady. This was the first video broadcast, and within four months, GE was transmitting images that were three times larger.

That same year, RCA divided its radio affiliates into RCA-Red and NBC-Blue, and RCA began broadcasting out of Schenectady the first regular schedule of U.S. television programming. In 1929, RCA purchased the Victor Talking Machine Company (originally an Edison-owned company) for $154 million.

David Sarnoff—an ambitious and visionary entrepreneur—was never pleased that RCA was controlled by GE and Westinghouse. He believed that both GE and Westinghouse were not capitalizing on the consumer and home markets and that they had focused too much on industrial and military radio applications.

Using his government contacts, Sarnoff was able to convince the U.S. Justice Department to launch an antitrust investigation into the "radio monopoly." In 1932, just before Roosevelt took office, the courts ruled that GE and Westinghouse should be required to divest their interest in RCA and make RCA an independent company. Sarnoff happily took control and led the company; eventually his son, Robert, succeeded him.

By any measure, GE and Westinghouse failed to get a fair return from this forced divestiture. GE received only $1 million and the new RCA headquarters at 570 Lexington Avenue in New York City, which in the 1950s became GE's headquarters. RCA moved to its famous Rockefeller Center building. Even worse, from the perspective of GE and Westinghouse, the parent companies lost their highly valuable radio and television patents—including those covering color television—and were prohibited from participating in new and rapidly growing markets.

WHY THE BROADCASTING MARKET WAS ATTRACTIVE TO GE

During my tenure as GE's corporate planner from 1980 to 1983, my department did an analysis of the types of businesses in which GE was most successful. Based on this work, it was clear that the broadcasting business was very attractive to GE because it possessed many of the same characteristics as the electrical business.

Both were network and technology based, which allowed GE to build a competitive advantage through (1) technological expertise and (2) a strong patent position. In addition, GE could sell to regulated customers, which provided a risk buffer and allowed the company to maintain high margins. There was a significant opportunity to develop and sell high-value radios, and later, televisions, that in turn would require new programs and more sophisticated systems, and thus create another version of the highly successful Benign Cycle strategy.

In fact, this is exactly what Sarnoff did with his "liberated" company. As a result, RCA was a very successful and profitable business until it changed its strategy in the 1970s.

Though both Swope and Young had strong contacts in the government and the public sector, it was clear that David Sarnoff was by far the more skilled politician. Taking advantage of public sentiment against Big Business, he was able to gain control of a major company in a rapidly growing market for almost nothing.

Another irony of GE's long and complex history: RCA later would play a major role in the success of Jack Welch. This will be discussed in detail in the chapters dealing with the Welch era.

OWNING EQUITY IN GLOBAL COMPETITORS

Swope started his GE career by establishing International General Electric (IGE), GE's wholly owned international subsidiary that was responsible for all exports and foreign licenses. During his tenure, Swope encouraged IGE to take equity positions in many of its foreign allies.

In Germany, for example, IGE took a 40 percent position in Allegemeine Elektizitäts-Gesellschaft (AEG, German General Electric), and it had three members on the AEG board, including Swope. IGE also acquired 16 percent of Osram, a major German electric lamp company, and 60 percent of Telefunken, a major player in the emerging radio industry.

And Germany was only one case among many. IGE took equity positions of various sizes in key electrical manufacturers around the world.

Table 4-1 depicts the largest percentage that IGE held in these major electrical companies and the year that this maximum share was owned.

Through this equity ownership, IGE exercised a strong influence on these partners, which provided GE with the means of controlling their competitive actions and prices. Although GE was especially aggressive in its overseas expansion, it was far from unique; most major American companies followed much the same strategy at this time.

THE PHOEBUS AGREEMENT

Also at this point in history, international cartels—aimed at fixing and controlling prices—were legal and were even promoted by governments around the world.

IGE was the reputed leader of the Phoebus Agreement, an international lighting cartel and the international equivalent of the National Electric Lamp Association. The following quote is from a 1920s-era antitrust document; it names the parties to this agreement and describes the enormous control and power they exercised:

Country	Company	Percent Owned	Years
Belgium	SEM	27	1927
England	AEI	59	1929
France	Alstrom	17	1931–47
	CFTH	10	1934
	Cie des lamps	37	1921–34
Hungary	UIL	13	1930
Italy	CGE	99	1938
Spain	GE Espanola	52	1941
	S.I.G.E	18	1930–43
Japan	Shibura Eng.	32	1920–32
	Tokyo Electric	57	1920–32
	Toshiba	31	1939

Table 4-1 The year and the largest percentage of GE's ownership of major electrical companies. For instance, GE owned 27 percent of Belgium's SEM until 1927.

> **A trade combination existed with the Electric Lamp Industry, viz., the Electric Lamp Manufacturers Association, which had been created primarily in the interests of three firms: the British Thomson-Houston Company, the General Electric Company, and Messrs. Siemens Brothers. The Association included from 90-95% of the industry, and controlled factors and retailers, fixed prices, and regulated output.[2]**

Cartels were defended by their advocates on the basis that they enabled smaller companies to survive and even prosper, as well as helped emerging markets to grow. In addition, they were not exactly like monopolies because there were competing cartels in each of the major industries, so no one cartel controlled the entire industry. To a certain extent, cartels served the same functions as alliances and joint ventures, which are still used today.

And, of course, there are cartels today. OPEC—the Organization of Petroleum Exporting Countries—is one of the best known and most powerful cartels in the world. It does all of the things that the Phoebus Agreement sought to do. It controls output and prices, and it decides which parts of the world will get its output. Today, most developed nations have antitrust laws that prohibit cartels in the name of stimulating competition, but some nations allow them to operate and even support them. In many cases—for example, in China and Dubai—the companies are owned by the government, which, of course, creates a far more powerful type of cartel.

In most industries today there is a wide variety of partnerships and cross-licensing arrangements that have some of the characteristics of a cartel. They are legal because, in most cases, they don't control output and pricing. Obviously, there are benefits to either providing or obtaining licenses, participating in trade associations, and creating teams and partnerships; the key is to recognize the distinction between *sharing* and *colluding*. Companies that fail to make this distinction run into trouble, and—as a result of illegal cooperation, price fixing, and other unethical and illegal acts—may be forced to liquidate those relationships.

Partnerships and alliances have always been integral parts of the GE culture. Recognizing their importance, Swope even tried to make cartels legal in the United States in his Swope Plan, which became the nucleus of the National Recovery Act.

TAKEAWAYS
Adaptability

Clearly, Swope and Young "took care of business." They instituted a complete and effective strategy to grow the electrical industry and to remain its leader. This involved all of the key elements of strategy. Like Coffin, they took advantage of what the laws permitted and used the laws effectively to grow the company. Their strategies are a textbook model for growing a market and industry.

- *Recommendation.* Review your strategy from the top to the bottom and make sure that it is internally consistent. Be sure that the programs fit the strategic priorities and the differentiators that you have selected. Continually test the legality of the programs and make sure they are within the law now; however, be prepared if the laws change in the future. The failure to attend to this obvious obligation has been a major contributor to the travails of many companies that have gotten into legal trouble in recent years.

Diversification and Decentralization

GE's Second Stage, 1940 to 1970
Wilson/Borch

HIGHLIGHTS

- *Winning the war*. General Electric and other major companies refocused their resources from consumer and industrial products and systems to the building of weapons, guidance systems, and propulsion systems and to the development of nuclear power. By the end of World War II, GE was no longer an electrical systems company but a highly diversified, technology-based giant.
- *Decentralization*. Unlike many other companies, the Cordiner/Reed team (1950 to 1963) decided that GE should remain diversified and not revert to focusing on just electrical systems. The company instituted a new organizational and management-by-objectives system to permit the top management to deal with the complexity and variety of participating in 21 industries.
- *Professional management*. Recognizing the need to develop professional managers who could manage in a variety of businesses, the company initiated the first company owned and operated manage-

ment development center to teach and apply best management and leadership techniques. In addition, the Cordiner/Reed team provided free consulting help to assure that the company was able to achieve both a return of 20 percent on its investment and 7 percent on its sales.

- *"Boulwarism" and the conversion of Ronald Reagan.* The Cordiner/Reed team was concerned about the increasing power of Big Government and Big Labor, and it responded by creating an innovative labor and government relations program that enabled the company to avoid being controlled and dominated by its unions and to counter unfriendly laws and regulations. Part of this program included the hiring of a future U.S. president, Ronald Reagan, to preach the gospel of free enterprise and the negatives of government bureaucracies and labor unions. Reagan became so convinced while making and conveying this message that he converted from being a liberal to being a conservative.
- *"Great Electrical Conspiracy."* Unfortunately, GE and its key electric utility business executives were convicted of price fixing. This prevented Cordiner from appointing his successor and caused the company growth to plateau at $5 billion.
- *Nine major ventures.* The new CEO, Fred Borch, was forced to undertake nine new major ventures simultaneously to stimulate growth. These included four product and five service ventures.

CHAPTER

Winning the War

BY 1940, it was clear to most American leaders that the United States would have to enter the war and fight alongside its few remaining allies. Hitler had already conquered France and Stalin's Russia. Mussolini's Italy was part of the Axis alliance. England was being devastated by a ferocious air bombardment.

President Roosevelt was still having a very difficult time persuading the American people of the necessity to join the war, but he was able to provide weapons and supplies to England through the Lend-Lease legislation. With this stimulus and others, American companies began converting their production capacities away from consumer, commercial, and many industrial applications in favor of military equipment and weapons.

During its first 60 years GE had focused on stimulating the demand for electricity and making GE an innovative market leader. World War II transformed the company from an electrical industry leader to a highly diversified corporation. In the context of a global conflagration, the normal rules of commerce were suspended in such aspects as marketing. The company simply took direction from the military, and it used its considerable talents to design and manufacture an astounding array of weapons and systems.

The postwar era subsequently proved to be a bonanza for most American companies. Pent-up demand was enormous, since production of most non-war-related goods had been suspended during the war. In addition, there was almost no foreign competition, and the U.S. government launched a number of massive initiatives to reconstruct Europe and Japan. Finally, the population was becoming more educated and increasingly affluent. For most American manufacturers, the biggest challenge was keeping up with the great demand.

During the war, GE's top leaders—Charles Wilson and Philip Reed—became senior government officials, and Swope and Young served in the interim as the company's caretakers. In 1945, Wilson and Reed returned to lead a very different company—one more diverse and complex—and they had to address major changes in the workforce (see Exhibit 5-1).

Let's take a deeper look at this key period in GE's history.

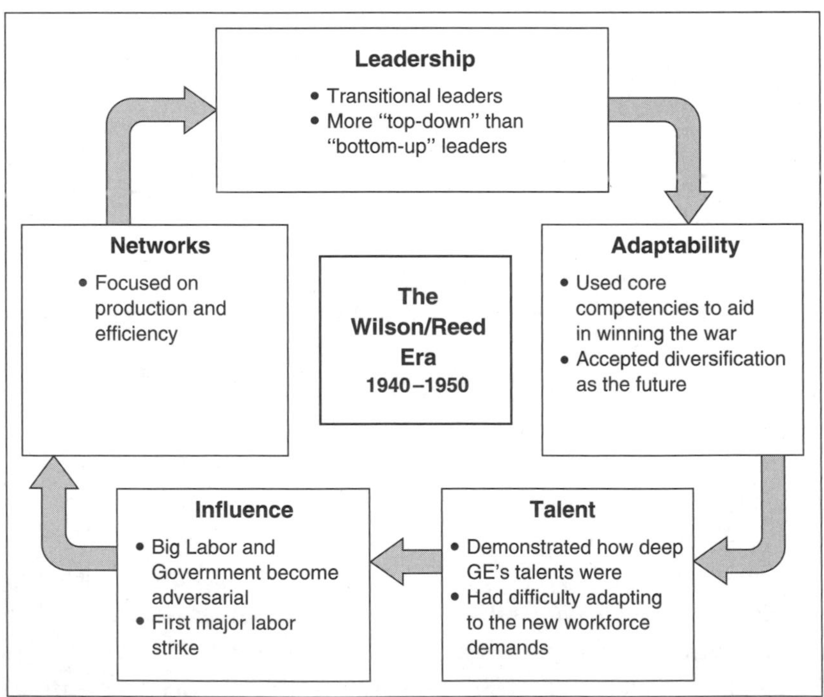

Exhibit 5-1 LATIN and the Wilson/Reed era.

OFFICE BOYS AND PATENT LAWYERS

In 1940, Swope and Young turned the company over to another team. Charlie Wilson was named president, succeeding Swope, and Phil Reed became chairman. Charlie Wilson was known as "Electric Charlie" because the CEO of General Motors was also a Charles Wilson, and he had been nicknamed "Engine Charlie."

Wilson had joined Sprague Electric Works, a GE subsidiary, as an office boy at the age of 12. He moved up through the ranks, and he augmented his on-the-job training with night courses in accounting, engineering, and mathematics. Wilson was a strong production and manufacturing expert. He became the vice president in charge of consumer products, the division that included both small and major appliances.

Phil Reed was both an electrical engineer (BSEE University of Wisconsin) and a lawyer (LLB Fordham University). He specialized in patent law and joined GE's legal department in 1927. He became chairman of the board at the age of 40.

In their initial term in office, Wilson and Reed served as the GE leadership team for only two years. In 1942, Wilson was appointed vice chairman of the War Production Board. Reed also left to serve as a "dollar-a-year man" in the Office of Production Management and as a member of the U.S. Mission for Economic Affairs.

Gerard Swope and Owen Young were coaxed out of retirement to lead the company during the three years Wilson and Reed were serving the government. This was a very unusual situation; historically, GE executives had almost no operational responsibilities after retirement. Unlike other firms, retired GE executives were not even permitted to remain on the board of directors. But the war created an unprecedented situation, and Swope and Young were asked to return.

At the end of the war, in 1945, both Wilson and Reed assumed their previous positions: Wilson as president, and Reed as chairman. Wilson remained for only five years and left the company again to do public service. Reed continued to serve as chairman until 1959.

USING KNOW-HOW AND SKILLS TO HELP WIN THE WAR

For the duration of World War II, American companies did not have to worry about the usual concerns they had worried about prior to the war, such as what to produce and how to compete. Their only task was to apply their company's talents to provide the military with what it needed to win the war. In short, GE's strategy was simple: *help win the war* by applying all of its accumulated resources.

It was a time when the company's leaders had to figure out GE's core competencies and how they might be redirected toward this new purpose. A few of the results of this self-scrutiny and redirection are summarized below.

Propulsion, Radar, and Communications Systems

Using their propulsion-related skills, GE's engineers developed new propulsion systems for more than 1,700 Navy fighting vessels. Their electromechanical turbine skills resulted in the production of more than 255 drive systems for Navy destroyers. The company produced the first radar system, and it also provided radio communications equipment. Naval gun directors were developed and added to the United States' arsenal of weapons.

First American Jet Engine

The English government had built prototypes of jet-propelled aircraft, and GE helped to make them operational. This enabled GE to be a major provider of military jet engines and later to move into the commercial jet engine business.

Nuclear Physics

The company's R&D lab contributed to the development of the atomic bomb, and later it applied this technology to the development of electrical nuclear power and the nuclear submarine programs.

WILSON AND REED RETURN TO A MORE COMPLEX COMPANY

In 1945, when Wilson and Reed returned, they found a company that was far more diversified and complex. GE now produced products and services in 21 industries, up from 3 when they left. The company had demonstrated its ability to create new products and apply its deep technologies in many areas.

Of course, GE was not alone. Other major companies followed more or less the same pattern. By the end of the war, Westinghouse had also become a highly diversified company, and it was a direct competitor in many of GE's new emerging growth areas. In the auto industry, Ford and General Motors had become highly diversified as well. For a brief period, they found themselves competing against GE in many markets. Both Ford and GM ultimately elected to divest these new ventures, however, and concentrate on their core automobile businesses.

THE NEW GE

Unlike some of its competitors, GE decided to remain diversified. Following is a list of some of the many new products, systems, and services that the company now offered.

Propulsion Systems

These were developed to power ships, aircraft, and locomotives. This made the company a leader in military markets that served the Air Force and Navy, and it led to the creation of its aircraft jet engine business, which is still a leader, and its large aerospace and defense businesses, which were sold off by Welch in the 1980s. These technologies were used to create the land-based gas turbine for electrical generation.

Electronics

During the war, GE had developed a military and industrial electronics capability. This led to the creation of a number of new electronics-based businesses, including industrial controls, industrial computers, and numerous telecommunications businesses. In addition, the company had developed the ability to substitute electronics for many electromechanical devices.

Nuclear Power

Nuclear power became a major new opportunity after the war. GE led in the development of the boiling water reactor (BWR) for electric utility applications, and it was a major contributor to the development of the pressure water reactors for Admiral Hyman G. Rickover's nuclear submarine fleets.

Industrial Automation and Productivity Systems

GE became highly skilled in automating plants and using electronics and computer know-how to increase productivity. These skills enabled the company to move into the industrial automation markets and to use these talents to improve its own manufacturing and production facilities.

Materials

GE used its chemical and materials knowledge to improve silicones and to make new materials that could be used in military applications. These were the core competencies that led to GE's innovations in plastics and artificial diamonds.

As noted above, when World War II ended, and the Wilson/Reed team returned, GE and almost all other U.S. companies faced a dramatically different world.

CAPITALIZING ON PENT-UP CONSUMER, INDUSTRIAL, AND PUBLIC DEMAND

Prior to the war, the United States was still mired in the Great Depression. All consumer, industrial, and commercial markets were severely depressed. The case can be made that had it not been for the war, the American economy—and economies around the world—might not have recovered in any recognizable form. For all of the war's many evils, it served to jumpstart the domestic American economy and, eventually, the world's.

Since no consumer goods were manufactured during the war, almost all of the consumer goods sectors had high pent-up demand. Meeting one consumer need often created another demand. For example, housing was in desperately short supply following the war. Developers drew on the techniques of mass production to begin building houses on a massive scale. Long Island's Levittown, for example, drew directly on the cookie-cutter techniques that had been developed during the war to produce thousands of planes, ships, and military vehicles.

The building of new homes, in turn, stimulated demand for household appliances, as well as a new major contractor segment for GE. Automobiles flew out of the factories into the showrooms and into consumers' new garages.

The electronics and telecommunications breakthroughs that had been developed to produce weapons and military systems were applied to consumer and industrial markets. This led to explosive growth in the radio and television markets. Radar technology led to the development of microwave technology for cooking. All of these trends enhanced GE's consumer businesses.

Entire cities were created, and massive highway and telecommunications networks were built. In short, the issue was not *what* to build but *how* to build it and get it to market as quickly as possible. This caused a huge surge in the construction of manufacturing and commercial buildings, providing GE with major growth opportunities for its industrial and commercial businesses and creating a need for new electrical systems. Nuclear and gas turbines were added to the GE mix, and these businesses also grew dramatically.

THE BIRTH OF THE EDUCATED MIDDLE CLASS AND THE "AFFLUENT SOCIETY"

The GI Bill—which allowed returning World War II veterans a college education paid for by the government—enabled millions of soldiers to go to college and get degrees that previously had been out of reach for them. This created a new middle class that was more sophisticated, educated, and affluent. This, in turn, stimulated demand for new, more sophisticated, and higher-end consumer goods.

GOVERNMENT BUSINESS AND R&D MONEY

Another result of the war was that GE, like many other companies, learned to work with the government and use public money to develop new systems, products, materials, and electronics. Government programs enabled the company to develop new products that would ultimately be used in industrial, consumer, and commercial applications. Many of the high-tech products that we are using today came about as a result of these programs.

Although government business had a low return on sales, it had very positive cash flows, and it required little in terms of investment dollars because the government often owned the facilities and made all the investments. This gave U.S. companies such as GE a major competitive advantage.

NO FOREIGN COMPETITION

An especially attractive feature in all of this growth was that, for the most part, only American companies could take advantage of the opportunities. European competitors, for example, had been devastated by the war and for the time being were unable to compete.

In addition, the Marshall Plan and other government-funded programs stipulated that only U.S. companies could participate in the supply of these programs. This meant that GE and other American companies had exclusive access to huge amounts of government funding.

DON'T WORRY ABOUT WHAT IT COSTS

Another key change was the power of labor unions and the increasing influence of Big Government. Labor unions had gained power in the late 1930s because of the combination of the Depression and the New Deal. During the war, the federal government had nationalized all of the industries, telling them what to make and when to make it. In most cases, costs were not an issue. Labor unions were not permitted to strike, and wages were frozen.

After the war, the industrial and business leaders' major challenge was to reconvert the production and supply chains back to the traditional focus on consumer, industrial, and commercial products and systems while continuing to meet their military responsibilities.

This meant that the focus was on manufacturing capacity and utilization rather than on selling, marketing, or even competing. Customer demand for almost all products was so much greater than the supply that pricing was not an issue. This was a period when companies and their leaders didn't need to have long-term marketing and competitive strategies; all they needed to do was build factories, hire workers, and produce and deliver products. This is one major reason why the art of strategic planning effectively disappeared and wasn't reinstituted until the 1970s.

Because companies were so desperate to get the products out the door, they were not very concerned about costs, especially labor costs. Most of the companies just gave the unions what they wanted, and sometimes even more. GE, as will be explained below, was a notable exception.

Management was willing to complement wage increases with longer-term benefits such as health insurance, life insurance, noncontributory pensions, and shorter workweeks. Today, in far more competitive contexts, many companies can't afford to keep the promises that they made in the heyday that extended from the 1940s to the 1970s.

GE'S FIRST MAJOR STRIKE

As noted in earlier chapters, Swope and Young created a highly cooperative and proactive labor climate over the course of their prewar tenure. During the war, as noted, labor unions were forbidden to strike, and most key players in the economy were focused on the national goal of winning the war.

After the war, however, the climate began to change. GE unions began to demand more and became more conflict oriented. And even though Wilson had worked his way up through the organization, he was not sympathetic to GE workers' demands for more money and better benefits. Concluding that these demands were unreasonable, he decided GE should be willing to withstand a strike.

The result, in 1947, was a major, bloody strike: the first and still one of the most hostile in GE's long history. In Philadelphia, police were called in to attack the strikers, reminiscent of the auto strikes of the 1930s.

This strike only strengthened the resolve of the United Electrical Union, which was dominated by socialistic—if not communistic—leaders. It also changed the union-company relationship from cooperative to highly adversarial, and ultimately it led to GE's adoption of "Boulwarism," discussed in the next chapter.

Wilson decided to return to government service in 1950. Lasting only five years, his was the shortest tenure of any GE president or chairman. He selected his executive assistant, Ralph Cordiner, to succeed him. Cordiner had served under Wilson at the War Production Board and therefore had Wilson's confidence. Phil Reed remained part of the Cordiner team until 1959.

Perhaps the best that can be said about the Wilson era is that Wilson didn't stay around for long, and he selected a very strong and capable successor who was able to address the complexity of a changing world and enable GE to prosper as a diversified company.

TAKEAWAYS

Leadership

Wilson was a self-made man, and his example illustrates both the pros and cons of developing your own leadership. Because he had joined the company in 1912 and had worked his way up through the ranks, he understood the old GE perfectly and probably would have been well equipped to lead the company. But his experience proved totally inadequate for the significantly changed company he had to lead after the war.

Leaders can try to change the world, but first they must be suited for the real-world environment around them. If they are not, then they need to be replaced. Fortunately, Wilson recognized this fact and left of his own volition.

- *Recommendation*. Look at the changing world and markets you serve and ask if you and your leadership team are suited for the anticipated changes. If not, then prepare an appropriate succession plan on an accelerated timetable.

Adaptability

Building on strengths. This is simply another way of stating the importance of focusing on your core competencies. GE clearly demonstrated, during and after the war, that many of its materials, chemical, electronic, and electromechanical skills could be applied in new and exciting ways.

- *Recommendation.* Review all of the internal skills and abilities that you have and determine if they can be applied in new ways. Carefully evaluate if you can use these abilities to create new products, services, and even entirely new businesses. Be creative first and critical later. Of course, a careful evaluation will be required before you make the final decision. Be selective and pick only those opportunities where you can be a leader. Don't try to do too much too soon. This will be explored further in Chapter 6, when we discuss the Borch ventures.

Talent

The war interfered with GE's ability to train and develop people, but it also demonstrated that GE had a deep enough bench to get things done, even when its youth and senior management were enlisted to serve their country. This was strong evidence of the effectiveness of the womb-to-tomb human resource programs of Coffin, Swope, and Young.

- *Recommendation.* Take a look at how deep your bench really is in critical areas. Do you have enough talent to compensate for a major loss of key people?

Influence

Even though Wilson took a major strike that may have been counterproductive and unnecessary, he certainly demonstrated a willingness to take a stand against unreasonable union and government demands. This philosophy, if not this particular outcome, became a foundation of future GE responses to labor and government policies. In addition, it has enabled the company to avoid the trauma being experienced today by many major U.S. companies, which in the past simply gave the union and government a pass and raised their prices to cover for their actions.

- *Recommendation.* Identify trends that can impact your ability to control your company's destiny. These may come from a variety of stakeholder groups, whose demands are unreasonable and potentially detrimental to your ability to lead and keep the organization vibrant. We will discuss stakeholders in Chapter 8.

Networks and Systems

The company's performance in applying its talents to create new systems and products for the war was nothing short of amazing. It demonstrated how well-conceived and implemented GE's management systems had been in the past.

- *Recommendation*. Take a look at your current management, financial, and strategic systems, and determine how effective they are and whether they will continue to be effective, or even relevant, in the future. Identify those areas that appear to be more about words than actions and refocus on *actions*.

CHAPTER

Decentralized Growth

EVEN THOUGH the 1920s were great times for American manufacturers, the 1950s were even better as the great post–World War II management boom became a reality.

The United Nations was formed and sited in New York City; the ambitious goal of this organization was to help prevent another global conflagration and the associated devastation. Europe and the Far East were being reconstructed with U.S. funds. The demand for innovative consumer and industrial goods continued to be enormous, and only U.S. companies were in a position to meet it.

In retrospect, this was a period when many American corporations became complacent and lax—"fat and happy," in less generous terms. Many companies instituted a version of what might be called the "field-of-dreams strategy": If we build it, the customers will come.

In other words, we can build plants, make products, and sit back and take orders. This caused an atrophying of the strategic thinking, marketing, and forecasting skills that would eventually be needed in the face of real global competition. Corporate skills, like muscles, must be exercised.

Cordiner and Reed took over the leadership of GE, and they focused on developing sophisticated management systems to help the company cope with these major growth opportunities and with the diversity of corporate interests they had inherited.

They continued the tradition of building a strong, deep bench by expanding and enhancing training at all levels and by adding new functional training programs. But among their most significant achievements were the development of the "professional management" concept and the creation of Crotonville, the first and most extensive company-operated management development institute.

GE leaders once again demonstrated their willingness to share the wealth with their employees by instituting new health, pension, and savings programs. These programs included one of the country's first corporate matching-gift programs that permitted employees' contributions to their colleges to be matched by similar gifts to their colleges from GE. The company also created the GE Foundation to encourage and systematize charitable contributions.

That said, Cordiner and Reed had very different perspectives on the government and unions than did Swope and Young. Cordiner viewed Big Government and Big Unions as major threats and adversaries who desired to take away their management controls and prerogatives. As a result, he embarked on extensive union-bashing and communications programs to neutralize the power of both Big Government and Big Labor. He instituted a highly successful program, called "Boulwarism," designed to offset the power of both unions and government. It included the hiring—and the philosophical conversion—of a future U.S. president.

On balance, the period from 1950 to 1960 must be judged as highly positive for GE, since the company grew, and grew profitably. Unfortunately, many of these results were undercut by the "Great Electrical Conspiracy," which hampered the company's ability to select its leaders and imposed a major drag on the company's growth.

The next three chapters describe the Cordiner/Reed era in terms of (1) growth strategies, (2) the onset of management by objectives, and (3) the company's willingness to take on Big Government and Big Labor.

THE CORDINER/REED ERA

In 1950, Charlie Wilson selected his executive assistant, Ralph Cordiner, as his successor to lead GE, while Philip Reed remained as chairman.

Ralph Cordiner was an appliance salesman who worked his way up through the sales and merchandising organization for the Edison General Electric Appliance Company. In 1939, he left GE and became president of Schick Razor. Three years later, he rejoined his former boss, Charlie Wilson, at the War Production Board. When Wilson returned to GE, Cordiner returned with him as his executive assistant.

In 1950, the embattled Wilson decided to return to government service. He turned over the company to Cordiner, who served as president from 1950 to 1958, and as chairman from 1958 to 1963.

MANAGEMENT BY OBJECTIVES (MBO) IS BORN AT GE

Unlike other major companies that narrowed their product lines after World War II, Cordiner and Reed decided to continue to pursue the diversification route. To their credit, they recognized that managing a diversified and complex company required a different management approach and organizational structure (see Exhibit 6-1). They therefore retained the services of academic and consulting experts to determine what changes needed to be made.

The GE team decided to embrace a new management concept, which became known as "management by objectives" (MBO), and to break the company into numerous decentralized product departments. Product departments became the building blocks of the company. They were assigned the responsibility to develop competitive and business strategies and plans to meet the overall corporate financial objectives: 7 percent return on sales and 20 percent return on investment.

This represented a dramatic change from the company's traditional centralized organization. Before MBOs, corporate management was responsible for setting the objectives and developing the strategies, and the operating units were expected to execute them with little or no deviation. In effect, the shift transferred power from the centralized functional units to the product department general managers.

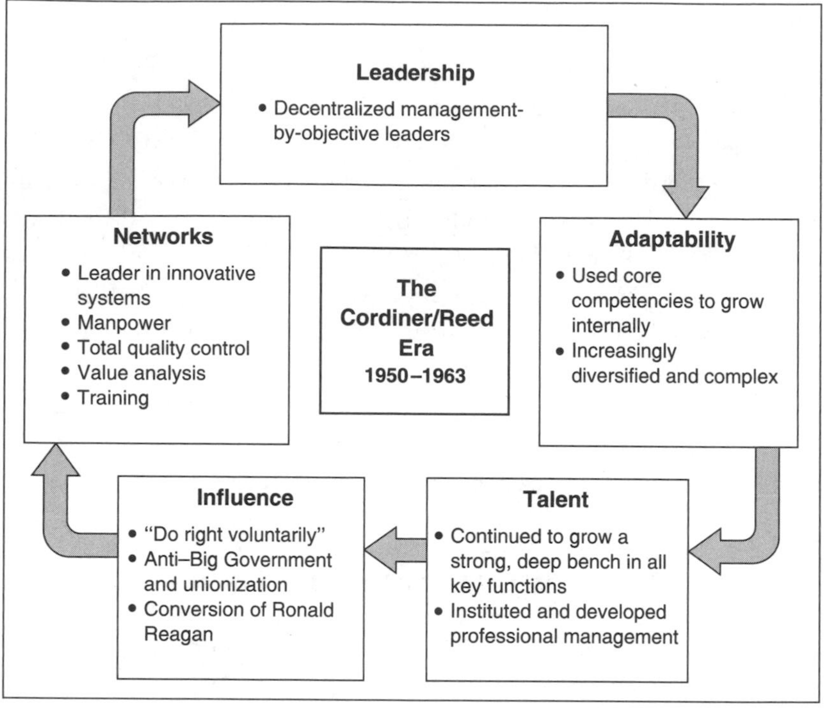

Exhibit 6-1 LATIN and the Cordiner/Reed era.

DECENTRALIZATION

Cordiner divided the company into three layers of management—groups, divisions, and departments—for each of the major industry sectors. The major groups included consumer, industrial, and electric utilities. Each of the departments was required to have its own engineering, sales, manufacturing, finance, and employee relations operations. No deviations were permitted, so each organization looked the same on paper. When a department exceeded $50 million in revenues, it was split into smaller departments.

The result was that by 1956, General Electric manufactured 200,000 separate products and had 350 lines of products in nearly 100 product-manufacturing operating departments, which averaged between $30 and $40 million in revenues. The company's product mix was 35 percent consumer products, 25 percent user products for business and industry, 20 percent highly engineered defense, electronics, and atomic products, and 20 percent components and materials produced chiefly for other manufacturers.

BROAD AND EMPLOYEE STOCK OWNERSHIP

Cordiner was a strong advocate of having a very large number of shareholders so that GE could not be controlled by any one individual or investment group. The company decided that when the stock price reached $100, it automatically would be split to keep it within reach of the small individual investor. This continues to be the GE stock-splitting policy.

In order to encourage employee stock ownership, the company implemented a stock bonus program that permitted employees to invest systematically in GE stock. For every dollar they invested, the company would add another 50 cents. This program—which is very similar to the current 401(k) programs that are so popular today—was arguably 40 years ahead of its time.

OUTSIDE BOARD OF DIRECTORS

Cordiner wanted to have a board of directors that included a diverse and experienced group of outsiders. As he put it:

> **To assure that the interests of the owners will be protected, General Electric has 19 men, of whom only two (the Chairman and myself) are company executives. They are national, and come from a wide variety of businesses and industries, including education, food, agriculture, mining, manufacturing marketing, banking, and transportation.[1]**

Again, this approach—although certainly not unique to GE—can be seen as well ahead of its time. Today, many companies are scrambling to replace insiders with outsiders on their boards.

INTERNAL GROWTH

Cordiner urged the company's decentralized management to be risk takers and to develop new products and businesses based on their internal strengths, or, as it is now put, "core competencies," rather than on acquisitions or alliances. This required that the company balance the short and long range—that is, achieve the short-term numbers but look longer range for new opportunities and threats.

THE BUILDING CONTRACTOR AS A NEW CHANNEL OF DISTRIBUTION

Since housing construction was booming, GE created a new distribution channel to sell directly to home and apartment builders. The objective was to get GE appliances installed so that when consumers needed to upgrade, they would automatically select GE or Hotpoint brands. In addition, GE established its own appliance service business so that it would not have to rely on retailers or independent contractors.

The consumer group's major appliance division continued to add innovative products to its cooking, dishwashing, and refrigerating product lines. This included developing new technologies such as the microwave oven and the induction cooker, improving the quality and beauty of the appliances, and helping to make the kitchen a family room.

In addition, innovative cooling and heating products were added to the line. A heat pump, Weathron, was designed to permit users to both heat and cool their facilities. Room air-conditioners were developed to permit consumers to cool individual rooms, thereby supplanting old-fashioned fans.

CREATING INNOVATIVE SMALL APPLIANCES

GE's small appliance department—headed by an innovative merchandiser, Willard Sahloff—developed ways to brush your teeth, dry your hair, cook your toast, and brew your coffee.

Using the product-obsolescence approaches that had been so successful in the automobile industry, the consumer was encouraged to continually upgrade these appliances by means of new features, more attractive packaging, or both. Sahloff also moved GE into the traditional department stores, thereby adding to the sales and distribution network.

Radios, portable televisions, and stereos were also added to the product portfolio, with the company using the appliance retailers and selected department stores to sell these new products.

The combination of product innovation, strong retailer franchises, aggressive advertising, and fair-trade pricing enabled both the major appliance and small appliance businesses to be very profitable and to continue to be leaders in their respective markets.

BACKING FAIR TRADE AND FIGHTING DISCOUNTING

Underpinning GE's ability to maintain control of both who sold the company's products and the prices they charged for those products were the fair-trade laws. These laws permitted the manufacturers to select those whom they wanted to sell their products and to prevent anyone from selling their products without their permission. Thus manufacturers such as GE could prevent price erosion and the dumping of their products. These laws created pricing conditions that were consistent with the agency and franchising pricing used by Swope and Young.

In the early 1950s a new retail trend called "discounting" appeared on the scene, which threatened the company's ability to control both its retailers and the prices they charged. The first discounter, Masters, sprang up in New York City. Masters sold its products to New York City civil servants only, using a "club plan" similar to today's Sam's Club and Costco. It was highly successful because its prices were lower than those of the authorized dealers. Its success encouraged others to follow the same practice. Another New York discounter, E.J. Korvette, was one of the first companies to sell directly at a discount to the public.

The major manufacturers, led by GE, took legal action to prevent these discounters from obtaining and selling their products. Many of the products sold in discounters at the time were purchased from "franchised retailers" who wanted to move excess inventory. Lawsuits followed. The discounters ultimately won the battle, and fair-trade agreements were declared illegal.

Arguably, the loss of fair-trade agreements and pricing was the single biggest contributor to the decline and ultimate fall of American consumer products companies. Retail margins were cut, and the U.S. manufacturers' profit margins were squeezed. Since discounters didn't provide after-sales service, companies such as GE were required to expand their own direct-to-consumer service organizations. The discounters provided retail distribution for the newly emerging foreign brands, especially from Japan and Korea, which were able to price lower than their U.S. competitors. The ultimate results are now clear. Today, foreign brands dominate the market. The GE brand still exists on consumer electronics products, but Thomson of France is the owner and producer of these lines. GE's major appliance service became a key portion of its profitability.

MAKING ELECTRIC UTILITIES EVEN MORE DEPENDENT

More appliances—more heating and cooling devices, more radios and televisions—meant that the electric utilities had to continue to expand their generating capacity.

For GE and competitor Westinghouse, this was another golden opportunity. Using the technological know-how they had developed during the war, the two companies aggressively developed nuclear reactors and gas turbines, and they also worked at increasing the size and efficiency of the traditional large coal- and oil-fired plants. In addition, GE and Westinghouse developed new and more efficient transmission and distribution systems to ensure that power was available at the right place at the right time.

Continuing the Coffin and Swope relationship-based strategies, GE offered electric utilities special services to ensure that the utilities would continue to grow and be profitable. These included the following, for example:

1. *Free forecasting.* GE provided electric utilities with free consumption forecasts, enabling those electric utilities to predict demand and therefore build adequate capacity. GE convinced the electric utilities that they needed to have a minimum of 17 percent excess capacity in advance of demand. This became an industry standard. It certainly ensured that utilities would have enough capacity to satisfy demand except in truly extraordinary circumstances. It also enabled GE to "level-load" its manufacturing plants by giving the company a clear sense of what kinds of orders would soon be in the pipeline.
2. *Rates based on ROI.* GE helped electric utilities convince state regulators to keep setting electric rates to generate a specific rate of return on investments (ROI). This continued to enable GE and

other key electric products and system companies to sell more advanced and improved electrical systems to the utilities, since the more they bought and installed, the higher their returns would be.

3. *Privately owned utilities preferred to government-owned ones.* GE continued to promote privately owned electrical utilities over government-owned-and-operated systems.
4. *Training at all levels.* GE bundled training into its product and systems contracts to ensure that the equipment and systems were properly and safely operated and maintained. Utility executives received the opportunity to participate in GE's state-of-the-art management and executive programs. Many of the electric utility executives were graduates of GE's training programs and therefore had the GE monogram engraved in their minds.
5. *Reduced electric utilities' nuclear risk.* GE instituted "turnkey nuclear pricing" to sell nuclear systems and reduce the risks to the utilities. In other words, GE quoted one price to design, build, and install nuclear systems. This enabled the utilities to get access to this new technology with little or no risk. Obviously, it stimulated demand for nuclear plants and forced GE's key competitors to adopt this same "all-in" pricing strategy.

GE's electric utility relationship strategy was highly successful. Electric utilities prospered and grew. Utility stocks, such as AT&T's, were considered so sound that they became the quintessential "widows-and-orphans stocks." The country prospered in part because of its ample and reliable supplies of electricity. And, not surprisingly, GE and its competitors in this field grew and prospered. In short, it was a win-win situation. This lasted until the Great Electrical Conspiracy, which I will describe further in Chapter 8.

MISCALCULATING THE TURNKEY COSTS

Unfortunately, GE lived to regret its turnkey nuclear pricing strategy. The company didn't properly evaluate the total costs of getting the needed regulatory permissions or of dealing with the very militant construction workers' and teamsters' unions. In addition, reactors were not standardized, so each facility necessitated a unique design, which in turn imposed extra costs and created increased safety risks.

For all these reasons and more, the overall costs of the nuclear plant business far exceeded estimates, and the company lost huge sums of money. Unfortunately, turnkeys had become the industry standard, and all of the major nuclear reactor systems producers lost hundreds of millions of dollars.

GE and other producers continued to lose money on nuclear plants until the 1970s. Strangely, the only reason the U.S. nuclear industry became profitable at that point was that no new reactors were being built. Because each of the reactors was unique, only the original manufacturer could provide the parts and services to maintain, repair, and upgrade existing nuclear facilities. This is an excellent example of why having a large installed base in a technology business is so important, and it was one of the reasons that Toshiba was willing to pay more than $5 billion for the Westinghouse nuclear business in 2006.

The United States still generates only 20 percent of its electricity from nuclear power. Highly visible accidents—such as the near disaster at Three Mile Island—certainly hurt the nuclear industry. But equally to blame was the lack of standardization in the industry, and GE owns part of the blame for this failure.

WRONG TECHNOLOGY, AGAIN

Let's look a little more closely at this episode and at the lessons it contains. In the period in question, there were two competing technologies: boiling water reactors (BWRs) and pressure water reactors (PWRs). GE backed the BWR technology while the rest of the industry, led by Westinghouse, used PWR. Note the parallels to the Edison/Westinghouse conflict over AC versus DC at the beginning of the twentieth century.

PWR technology had been developed for nuclear submarines, and it was more popular than BWR. More than 75 percent of the units sold were PWR designs. GE, even though it also provided PWR units for the naval submarine program, backed the BWR design. Today, it appears that GE selected the wrong technology, but—unlike Villard, who admitted defeat and moved the company into the AC systems business—the Cordiner team and its successors continued to aggressively promote BWR.

Meanwhile, France and Japan—two energy-poor countries that are large consumers of nuclear energy—took a very different approach to nuclear power, requiring that all nuclear plants in their countries be standardized. This has enabled both countries to generate in excess of 90 percent of their electrical needs using nuclear energy.

Ironically the popularity of nuclear power is again on the rise, and it is possible that the industry will be reborn and grow.

In fact, it is almost certain that the United States will once again build nuclear reactors as a means of decreasing its unhealthy dependence on imported oil and gas. If it does so, however, it will require a standardization of reactor technology and the development of a complete system that includes enrichment and the safe disposal of spent fuels, neither of which was dealt with in the original nuclear programs.

GROWING FROM WITHIN: PROS AND CONS

Cordiner urged all of his product departments and divisions to create new products using the skills and know-how of the research and development center and their own unique skills.

Cordiner wrote in compelling and cogent ways on this subject. In 1956, for example, he wrote:

> **What has happened is that, although the company started with the basic technology of electrical engineering, the technologies diversified as its engineers ran into technical barriers. For example: our designs very early encountered technical limits in insulating materials. The company needed insulating capacities that were not commercially available, and was thus obliged to enter into chemical research, in order to develop its own special materials.**
>
> **Likewise, many of the company's products from lamps to turbines have been limited primarily by the kinds of metals that have been available. So, in order to produce more efficient turbines and to provide customers with a lamp that will give more light for his or her money, GE has engaged in metallurgical research and has become a producer of special metals.**
>
> **Thus, as we overcome new scientific and technical barriers, we see a merging of old technologies, the rise of new technologies, and the growth of fresh businesses which have an actual, but not**

always obvious, basis in the primary technology of producing and utilizing electric power.[2]

The 1955 General Electric annual report highlighted many of the new products that resulted from GE's internal developments and know-how:

- *Gas turbines* for electrical generation and for propulsion systems used in ships and locomotives. (Note that the applications of gas turbines were not focused on just electric utility applications; they were also targeted for propelling ships and locomotives.)
- *Silicones* to be used for consumer and industrial applications.
- *Industrial X-ray equipment* to identify structural product and building defects.
- *Industrial electronics, controls, and automation systems* mainly for commercial and industrial applications.
- *Computers* for managing the electrical systems grids.
- *Artificial diamonds* mainly for grinding and abrasion.[3]

COMPETING AGAINST YOURSELF

One of the major limitations of this approach was that in some situations departments competed against each other. For instance, the jet engine department and gas turbine department developed two different versions of the gas turbine and found themselves competing against each other in some markets. This wasn't resolved until much later during the Borch era; meanwhile, the result was customer confusion and the loss of business to competitors.

Another failing of this uncontrolled product innovation and development approach was that GE often failed to really understand the external factors that separated winners from losers. The GE heat pump provides an excellent example. GE erroneously assumed that the heat pump could be used anywhere in the United States regardless of the weather. GE decided to demonstrate the technology by building it into the company's new showcase facility in Crotonville, New York. Unfortunately, the company failed to recognize that the heat pump, or "Weathron," as GE called it, was not particularly efficient—or even operational—in cold, snowy climates with dramatic temperature swings.

Crotonville proved to be an embarrassing promotion: The units not only failed to either heat or cool the new management center but they were also very ugly and became a constant reminder of a failed strategy. They ultimately had to be removed, to be replaced by a traditional forced-air heating and cooling system.

CONTINUING TO SERVE THE NATIONAL INTEREST

Most companies that did business with the government found it to be a mixed blessing. Margins were good, and demand was predictable—at least up to the moment that the government unilaterally canceled a contract.

But some companies, including GE, felt that additional factors had to be considered. As Cordiner put it:

> **General Electric prefers commercial, non-defense business because it is generally more open for the "Company-determined" innovation and is more profitable.**
>
> **But because of the Company's unique technical capacities, it is called upon regularly to develop and produce complicated equipment and systems for the armed forces. The company's policy is to concentrate its efforts on those defense projects where it can make a distinctive technical contribution—generally the advanced scientific weapon systems and the unsolved problems in military technology.[4]**

Decades later, Jack Welch made his mark in part by exiting *all* of these government businesses.

BUSINESS COMPUTERS: A MISSED OPPORTUNITY

In 1956, GE won a contract to produce the Electronic Recording Machine Accounting (ERMA) computer system for the Bank of America. The $31 million ERMA contract was the largest nongovernment computer contract that had been awarded up to that time, and GE beat out 28 other companies to get it. But there was one problem: Ralph Cordiner strongly opposed GE's entrance into the commercial computer market.

Prior to 1956, GE's involvement in the then-fledgling computer industry was limited to the production of vacuum tubes, relays, small motors, and other components for IBM. The ERMA system represented a quantum leap forward for GE. Simply stated, it was a checking account bookkeeping system, consisting of computers and automated check handling and sorting equipment, for one of America's more prestigious banks—in other words, a complex but industry-defining opportunity.[5]

It is still unclear why Cordiner vetoed GE's entry into the computer industry. What *is* clear is that this was a major missed opportunity. Cordiner's successors tried to rectify his mistake, but by that time, IBM was too strong.

NEUTRALIZING THE WARLORDS

Another Cordiner challenge lay in taking back the company from the major location "warlords." During the prewar and war eras, the management of the major electric utility locations—Schenectady, Philadelphia, and Pittsfield, in particular—had extraordinary power in the company, and they resisted any major changes. In fact, many of these leaders were unreceptive to GE's diversification strategies. This represented a clear threat to Cordiner's authority.

To neutralize the power of the electric utility warlords, Cordiner took several important steps:

1. He moved GE's corporate offices out of Schenectady and relocated them to 570 Lexington Avenue, New York City.
2. Since the warlords controlled the Elfuns and their meeting place, Association Island, Cordiner closed Association Island, and he built his Management Research and Development Center at Crotonville, New York.
3. He reorganized and changed the company power structure.
4. He put more emphasis on the rapidly growing consumer and commercial businesses.

LEADING LIKE AN OUTSIDER

Cordiner behaved less like an insider and more like an outsider who had acquired the company and was determined to put his own stamp on it.

In some ways, Cordiner *was* an outsider. He had left GE, had become the Schick Razor CEO before the war, and then had joined Charlie Wilson at the War Production Board. This outside experience seems to have broadened his vision, increased his confidence, and otherwise served him well.

Seen through this lens, Charlie Wilson was an insider in the sense that he grew up entirely within the company (although he was a consumer executive in Bridgeport, Connecticut, and he was not part of the powerful electric utility and industrial business group in Schenectady). Perhaps Wilson would have benefited from more outside-world experience. On the other hand, Jack Welch's profile was something like Wilson's, and no one would say that Welch was a captive of old ways of thinking.

TAKEAWAYS
Adaptability

Homegrown businesses. Cordiner elected to grow his own businesses and not rely on acquisitions and mergers. He instituted a system to identify and use abilities, skills, and know-how to grow.

- *Recommendation.* Take some time to identify what your company is *really good at* and determine if these strengths can be translated into businesses and new ventures. Be selective. Make sure that they are *real* strengths and not just perceived ones.

CHAPTER

Professional Management

A KEY ELEMENT of Cordiner's decentralized growth was to develop and maintain a deep bench of professional managers who would be able to identify new growth opportunities and deliver the promised results. Like other GE leaders, Cordiner and Reed were both committed to developing employees at all levels, and they invested heavily in training. They even built a special "temple" dedicated to developing the best management possible.

PROFESSIONAL MANAGERS AND NOT OWNERS

Cordiner made it clear that the GE managers were "employees hired by the share owners through their elected directors to manage their business in the balanced best interest of all concerned."[1]

This is a very important point because many of the managers had started to believe that it was "their company" and they could run it as they saw fit, without concern for the investors, customers, and employees. Cordiner, obviously, disagreed.

THE BIRTH OF THE PROFESSIONAL MANAGER

Cordiner recognized that managing a diversified, decentralized company would require a different type of manager. He believed that management was a profession—like engineering, accounting, and science—and that there were fundamental managerial principles that could be taught and therefore *should* be taught.

Professional managers, like engineers, were to be provided with the tools and skills to attack any problem and manage any type of organization, regardless of its size, maturity, and technology. This philosophy too had its pros and cons. On the one hand, a broader range of managers received high-quality training. On the other hand, it led to the belief that "a great manager could manage anything." This was ultimately proven to be wishful thinking, which caused GE many headaches and heartaches.

PROFESSIONAL MANAGEMENT BECOMES A RELIGION

In some ways, Cordiner made professional management like a secular religion:

1. He enlisted the best minds to identify and document the best principles of management.
2. He built his own temple (Crotonville) to conduct research, development, and teaching.
3. He issued his own bible, which became known as the "Blue Books," and eight commandments.
4. He "ordained" high priests and missionaries.
5. He audited and reviewed managers' performance to ensure that his prescribed management principles and techniques were being applied.
6. He rewarded and punished managers based on their adherence to (that is, their implementation of) the eight commandments.

TAPPING THE BEST MINDS; IDENTIFYING AND DOCUMENTING THE BEST PRINCIPLES

Cordiner hired Harold Smiddy, a well-known "management scientist," to lead the overall effort. Smiddy was given the financial resources to tap the minds of the best management professionals available. At that time, these were key academics such as Peter Drucker, and major consultants such as H. B. Maynard, McKinsey, and Booz Allen Hamilton.

I should note that this is a continuing GE policy today: Invest what it takes to make changes and tap the best expertise.

A TEMPLE IN CROTONVILLE FOR RESEARCH, DEVELOPMENT, AND TEACHING

Cordiner needed to disconnect from the past, so he created a new management center located in a relatively isolated part of New York State north of New York City. He built a very unpretentious living area and a building for consultants, trainers, and classrooms. One of the more innovative rooms was the "Pit." Shaped like a medical amphitheater, it was intended to promote a vigorous exchange of views.

Crotonville was staffed with a cadre of teachers, writers, and management scientists. The primary reasons that Cordiner and Smiddy wanted to develop their own facility—instead of sending their executives to business schools—were these:

- GE planned for large numbers of people to go through the program.
- GE believed that it was so different from other companies that it required writing and using its own case studies rather than using those already generally available that had been drawn from other companies.
- GE wanted to control the topics, design, and execution of its courses.
- There were really no other facilities or programs that were comparable.

Using the input of academics, consultants, and its own internal talents, Crotonville put together a very intensive, continuous 13-week program for 80 carefully selected employees.

In the first run of the program, participants were not permitted to return home—or have contact with their offices—during the entire 13-week period. In other words, they had to disconnect completely from their business and their families. This intensity and complete isolation caused a great deal of stress, and the participants felt cut off from the external world. It is reported that one of the first participants committed suicide because of the high levels of stress.

THE EVOLUTION OF CROTONVILLE

After this first session, the course remained 13 weeks, but there were planned breaks, and participants were able to go home several times during the session. The key topics covered in this three-month program were the development of employees, the use of persuasion rather than command, how to improve teamwork, integration, the key measures expected, and how to use different types of compensation systems to motivate the team.

Because the company's leaders were concerned about the growth and power of Big Government and Big Labor, and because they were terrified that socialized planning might be introduced in the United States—as it had been in Britain and other European countries—there were numerous sessions on economic, social, and political changes.

CROTONVILLE COURSE DESIGN

The course design was clever and innovative. In the morning, participants heard lectures by national figures—well-known politicians, government officials, economists, and sociologists—to get an outside perspective. In many cases, these were individuals who advocated national planning or otherwise increasing the power of labor or government. The goal was to give participants insights into the minds and actions of adversarial groups rather than of only those that held the same beliefs as GE.

In the afternoons, there were sessions designed to analyze what the group had heard from the outsiders. GE perspective and policies were provided and discussed to ensure that the participants understood where GE stood on each issue.

While serving in the U.S. Army, I studied the art and science of brainwashing, and I even wound up giving lectures on the topic. When I returned to GE, I concluded that the Crotonville approach bordered on brainwashing. The combination of the intensity, isolation, and indoctrination of the GE perspective was very similar to the approach used by the Chinese and Viet Cong in brainwashing U.S. prisoners. There was no disputing the effectiveness of this technique by the enemy: Many soldiers were converted into antiwar advocates. And Crotonville, too, was effective.

Cordiner described the results he expected from this major financial and personnel investment in Crotonville. In 1956, 4,000 managers and professionals took the Professional Business Management Course, and this number was projected to reach a cumulative total of 25,000 by 1959, some 11 percent of the workforce.[2] It was an unprecedented commitment—and set a standard that later GE leaders felt constrained to follow. For example, this intensive commitment of people, money, and resources to executive development was continued by Welch in his Work-Out and Six-Sigma programs.

THE GE PROFESSIONAL MANAGEMENT BIBLE

Cordiner recognized the need to have his own bible as well as his own missionaries to spread his secular gospels. Consultant Smiddy developed a series of what became known as the "Blue Books," large, hardcovered, expensive books with blue covers.

These books summarized the four key elements of professional management: plan, organize, integrate, and measure—or POIM, as they were christened. These were distilled from the best business minds, and they were very consistent with what Drucker had advocated in his 1954 watershed book, *The Practice of Management.*

In addition, Cordiner's own 1956 book, *New Frontiers for Professional Management*, was distributed to all of GE's key managers and professionals. It consciously reinforced the philosophies outlined in the Blue Books.

SELECTION OF MISSIONARIES

If the Blue Books were the GE management bible, then Cordiner needed individuals to spread the gospel of the books—and those individuals had to be (or appear to be) true believers. GE therefore hired individuals who proved capable of teaching and spreading the word. In addition, many of these missionaries came from GE's newly formed Management Consulting Services.

THE MEASUREMENT SERVICES

Cordiner recognized that change could be achieved and sustained only if managers were rewarded for results—and they could be rewarded only if there were effective performance measures. He therefore instituted the eight key result areas, which could be considered another part of the management religion. I think of them as GE's "Eight Commandments of Professional Management."

THE EIGHT COMMANDMENTS AND MEASURES

1. Profitability
2. Market share
3. Productivity
4. Product leadership
5. Personnel development
6. Employee attitudes
7. Public responsibility
8. The balance between short-range and long-range goals

Recall that General Electric suffered a traumatic event in its first year of operations. This was the Panic of 1893, which almost bankrupted the company. Since that time, General Electric has embraced two key measures of financial performance: return on investment (ROI) and cash flow. These measures have enabled the company to achieve consistent returns and enjoy positive cash flows throughout its history.

But Cordiner wanted GE managers to address more than just the financials. Let's review what he wrote in his book about business measures:

> **The traditional means of profits such as return on investment, turnover and percent of net earnings to sales provide useful information. But they are hopelessly inadequate as measures to guide the manager's effectiveness in planning for the future of the business—they are where his decisions have the most effects.**
>
> **A survey of the measurement already in use in the Company showed that they were at once too numerous, and yet not necessarily guiding decisions on the balanced basis toward the main objectives of the Company.[3]**

Cordiner initiated this study, and he established a "Measurement Service," described as a "permanent organization component in Accounting Services." This organization was charged with establishing the specific criteria to be used, communicating them to operations, and then periodically checking to see if the measures were being met.

Professional management and the eight key results were vital parts of the GE management system until the mid-1960s. They led to many positive results, but they also caused many problems. The intent was honorable, but the reality was less satisfactory, especially when managers were placed in situations without the proper experience and understanding of the business and they relied heavily on ungrounded measurements. Again, the assumption that a manager could manage anything was proven wrong, but the company took far too long to admit it.

TOO MANY MEASURES . . . SOME CONFLICTING

GE has been "measurement happy" since that long-ago time. I once observed to a management group that GE continued to add to the measurements and never threw any away.

Some of the parameters included in the Cordiner gospel were not easy to measure. For instance, market share must be defined in the context of a served market. Very often, the definition of the "served market" was gerrymandered to make the performance of the general manager and the department look better than it really was. Arguments over served markets and share often caused major conflicts between departments and the corporate staff.

Other measures—such as employee attitudes and public responsibility—were never clear and therefore only added to the confusion. In reality, the only measure that was used was *profitability*. The system looked good on paper but wasn't very helpful. Unfortunately, these measures continued to be used and became part of the GE psyche.

Cordiner was successful in destroying the warlords' power and using his management courses and audits to remold the company into a single entity. But in so doing, he also made enemies. Many of the managers and business executives resented, even hated, the rigidity of the system. When they finally got the opportunity to rebel, they did so with a vengeance.

EXPANDING AND STRENGTHENING THE GE FARM SYSTEM

Ralph Cordiner wanted to be sure that all of the key functions of the business were staffed with highly competent, well-trained professionals, so he significantly expanded the number and type of functional training programs. One way he did so was to create broad and deep relations with the academic world.

Corporate Functional Services Organizations

Corporate Functional Services organizations were established for each of the business functions. These organizations were responsible for providing consulting, auditing, college recruiting, and companywide entry-level and advanced training and development programs.

Functional consulting was provided free of charge to the product departments to implement the programs that they were expected to implement. These consultants worked with their assigned functional management to develop and offer training programs. These programs were often highly unique. For instance, GE was a leader in total quality control, value analysis, performance appraisal, and interviewing. In many cases, the courses were adapted to fit the specific needs of the business.

Functional audits were conducted as well. These audits evaluated whether the departments were executing the prescribed programs and if the measures were being achieved. Each function had its own audit team, and the audits were comprehensive.

On a personal note: I served on a human resource audit in Waynesboro, Virginia, and it included evaluating employee attitudes, union activities, communications, delegation, and community affairs. Detailed reports were prepared and provided to senior management and the department. Schedules and milestones for follow-up were developed to make sure that the recommendations were being implemented.

Unfortunately, corporate staff and department management became highly adversarial in this period. Even though the intent was good, the results were often negative. The department-level management often was not impressed with the consulting and audit teams, discovering that there was truth in the old adage "You don't get something for nothing." As a result, product department general managers often hired their own outside consultants, in many cases explicitly to challenge the recommendations of the company services teams.

Corporate Functional Services were also responsible for centralized college recruiting. They established strong relationships with the placement offices of all of the major colleges and universities in their areas of expertise (see Table 7-1).

Training Functional Leaders and Professionals				
Engineering	**Marketing/ Sales**	**Manufacturing**	**Finance**	**Human Resources**
Entry level	Marketing	MTP	FMP	ERTP
Advanced	Technical marketing	—	—	Legal
Creative	ASP	—	—	—

Table 7-1 GE functional entry-level training programs initiated during the Cordiner era. (See pages 110 and 111 for a guide to the acronyms.)

Expanding the Functional Services Training Programs

Each functional services organization developed and operated companywide training and education programs. It is interesting to note that even though Cordiner was the disciple of decentralization, he recognized the need to have one "company image and collegial relationships."

Cordiner's team enhanced traditional training programs. For example, engineering was expanded to three programs:

1. The "test program" was renamed the "Engineering Program," and it became a companywide offering.
2. The Advanced Engineering Program was added to attract advanced degree holders and provide recruits for the General Engineering Labs and in Corporate R&D.
3. The Creative Engineering Program was introduced to stimulate more creative thinking and innovative products.

As for finance, the Business Training Course became the Financial Management Program (FMP), and it focused more on developing the financial and accounting skills of its members. The FMP's top graduates were often given the opportunity to join the Traveling Audit Staff, which required a very heavy travel schedule for at least a three-year period. Almost all of the key financial executives and officers were graduates of both the FMP and the Traveling Audit Staff, and if an FMP graduate elected *not* to join the audit staff, he or she quite often left the company thereafter.

As for manufacturing, Cordiner recognized the need for manufacturing specialists, so he initiated a Manufacturing Training Program (MTP). Trainees did assignments in all areas of manufacturing, including plant engineering, industrial engineering, purchasing, quality control, and product planning and control.

CUSTOMERS FIRST

Cordiner was a salesman. He made it clear in his book that "customers were first" and that if you couldn't sell your products, you didn't have a business. He recognized, however, that sales and marketing were not the same, so he established training programs in these areas:

- *Marketing Training Program (MTP).* This marketing program was a one-year program, with three-month assignments in four locations. The students were MBA graduates.
- *Technical Marketing Program (TMP).* This program focused on one business, primarily one that needed a technical background. Participants in TMP tended to be engineering graduates who were more sales oriented than technically oriented.
- *Advertising and Sales Promotion Program* (*ASP*). Recognizing the need to have its own internal advertising and promotion organization, the company instituted this program to provide creative—but practical—advertising and promotion geared to a "GE type of customer."

MOVING FROM PERSONNEL TO HUMAN RESOURCES

At many companies, the "people function" has always been a professional stepchild. Most such internal organizations have been focused on personnel issues, or what some called "health-and-happiness concerns." The individuals who work in this area have often been the intermediaries between management and the employees, and their primary role has been to keep the workforce happy. Some have even called the people in this function the "chaplains of industry."

Cordiner and his associate Lemuel Boulware decided that the company would need a cadre of tough-minded, talented people who could work with employees and help neutralize the power of the unions. In that spirit, they instituted the Employee Relations Training Program (ERTP).

The majority of this program's members had law or master's degrees. The trainees were assigned primarily to manufacturing components, and they took the manufacturing courses mainly to ensure that they clearly understood the problems and issues in the manufacturing organizations and were prepared to address the unions and community issues.

I was a member of this program, after graduating from the financial program, and I had all my assignments in manufacturing, including several foreman assignments. One of the attributes of many of the trainees—including me—was that they were more business people than social scientists. The manufacturing courses gave me a clear perspective on the workers and their relationships with the unions.

And from those courses it was clear—to me at least—that actually liking people was an impediment to success in this particular area. Liking people and having them like you was not what it was about.

COMMON CHARACTERISTICS OF ALL GE TRAINING PROGRAMS

All of the GE training programs had several common characteristics. They were companywide; targeted talented recruits; lasted for three years; had tough, demanding courses; and continually evaluated both the on-the-job and class performance of the trainees.

- *Companywide.* Cordiner wanted to preserve the cohesiveness of the company and not allow decentralization to fragment it. All of the programs were companywide, therefore, and operated at the company level.
- *Talented recruits.* The recruits were all bright, hardworking, and committed people. GE was not interested in hiring "crown princes," but rather it wanted people who would work hard to get ahead. Most of the recruits came from middle-class and blue-collar backgrounds.
- *Three years' duration.* Except for the one-year, MBA-oriented Marketing Training Program, the training programs were three years in duration and included six-month assignments. Most of the programs required a move to two or three locations.
- *Tough, demanding courses.* These courses were designed at the college level and in some cases even at the graduate level, and they combined theory and GE practices. They were taught by operating people and not academics. Some of the courses, such as the engineering and the financial management courses, had examinations, and the participants received grades, just as they would have if they were in college.
- *"Up-or-out" philosophy.* All of the trainees were evaluated every six months. If they didn't measure up, they were asked to leave. Grades were also used to determine if a trainee would continue to be promoted—and employed.

Functional training programs have been part of the GE culture since its beginning; Cordiner made them more comprehensive and more professional. The objective was to develop individuals who blended professional *and* GE expertise. They were all taught the GE Way.

The ultimate objective was for trainees to become part of the GE corporate family and be willing to dedicate their lives to the company. Projecting this image of GE employment reinforced the womb-to-tomb mindset even though the programs were founded on an up-or-out mentality.

MAKE CHANGES, AND DON'T WORRY ABOUT THE CONSEQUENCES

One of the problems I found with the programs was that assignments were only six months in duration. This was just enough time for the trainee to make changes—and then leave.

In many cases, the changes were not well thought through, so the next trainee was stuck with undoing many of the problems created by his or her predecessors. GE frequently experienced the same problem with some of the general managers who would make major and disruptive changes when they arrived—changes that would cause major problems in the future—and then leave before those chickens came home to roost. It is interesting to note that Jeff Immelt, the current CEO, has recognized this problem and has instituted policies to keep key professionals and managers on the job longer so that they live with the results of the key decisions they make.

TAKEAWAYS

Leadership

Diversification, decentralization, and management by objectives. Cordiner and his team recognized that if they were to continue to be diversified, they could no longer be led from the top down. They adopted a new and relatively unproven way to manage: MBO. This was a risk, but they recognized that the organization and its measures had to be consistent with the strategy that they decided to pursue.

- *Recommendation.* Take a look at your organization and its reward system and make sure that they fit the strategy you have elected to implement. If they are not consistent, you must either change the strategy or the execution programs.

Talent

Professional management. A key part of making decentralization work was to have skilled, trained, competent managers at all levels. This required intensive and continuing training. The major flaw in this conceptual framework was the belief that managers were interchangeable and—with management training—could succeed in any situation or industry.

- *Recommendation.* Determine what skills are most critical in your specific markets and industries and be sure that your key managers and professionals are developed to operate in these environments. Make sure that you don't get trapped into a great-manager-can-manage-anything mentality.

Functional training and development. Business requires a *team* effort. The team must have the right talents in each of its critical functions. GE elected to develop its own talent base, function by function by function. It has been successful, on balance, but it is time-consuming and expensive. Few companies can afford the size and extent of GE's programs.

- *Recommendation.* Be sure that you determine which are the most critical functional skills for your organization and see to it that you develop at least those skills in your personnel. Remember that functional needs change over time and that a cookie-cutter, one-size-fits-all philosophy is unlikely to succeed.

Networks

Too many conflicting measures. Cordiner identified what he considered his eight key measurements or key results. Unfortunately, these measures are not all equal, and some are even in conflict. I believe that GE has too many measures and would be far better off focusing on just a few.

- *Recommendation.* Yes, measurement is critical, but be sure that you are selective in using measures to control your organization. Avoid complex and contradictory measures and rewards. Just as you can't be all things to all people, you can't satisfy all measures equally.

CHAPTER

The Conversion of Ronald Reagan

Let's introduce the main theme of this chapter—Ralph Cordiner's antipathy for Big Government and Big Labor—by citing Cordiner's own words on the subject:

> **The Company faced the same external challenges as the rest of business, although perhaps they have a special significance for large corporations. Among the most important of these were four troublesome conditions that still stand as active and potential roadblocks to economic and social progress.**
>
> **They are:**
>
> 1. **Excessively high taxes which are structured to penalize success and initiative;**
> 2. **Growing, unchecked union power which too often tends to seek its own ends, regardless of the consequences for the great majority of the people;**
> 3. **A fantastically growing federal government, highly centralized, tending to exert more and more control over the national economic life, and**

4. **The latent suspicion of "big business," a tempting target for demagogues who hunt for votes regardless of the economic and social consequences.**[1]

Cordiner instituted a very strong program to counter these trends. He hired a former associate, an appliance salesman named Lemuel R. Boulware, to develop programs to educate management about these critical issues so that it would be able to effectively communicate the negative impacts of big unions and big government.

RONALD REAGAN: SPREADING THE MESSAGE

Boulware hired a somewhat faded Hollywood actor, Ronald Reagan, to serve as the host of the *General Electric Theater* television show and—more important—to become his internal missionary to spread the word of the threat of organized labor and big business and to stress the merits of free enterprise.

Reagan traveled to GE factories around the country, where he spoke to both employees and managers at corporate banquets, thereby gaining a valuable political apprenticeship. His speeches were part patriotism, part pro-business pep rally. And though he was a Democrat—and a former union president—his message was becoming increasingly conservative. By the time *General Electric Theater* concluded its eight-year run in 1962, Reagan claimed to have visited all 135 of GE's research and manufacturing facilities and to have met some 250,000 individuals.

The combination of the influence of Lem Boulware and the speeches he gave led Reagan to convert from being a liberal Democrat to being a conservative Republican. This is how he described his conversion:

> **I began to talk more and more of how government had expanded and was infringing on liberties and interfering with private enterprise . . . . It finally grew to the point that one day I came home from a speaking tour and said to Nancy, "I go out there and make these speeches which I believe—they are my own speeches—and then every four years I find myself campaigning for the people who are doing the things that I am speaking against." And I said, "I am on the wrong side."**[2]

THE MOVE TO NONUNION, CORPORATE-FRIENDLY U.S. LOCATIONS

Cordiner moved his manufacturing facilities out of their traditional GE locations into new and nonunion locations. Several criteria were used to select the sites for the new plants. These included low labor costs, low unionism, and friendly state and local governments. Cordiner wanted to avoid the problems that he was having in the traditional GE Works—in places such as Schenectady, Lynn, Bridgeport, and Philadelphia—which were strong bastions of unionism and where the local communities had come to believe that GE owed them something because they were there.

This push was one of the major reasons why the company built its "factory of the future" in Louisville, Kentucky, to produce its GE-branded major appliances. But the IUE was more aggressive and proactive than the company. By the time the plant opened, it was highly unionized, and it became one of the most militant of all GE locations, even more than those in the Northeast.

Nevertheless, moving plants—even moving them overseas—became a common practice at GE, as well as at other companies, and it dramatically changed the relationships of the company with its local communities. In one sense, this gave GE more leverage, but it also made the traditional GE communities (Schenectady, Lynn, and Syracuse) more hostile and may have even accelerated plant moves.

"BOULWARISM": "DO RIGHT VOLUNTARILY"

The theme "do right voluntarily" summarized what the company planned to do with unions. In particular, GE intended to fight so-called pattern bargaining, in which the first group to settle set the "pattern" that all similar agreements would follow. This was, and still is, the auto industry's approach. As Boulware himself put it: "Pattern settlements played into the hands of union officials, who portrayed an employee needed to 'triumph over greedy and vicious management'" and who accordingly had to drag an unwilling company into doing the right thing by its employees.

Boulware believed that such tactics discredited both capitalism and the company in the eyes of employees. He further believed that those tactics nurtured employee resentment and hurt productivity by appearing to give credit to the unions for wringing from the company what it had been willing to give at the very outset of negotiations.

Fair But Firm Offers

Accordingly, Boulware abandoned the pattern idea. Instead he painstakingly researched each opening GE offered. Soon after that, he presented an up-front, fleshed-out competitive "product" (that is, a contract) that he termed "fair but firm"—an offer he felt would be at once attractive to the employees and fit within the limited means of the company and its customers.

Do Your Homework

Under the tutelage of Lem Boulware, the company did extensive research into the needs and wants of both its unionized and nonunionized employees. Based on its findings, the company created a wage-and-benefits package that it believed was fair and would satisfy the employees. This included wages, insurance, education, and pension packages. In many cases, these programs were unique and well above industry standards. The offer would be made to the unions prior to negotiations, and then the company would stand fast. Nonunion workers were also offered the package and were told they would get the new deal regardless of the unions' decisions about accepting the contract.

Though the company continued to negotiate, GE management made it clear that this was its best offer, and though some minor changes might be made, the package would stand even if the unions decided to walk out and strike. Since there were many nonunion shops and the unions were not united themselves, it placed GE is a very strong competitive position and made union leaders seem to be unnecessary. This angered and frustrated the unions, and in most cases, they took the offer with only slight modifications.

Union officials bridled at this new management approach and argued that the offer was nothing but a rigid take-it-or-leave-it stand and that, for all its talk of "balanced best interests," GE was "playing

God." The company was simply not bargaining in good faith, said the unions; it could have offered GE employees much more out of its "swollen" profits without having to raise prices.

The process was christened "Boulwarism," which became known worldwide. Boulware maintained that he was not inflexible, that only one of his opening proposals wound up without amendment in the GE contract, and that he was always receptive to the idea of letting the unions provide "any old or new information proving changes would be in the balanced best interests of all." The ongoing Boulware versus the union officials' battle of ideas became public knowledge, and politicians, commentators, and editorialists began taking sides.

But GE's 1960 negotiations with the International Union of Electrical, Radio, and Machine Workers, AFL-CIO, misfired. It led to a three-week strike and subsequently to a ruling by the National Labor Relations Board (NLRB) that through Boulwarism, GE had committed an "unfair labor practice."

According to a 1969 U.S. Second Court of Appeals decision sustaining the ruling, GE had allegedly used "sham discussions" instead of "genuine arguments." In addition, GE supposedly conducted a communications program that emphasized "both powerlessness and uselessness of union to its members" and that "pictured employer as true defender of interest of employees, further denigrating union, and sharply curbing employer's ability to change its own position."[3]

Boulware retired from GE in 1961, and Boulwarism as an idea and policy passed into history. So too did the heyday of adversarial unionism fade away along with the tide of union membership, as both the nation's and GE's labor force became sharply deunionized in the new age of information technology and global competitiveness.

In retrospect, we can see that the Boulware approach became a key element in GE's labor relations programs, and it allowed the company to take actions that other companies could not take. The company was free to do what it believed was in the balanced interest of all of the key stakeholders. Overall, it should be noted, GE employees were satisfied with the company's offering, and GE continued to be competitive. I believe that GE's strong labor relations stance enabled the company to avoid giving away expensive benefits and wages, such benefits and wages being the underlying problem that other major companies, such as GM and Ford, are trying to undo today.

WHY DID BOULWARISM SUCCEED?

Let's examine why Boulwarism was successful at GE:

First, GE had always been interested in its employees and had provided forward-looking employee programs such as a suggestion system (1906), pensions (1912), and insurance (1920).

Second, the UE was a communist-led union that appeared more concerned with a "people's revolution" than with the conditions faced by the GE workers themselves. This perception was enhanced by the infamous McCarthy hearings.

Third, the CIO created a competing non-communist-controlled union, headed by Jim Carey. The new union—the IUE—tried to get the workers to switch from the UE to IUE, and this divided the workers. And there were other powerful unions at GE as well, including the Teamsters and IBEW. Having so many unions, each competing against the others, permitted Boulware and his successors to divide and conquer. This was different from the auto, steel, and transportation industries, which usually had one union to negotiate with within the industry.

Fourth, management did its homework, and it was willing to give the workers excellent benefits that were innovative at the time. In most cases, the workers recognized that GE benefits and offers were good, so they were not interested in striking. I can remember when I arrived in Schenectady for my first training assignment, I learned that the employees and community said that GE stood for "Generous Electric."

Fifth, GE refused to accept industry negotiations. It insisted that it negotiate *as a company*. In most cases, Westinghouse and other key electrical manufacturers followed the GE lead, but it was company by company and not an industry agreement. This too was very different than other industries.

Finally, the GE leaders showed that they were willing to move plants if they could not be profitable. There were many U.S. cities that were nonunion and wanted the new jobs, especially GE jobs.

On a personal note, I believe that unions have lost their clout and in fact are weak in almost all industries. Society is not interested in having workers strike and disrupt their habits. The unions have lacked strong leadership since the death of their true giants—people such as Walter Reuther, George Meany, Mike Quill, and John L. Lewis. Unions have learned that they need to consolidate and merge to increase their solidarity and clout, but so far, such unions engage only a very small percentage of American workers.

As I was writing this book, there was a major split in the AFL, and the new unions representing the service sector, who are primarily Hispanic and other minorities, split with the parent union. This is similar to what happened in the 1930s, when the industrial unions split from the AFL craft unions and formed the CIO. The manufacturing sector unions are very weak, so GE has continued to practice a modified form of Boulwarism, which in simple terms means do your homework, understand what workers need and want, and then give it to them "voluntarily."

The real problem for the unions is that all companies now manufacture in foreign countries, and they outsource a major part of their output. This enables them to switch product manufacturing to the most favorable location and thus negate the impact of strikes.

I think GE's labor relations strategy will continue to work until there is a major change in our society or a major crisis. I have always believed that the next unionization thrust will come when the professional-class workers organize. In 2005, an increasing number of professionals—including doctors, college professors, judges, psychologists, and other professionals—were joining or creating unions because they felt they needed someone to represent their interests against government and employers.

ALMOST FIRED

Before we leave our discussion of GE's union relations strategies and policies, I want to share a personal experience that demonstrated how GE controlled its union relationships in the 1950s and 1960s.

As a member of the Employee Relations Training Program, I was working as a foreman of the Pittsfield-based distribution transformer test and inspection operation.

The training program encouraged trainees to become involved in the community, so I joined the Junior Chamber of Commerce. One of its activities was a weekly radio program. I became one of the hosts of this program, and I decided it would be interesting to invite a union representative to come on the show.

At that time, Jim Carey, the president of the IUE, had decided to assign national union organizers to help the local union increase its local power. I invited the Pittsfield union representative to join me on my program. He was a fellow Fordham alumnus, and so I thought it would be a good interview. During the program, the representative discussed several of the major issues. My associates and I were pleased.

Next morning, I was summoned to the office of the GE union relations manager. He was irate that I would conduct such an interview and accused me of negotiating with the union and overstepping my authority. It was clear that I was going to either be fired or severely reprimanded. I explained my position and what had happened. Fortunately, reason reigned over emotion, and I was told never to do it again.

This incident reinforced my opinion that GE was not a democratic institution, and it was highly defensive of its right to deal with the union. It was a lesson learned; however, I never stopped being an independent thinker and doing what I thought was "right voluntarily."

PRIVATE VERSUS PUBLIC ELECTRICAL SYSTEMS

GE took very strong stands on a number of other public issues. One of the issues was the increasing growth of government-owned electric utilities, including the Tennessee Valley Authority (TVA).

These projects were part of the New Deal, and there was strong support for the nationalization of all utilities. GE was not really enthusiastic to have the government as its customer at this time. GE management, though it was very socialistically oriented, clearly understood that selling to the government would cause price erosion and decrease GE's bottom line.

At the same time, it's obvious that if you take a stand against a specific type of customer group or take sides on which group you will support, you run the risk of antagonizing the group you are not supporting. GE decided to go ahead and do this for several reasons.

First, as indicated above, the company recognized that if the government became the customer, then the company would be forced to compete on price alone and would lose its competitive advantage.

Second, it was concerned that if publicly owned utilities were successful in driving down overall prices, other utilities—possibly *all* of them—would be nationalized, and this would have a negative impact on GE's ability to offer value-added services. In fact, the next natural step would be nationalizing the *producers* of the equipment. Even though Swope and Young were interested in helping society, they were not interested in being nationalized, as had so many companies in many European countries.

Finally, price competition would permit foreign competitors to gain a stronger foothold in the United States, and this would completely change the balance of power.

It is interesting to note that one of the reasons that the "Great Electrical Conspiracy" was uncovered in the late 1950s was because of the bids to TVA. These bids were public record, and the electrical unions that were highly adversarial in the 1950s published the bids, which clearly showed that there was no price competition. It became obvious that the bidders were dividing the market and were giving orders to smaller companies to ensure that they stayed in business while keeping the giant share for themselves.

So being willing to support one group of customers against another is a double-edged sword. That act may come back to haunt you even decades in the future.

GE'S WATERGATE: THE GREAT ELECTRICAL CONSPIRACY

As we've seen, Cordiner was very successful in growing the traditional business, moving into new markets, developing new systems, and installing a very comprehensive human resource and public relations program. The company's revenues grew, and so did profits.

GE's management system became highly respected. Cordiner started to work on identifying his successor, and reportedly he planned to turn over command to President Robert Paxton. Paxton was a proven power systems executive, and was well thought of in the company.

Then came the price-fixing scandal, the Great Electrical Conspiracy. GE, Westinghouse, Allis-Chalmers, and other key electrical systems and products companies were indicted for fixing prices on TVA bids and other government contracts. The companies were found guilty and were required to pay fines. In addition, many of the senior executives of the companies were convicted and sentenced to jail. All of the GE executives were fired. The other companies were more forgiving and didn't fire their executives.

THE NEGATIVE RESULTS OF THE PRICE-FIXING SCANDAL

There were several highly negative impacts that grew out of the scandal. First, GE's strong relationships with the electric utilities—a key underpinning of the company's success in this market—were shattered. The electric utility executives were forced to become more adversarial in their dealings with the company. They were required to seek bids from foreign companies, such as Siemens, Hitachi, and Toshiba. As a result, the U.S. producers, including GE, lost their dominant position, and global competitors gained a stronger position in this market, which they have continued to hold.

In addition, GE lost many senior executives in the power systems business. Entire management teams in Pittsfield's power and distribution transformer and in Philadelphia's switchgear operations were fired, and it was difficult to replace the lost talent. Partly as a result, GE's revenues stalled at $5 billion and didn't move for more than three years.

I was a trainee in Pittsfield when the news broke about the potential price fixing. The IUE, the dominant union, passed out handbills describing the circumstances and showing how the bids on some contracts were within cents of each other and how companies always seemed to win some bids, almost always in proportion to their industry weight. Their documents clearly showed not only that the prices were fixed but also that the business was divided according to market share. In other words, GE and Westinghouse got the major share, and others, such as Allis-Chalmers, got a smaller, but representative, share.

The Employee Relations and Manufacturing trainees were required to give out the company explanation, which was obviously written by the legal department. The union representatives and the trainees both stood outside the gates and gave out their respective documents. The union documents were better written and easier to understand, so they soon ran out of their handbills.

Unfortunately the company documents were the opposite: very legalistic and defensive in tone. We had trouble even giving them away, and we were left with many copies. I thought this was funny, especially when the union representatives, who felt sorry for us, took some of our documents and handed them out so we could go to work.

I recall the weekend when all of the key executives in the transformer division were suspended. This included both the division and two department general managers and the marketing and sales vice presidents. By Monday morning, there was literally no one running the businesses at the top. All of the executives had been fired, and the division general manager position was given to the vice president of manufacturing. Obviously the manufacturing organization didn't know about the price fixing, and its executives were the only ones left.

Robert Paxton, assumed heir apparent to Cordiner, came to Pittsfield and gave a speech in which he said that he and Cordiner were completely unaware of the conspiracy. My manager, Orv Wilkinson, returned from the meeting and told me that he hoped that Paxton was telling the truth. It appears that he was *not* telling the truth, given that he subsequently resigned.

I call this incident "GE's Watergate," since Paxton was implicated, forced to resign, and was never able to succeed Cordiner. Cordiner's image was tarnished and was never the same. Unlike Nixon, Cordiner kept his job, although he was kicked upstairs.

TAKEAWAYS
Influence

"Do right voluntarily." Among American business leaders, Cordiner and his team had a very different perspective about the role of unions and government. They believed that these two groups were conspiring to take away their power to control their own destiny, and so they took aggressive actions to counter them. This included hiring and using the talents of a future president of the United States.

- *Recommendation.* It is vital that you clearly understand the power of all of your key stakeholders and recognize that these groups can change from friend to foe and even back to friend. One of the clear lessons of strategic thinking is to continually assess all of the key stakeholders and focus on those who can be allies or adversaries.

Doing your homework and taking a firm stand. GE was willing to do its homework, decide what it believed was right for both the employees and the company, and then take a strong stand, even if it meant a strike. This enabled the company to keep its labor costs under control and not give away benefits, which would have had a long-term negative impact.

- *Recommendation.* It is important that you know what the company can afford and not be blackmailed into giving away your rights or assuming unnecessary costs. This should include taking stands on all sociopolitical and economic issues, as well as those which impact your employees.

CHAPTER

GE Can Do Anything It Wants to Do

ALTHOUGH FRED Borch began his career at GE as a financial auditor, he spent most of his professional life in sales and marketing. He was a member of the Crotonville-based Management Consulting Services, vice president of Corporate Marketing Services, and in 1959 was appointed to lead the consumer products group. In December 1963, he was named president and CEO of GE (see Exhibit 9-1).

Borch recognized the need to jumpstart the company, and he knew that this would require risky ventures. Since he had a marketing background, he decided to launch a search for new growth opportunities that were market based but would still build on GE's core competencies and strengths.

EXTERNAL FIRST: THE "GROWTH COUNCIL"

Borch instituted the Growth Council, consisting of some of the best minds inside and outside the company. The council's mission was to identify market opportunities that were growing faster than the GNP

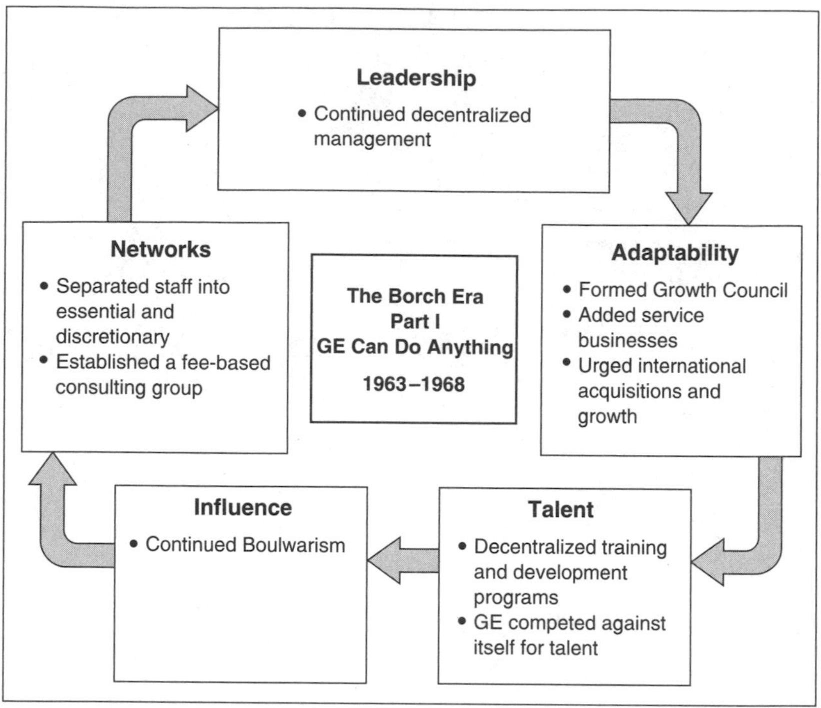

Exhibit 9-1 LATIN and the Borch I era from 1963 to 1968.

and in which GE had unique abilities and might gain a competitive advantage.

Borch recognized that the services sector often enjoyed higher margins and was less vulnerable to foreign price competition, so he insisted that both product and service opportunities be identified.

THE GROWTH COUNCIL'S PROPOSALS

Using the two key criteria of beating the GNP and playing to GE's strengths, the council proposed nine corporate-sponsored new ventures. Of the nine, four were product and system opportunities and five were service businesses (see Table 9-1).

Product Venture 1: Nuclear Energy

Cordiner had already made nuclear power a major GE venture, and the council recommended that GE continue to aggressively

Recommended Growth Ventures	
Product Opportunities	**Service Opportunities**
Nuclear energy	Entertainment
Computers	Community development and housing
Commercial jet engines	Personal and financial services
Polymer chemicals	Medicine
—	Education

Table 9-1 Growth Council's nine recommended product and services venture.

obtain BWR orders and maintain the unprofitable turnkey pricing strategy.

The theory was that the company with the largest installed base would ultimately be the winner. The council pointed out that there were other parts of the nuclear value chain that GE should evaluate and pursue if they looked viable. Two opportunities were highlighted. One was to provide enrichment services, and the second was to help utilities get rid of the highly toxic nuclear waste safely.

Unfortunately, the nuclear opportunity was never profitable, and growth stopped almost immediately with the Three Mile Island accident and the Russian disaster at Chernobyl. But GE remained in the nuclear power business even after the market collapsed. Recall that the nuclear business became profitable only when there were no new orders and the companies that built the reactors were able to capitalize on their strong repair and maintenance business. This was particularly true for GE, since it was the only company that could service the BWR units.

Product Venture 2: Business Computers (GE's Vietnam)

The 1956 Bank of America contract came close to putting GE in the business and financial accounting end of the computer business, but the deal was nixed by Cordiner.

Despite this setback, many in General Electric recognized the potential of using computers to streamline the company's accounting, financial, and operating systems. GE invested heavily in IBM computers, becoming IBM's largest private customer. The company was already in the industrial, process, and electric utility computer businesses, and it was a leader in automating many of its manufacturing operations. The aerospace group was a major supplier of computerized controls for military and defense applications.

Because the business computer market was still in its early growth stage and because GE had a large installed computer base, was highly skilled in using computers, and had developed proprietary software for accounting and business applications, the Growth Council recommended that GE enter the commercial and business computer market and compete with IBM.

GE established a new business unit in Phoenix, Arizona, and acquired Machine Bull in France. Unfortunately, the Growth Council made several major miscalculations that ultimately contributed to the venture's failure:

1. The council did not take into consideration the unwillingness of management information system (MIS) managers to switch from IBM.
2. The cost of switching was larger than the council thought it would be.
3. Leasing required huge cash flows.
4. The council did not anticipate fully the "Snow White and the Seven Dwarfs" phenomenon.
5. Good managers can't manage everything.

"No One Gets Fired for Picking IBM"

The first miscalculation was the difficulty of having the customers' information systems management and professionals switch to a non-IBM computer system. GE clearly failed to recognize that most of these information services managers and professionals had been trained by IBM, they were not familiar with other systems, and they were not inclined to be adventurous.

There was a common saying in information technology organizations at that time that underscores GE's challenge: "No one gets fired for recommending IBM systems, even if they're not the best." The conservative choice prevails.

The Cost Is More Than Just the Purchase Price of the Computer

Second, the expense and disruptive impact of changing systems were greatly underestimated. Unfortunately, GE learned this the hard way. Once the company decided to enter the computer market, Borch and his team insisted that all of the internal IBM systems be replaced with GE systems. This was very difficult and took much longer than anticipated. Not only did the equipment have to be changed but also the software had to be rewritten and the personnel trained on the new system. Further, the GE systems, in some cases, were not as good at the IBM systems. This negatively impacted GE's profitability and productivity.

A Leasing Business Requires Huge Cash Flows

Third, the Growth Council team failed to fully recognize the financial requirements and needs of leasing computers rather than selling them. IBM used leasing and extensive support services to create an almost impenetrable barrier to entry.

At this time, IBM didn't sell computers but only leased them to its customers. This meant that customers didn't have to invest their own capital to use computers, and IBM provided them with extensive installation, servicing, and software support. All of this meant that GE and the other competitors had to use their own money to play in the computer game, and it was a very capital-intensive way of doing business.

This was very different from the way GE sold to its electrical utility customers, for example. In that situation, the electric utilities had access to other people's money, improved their earnings by investment, and even paid their suppliers' progress payments during the production cycle. In short, the electric utility market was cash positive, not cash negative.

"Snow White and the Seven Dwarfs"

The team also failed to anticipate that several other companies that were able to produce computers—including Westinghouse, Honeywell, and Control Data—might simultaneously decide to enter the business computer market. Of course, that's exactly what happened, and these new entries—combined with existing competitors Univac, Siemens, and Hitachi—crowded the market. This competitive situation was described as "Snow White and Seven Dwarfs," with IBM playing the role of Snow White and the other competitors being the dwarfs.

All of these factors made the computer venture a very unprofitable and embarrassing situation for GE. Even with its French Machine Bull acquisition, GE never gained sufficient volume and share to be a viable player. And it wasn't just the financial costs that made this venture a significant negative for GE; many talented and high-potential managers left the company in frustration, and that had an even more serious impact over the long run.

Good Managers Can't *Manage Everything*

You will recall that one of the underpinning assumptions of Cordiner's philosophy was that a good manager could be taught to manage anything. The computer venture clearly demonstrated that this assumption was wrong.

Many of the GE managers assigned to the computer business had little or no experience in this type of technologically based, cash and capital intensive market, where they were competing against a very strong, well-entrenched, and cash-rich market leader. The lessons they learned at Crotonville didn't prepare them for the battles they fought, and GE lost hundreds of very capable people in trying. Initially, the company followed an internal selection strategy. The company then gradually went out and hired industry professionals, but doing so was not sufficient to stop the bleeding and the loss of key managers and professionals.

I call this "GE's Vietnam" because of the parallels between the tremendous effort the United States invested in a losing cause and the embarrassment of being forced to admit defeat and withdraw with major losses.

Product Venture 3: Commercial Jet Engines

Recall that during World War II, GE made major contributions to the development of the jet engine. GE and Pratt & Whitney (P&W) both recognized the potential of this new aircraft propulsion technology for powering commercial aircraft, but it was Pratt & Whitney that first worked on commercial aircraft applications—soon capturing 75 percent of that market—while GE focused on continuing military applications.

The Growth Council recognized the potential of the commercial jet engine applications, and as a result, GE created two separate facilities. The Cincinnati suburb of Evendale became home to the large commercial jet engine business unit, and Lynn, Massachusetts, focused on the smaller military engine.

Gerhard Neuman, a former World War II Flying Tiger mechanic, was appointed general manager of the commercial engine department. He was a very aggressive, competitive leader who was determined to be No. 1 in this market.

By this point, the major competitors in the segment were the General Motors' Allison Division and United Technology's Pratt & Whitney unit. Allison was not given the support of General Motors, since it had decided to divest itself of all its nonautomotive business units. United Technologies CEO Harry Gray, however, was determined to maintain P&W's commercial engine lead.

Two Groups of Decision Makers

Selling jet engines required convincing two groups of decision makers. First were the major commercial aircraft manufacturers—Boeing, McDonnell, and Douglas—that had to be convinced that the engines were right for their aircraft.

The second customer was the airlines. Airlines were not only interested in the best performance in terms of safety and reliability but they also wanted the lowest operating, repair, and maintenance costs. In most cases, both the airlines and aircraft manufacturers wanted only one engine supplier because it was expensive to employ the higher number of technicians with the technical skills to deal with more than one.

Since Pratt & Whitney commanded 75 percent of the commercial engine business, and since both the aircraft manufacturers and the airlines were satisfied with P&W's quality and performance, GE faced a major challenge to unseat P&W. GE therefore embraced a twofold strategy. First, it worked on developing engines that were clearly more efficient, cost less to operate, and were easier to maintain and repair.

But this was not enough. Success required a second unique strategy, which involved financing. Recognizing that the airline industry was very capital intensive, GE's aircraft engine business worked with GE Credit to provide an attractive financial program for the airlines. This involved *leasing*, instead of selling—and not just the engines. If the airlines agreed to require that GE engines be installed on the aircraft they purchased, then GE would *purchase the aircraft and lease it to the airlines*.

It was an audacious move, but the financing was so attractive that the airlines couldn't refuse. The offer effectively forced aircraft manufacturers to use GE rather than P&W engines. Over time, the market shares were reversed: GE then had 75 percent of the market, while P&W had the rest.

Another benefit of this financial approach was that GE also provided the repair, maintenance, and upgrading services for the engines, and it was able to increase its margins with a combination of labor and spare parts revenues.

This was a winning strategy, and it forced all of the other manufacturers to follow suit. In a sense, GE did to P&W in this market what IBM did to GE and other competitors in the business computer market—with comparable success.

Product Venture 4: Polymer Chemicals

In his book, Cordiner described how GE's materials businesses were created. In most cases, they were an unexpected result of trying to create a new and better way of insulating generators or transformers. In fact, the successful creation of GE's materials and chemical businesses resulted from a unique combination of invention and strategic leadership.

One of the major reasons that General Electric's materials businesses succeeded was a chemical engineering Ph.D. named Charlie Reed. Reed, blessed with both creativity and leadership skills, was able to put together a team of very diverse individuals and encourage them to create a business—one that has continued to be a major part of the GE culture. One of the by-products of this business, of course, was Jack Welch.

The strategy was simple but very effective. This business unit focused on using GE materials and chemical know-how to solve high-value problems faced by key industries. Conversely, the group explicitly avoided competing in the traditional high-volume commodity materials sector dominated by Du Pont and others. Reed's team developed a number of new materials, including Lexan and Noryl, and the business has been very profitable for many years.

The "Uniqueness" of the Plastics/Welch Culture

I always found it interesting that the plastics business teams stressed that they were *different* and not just another part of GE. True, they had that entrepreneurial swagger that is often associated with successful new ventures. In reality, though, they *were* part of the company, and they weren't unique in being "different." Most of the GE business units had their own distinct cultures.

In fact, I don't believe that there has been one "GE culture" since the company became highly diversified. Each business is so different that it develops its own culture and style. Unlike GM, Ford, or the pre-Gerstner IBM, there was no one GE style or culture. In fact, one reason the company has been able to be both diversified and successful is that *more than one culture is tolerated.*

To recap, the four product ventures turned in mixed results (see Table 9-2). Computers were a complete failure, and nuclear has never done what it was expected to do. Commercial engines became both a product and financial services winner, and polymer chemicals, although it took time, finally became profitable.

The Product Venture Results

Complete Failure	Didn't Meet Expectations	Successful
Computers	Nuclear	Aircraft engines
		Polymer chemicals

Table 9-2 Evaluation of the four product venture's results.

PRODUCT VENTURE CHARACTERISTICS

One of the common characteristics of these ventures was that they were going after huge potential markets, which required perseverance and financial resources to make them successful. All of them required long-term relationship building, and they forced GE to provide the customer not only with great products but also with the skills, financing, and management needed to be successful. You can see that these are very similar to the characteristics required in the electric utility industry, which was so well known and understood by the GE management. These are the types of businesses in which GE has been able to win.

THE GROWTH COUNCIL'S SERVICE VENTURES

Traditionally, GE viewed services as a means to sell products and systems rather than as businesses in and of themselves.

Borch wanted GE to create new, high-profit service businesses for a number of reasons. First, there were often higher margins in providing services than in selling products. Second, they were less susceptible to foreign competition. Third, they were less cyclical. Finally, they could be used in combination with the products businesses to create stronger customer relationships.

Again, as with the products initiatives, the goal was to identify services that (1) were growing faster than the GNP and (2) would build on existing GE capabilities and know-how.

FIVE SERVICE BUSINESSES RECOMMENDED AND IMPLEMENTED

1. Entertainment
2. Community development and housing
3. Personal and financial services
4. Medicine
5. Education

Service Venture I: Entertainment

Even though GE was required to divest its stake in RCA, it continued to own and operate several radio and television stations. The Growth Council concluded that there was an opportunity to create special programming for the television networks and independent stations and to provide films for distribution through traditional movie theater channels.

Consistent with the "grow your businesses" theme, the company created a new division, Tomorrow Entertainment, to produce movies and specials.

Show Biz Is Different

One of the first productions was *Marco*, starring Desi Arnaz, Jr. Put kindly, this was a total disaster, both financially and artistically.

It also demonstrated convincingly that GE management—traditionally, a rather staid group—was totally unprepared for the Hollywood lifestyle. To cite just one example among many: GE had a policy that all of its employees had to take a physical exam. The stars of the picture were asked to take these physical exams in the GE headquarters. They complied with the request, and then—male and female alike—shed all of their clothes and streaked buck naked through the halls of Corporate. Based on this episode and others like it, many of us concluded that GE was not ready for prime time.

More Miscalculations

But there were more serious problems ahead. GE's Growth Council failed to recognize that the motion-picture distribution business—and its associated theaters—were highly controlled and that a new studio had little chance of screening its pictures in these theaters. Further, the television market was small because the major studios or the networks themselves provided the programming.

The result was another unprofitable and poorly evaluated growth opportunity.

In the last few years, GE has continued to pursue this high-risk, high-reward opportunity. In 2003, for example, GE acquired Universal Studios, so it appears to still be pursuing the same game plan that Borch envisioned in his reign. The major difference, of course, is that Borch tried unsuccessfully to build it from within, while the Welch and Immelt administrations have been willing to make it an acquisition game.

Service Venture 2: Community Development and Housing

One of the more visionary ideas of the Growth Council was to go into the business of building complete communities, including all of the infrastructure, utilities, schools, retail, and homes normally associated with a community.

GE selected Columbia, Maryland, as its targeted location. It built an Appliance Park-East in the town, and it hoped to use this to attract other industry and to be the foundation of the community.

GE believed that it could supply the equipment to provide the electrical generation, transmission, and distribution, as well as transportation systems.

In addition, it planned to create "homes of the future" using GE appliances, heat pumps, communications products, and electrical devices. Innovative materials—invented by GE, of course—could be used to build the homes.

Finally, the company could provide financing to the home and commercial owners. In short, GE believed it could capture a significant percentage of the contributed value created by building a major new community—and then replicate the experiment in other locations.

Why It Didn't Work

First, GE failed to recognize the need to gain control of cheap land *before* it set out to build a community. Disney, for example, spent years assembling parcels of land before anyone even knew that the entertainment giant had plans to build Disney World and Celebration. It sounds obvious today, but it wasn't obvious to GE at the time: Once it becomes known that a major purchase of land is in the works, speculators move in and drive up the price of land.

Second, GE failed to understand how hard it is get the approval of local and state governments to build, especially on a large scale. Zoning restrictions proved to be a major obstacle to both the community development and modular housing ventures.

Finally, dealing with the highly militant, politically connected, and high-priced trade unions added not only complexity but also significant costs. Further, the company could not control these unions using its generally successful Boulware strategies.

In short, GE failed to think and plan strategically. The project failed to take off and had to be aborted.

Service Venture 3: Personal and Financial Services

The Growth Council recommended that the existing consumer services be extended to include other home-centered services, such as lawn care, painting, carpentry, and plumbing. The strategy was to systematize these crafts and services and thus make them more productive and efficient. Annual service contracts would be offered to consumers so that they could budget these expenses, and GE would be assured that the services would be utilized year-round.

Though some of these additional services were in fact offered, GE found that a large percentage of the profits were made from spare parts and that it was difficult to create more efficient systems that could effectively compete against the local service providers. As a result, GE didn't aggressively pursue the opportunity but rather concentrated on major appliance services and contracts.

One-Stop Financial Services

One of the best ideas of the council was the development of a one-stop financial services offering.

Financial services were at that time extremely fragmented. Banks were prohibited from providing insurance and investments. Investment firms could not offer banking services. Each was highly regulated at the federal and state levels. The council's vision was to build on GE's internal capabilities and create a fully integrated, consumer-focused financial package. In essence, it was a vision of the "one-stop financial services package" that has now become common.

The concept was to use the insurance, pension, investment, and lending skills of the company and create a package to be offered by the GE Credit Company (GECC). This included offering credit, health and life insurance, mutual funds, and investment advice based on GE's internal skills and systems.

GECC had two unique advantages. First, it was not regulated as were the banks, insurance, and investment companies with which it competed, so it could provide services that they could not provide. Second, the company could borrow money at very attractive rates, since it was able to use the parent company's Triple A credit rating.

This financial venture was the most successful of all of the recommended service ventures, and it became a major part of the company's portfolio when Welch became consumer sector executive and later CEO.

Even though the Growth Council started the company moving into this arena, it took more than two decades to make it a very significant contributor to, and factor in, GE's strategies.

Service Venture 4: Medicine

William D. Coolidge, a prolific inventor in GE's R&D lab, revolutionized medical diagnostics when he developed the modern form of the X-ray tube. Later, during the 1930s, GE purchased Pickering and enhanced its medical X-ray position.

The Growth Council envisioned building on the X-ray position in health care to broaden the offering. This would include providing financial and management services to hospitals and the addition of other medical systems that would tie in with its diagnostic position. In addition, GE believed that it could sell health-care services to other companies to manage their health-care programs.

Lacking a Champion

New internal ventures require a strong champion to make them happen. Unfortunately for GE, this health-care venture didn't have such a champion.

In fact, I recall that in the early 1970s, GE considered selling off the X-ray business because it had not kept a leadership position, and new technologies, such as CAT scanning devices, appeared likely to displace the traditional X-ray system.

But this venture later found a strong champion: Jack Welch. He invested heavily in new technologies, including magnetic resonance imaging (MRI). He relocated innovative executives into this business, and it has become one of the company's darlings. One of the leaders of this endeavor was current CEO Jeff Immelt, who continues to be a strong advocate of the health-care business.

Service Venture 5: Education

GE was an early leader in training and developing its employees, and it consistently looked at ways of improving the educational process. The council believed that computer technology and "programmed learning" systems could greatly enhance the educational process. It targeted preschool and elementary education as the two key segments.

General Learning, a new wholly owned subsidiary, was established and given the mission of using GE know-how and technology to improve the learning and efficiency of the educational processes. Since GE had no position in these markets, it acquired Silver-Burdett and several other textbook publishers to gain entry into this area.

A nursery school company was also purchased to uncover new ways of teaching preschool children. The market was still in its embryonic development stage, and there were few competitors trying to do the same thing.

Unfortunately, this was another venture that was not strategically evaluated. The company failed to recognize the power of the educational unions and the reluctance of state and federal educational agencies to support new ways of teaching.

In addition, every local school board had different ideas about what needed to be done. There were no standardized solutions that could be used, and teachers' unions and local school administrators showed little interest in having the educational arena privatized. In fact, they fought GE strenuously. For all these reasons, the new venture ultimately was sold.

LESSONS FROM THE GROWTH COUNCIL'S VENTURES

There are many lessons that we can learn from the Borch Growth Council and its offspring ventures (see Table 9-3).

Venture Scorecard		
Businesses That Failed or Were Transformed into New Businesses		**Businesses That Succeeded**
Businesses That Failed Completely	**Businesses That Were Transformed**	
Computers	Became Nuclear Services	Aircraft Engines
Entertainment	—	Engineered Plastics
Community Development	—	Financial Services
Education	—	Medical Systems
Personal Services	Became Appliance Services	—

Table 9-3 Two main groupings are depicted. Beneath them, column one identifies failed ventures. Column two identifies business that were transformed from the ventures. Column three shows the successes.

It is clear that the council was able to select high-potential growth opportunities. All of the ventures targeted sectors that have since become major industries, and in some cases they are still very attractive. In fact, some companies have been able to capitalize on these opportunities and build very profitable growth organizations. GE was too early in the market's life cycle and attempted to pursue too many ventures without careful strategic evaluations, while lacking the resources to do them all at one time.

GOING GLOBAL

In addition to embarking on these complex internal ventures, Borch challenged the business units to become more global. Several organizations accepted this challenge and made acquisitions to gain entry into the European markets.

Lighting increased its equity in Osram, the German lamp manufacturer, which was one of the original members of the Phoebus Agreement. Television acquired KUBA, a German television company, and major appliances acquired COGENEL, the General Electric of Italy.

It didn't take long to realize that these were major mistakes. Osram didn't add much to the lighting business and in fact became a distraction. KUBA was a market leader in black-and-white television, but it was deficient in the emerging (and quickly dominant) color television technology. The television business was unable to help it since it had a weak position. The same proved true of COGENEL.

In addition, it was apparent that GE's managers for the most part were not internationalists and were poorly equipped to lead foreign organizations. In fact, it was difficult to get managers to accept these jobs, in part because the jobs were considered to be detrimental to the careers of those who were up and coming. Finally, in their foreign operations, the GE executives tried impose the GE Way without adapting it to the different cultures. The combination of these factors contributed to failure.

TOO MUCH STAFF

Before we move to the second stage of Borch's reign, it is important to review another major issue that he had to address: the large, expensive, and adversarial corporate staff organization that he inherited.

You'll recall that Cordiner created a very large staff organization to provide consulting services to the decentralized units. Consultants were assigned to help operating managers—even if they didn't *want* the help. Though the consulting services were free, many general managers resented being forced to use the staff organizations. To make matters worse, often these same individuals conducted the management and functional audits. This clearly inhibited the ability of the staff personnel to gain the confidence of the business units, since they often used insider knowledge in their audit activities.

As a result, there were many confrontations between corporate staff and the operating management. When Borch decided to reduce corporate staff and not require operations to use their services, the operating managers could not conceal their glee.

Two Types of Staff Organizations

Since Borch managed the marketing consulting component of Management Consulting Services, he recognized that there were many very talented professionals in these corporate organizations. Instead of just eliminating the organizations and firing the staff, he came up with an innovative way to allow the staff professionals and management to keep their jobs but at the same time reduce costs. He divided the staff organization into two groups: Corporate Executive Staff and Corporate Consulting Services.

The Corporate Executive Staff included accounting, finance, legal, investor relations, executive manpower, and employee relations—in other words, the traditional types of staff organizations that were needed to operate the company.

All of the other discretionary staff organizations were combined into a new organization, Corporate Consulting Services (CCS). This organization was headed by GE's first female vice president, Marion Kellogg. Kellogg was a career GE employee with a national reputation for her innovative work in employee evaluations and appraisals.

CCS had six major components: engineering, manufacturing, executive education, marketing, advertising and sales promotion, and strategic planning. They operated the entry-level training programs, managed college recruiting, provided functional management and professional training and development programs, as well as providing onsite consulting to operating managers (when requested!).

Liquidate or Be Liquidated

CCS components had to sell their services to the operating management, and therefore they had to compete against external consulting and educational organizations. As a result, CCS fees had to be comparable to those charged by equally skilled external competitors. In other words, Borch wanted to make sure that when CCS was selected, it was because of the value it provided. In addition, CCS organizations were permitted to sell their services and programs to GE's customers, suppliers, and nonprofit educational and community organizations.

The underlying assumption was that if CCS had to sell its services and charge competitive prices, the size of the staff would be reduced, and only those who had unique skills and abilities would survive. Meanwhile, the product departments were urged to establish their own training programs, do their own recruiting, and be as self-sufficient as possible.

Another Miscalculation

Though Borch expected a reduction in staff, the opposite happened. In retrospect, he miscalculated the talents of the service managers and professionals. First, he failed to recognize that these service professionals had friends in the business units, and—in some cases, at least—were considered not only skilled but trusted. Though the rates they charged were comparable to outsiders, CCS consultants knew the GE systems and businesses, so they were often more productive and could do the job less expensively with higher quality.

CCS was not only able to cover its expenses but it was also able to make a profit. These profits were used to hire more staff, so—three years after the creation of CCS—the CCS staff organizations were larger rather than smaller. But this was good news: It demonstrated that the organization was skilled and added value both inside and outside GE.

GE Competing against GE for People

Since corporate college recruiting was curtailed and the number of companywide trainees was significantly reduced, many of the departments and divisions initiated their own recruiting programs. Almost inevitably, they began to compete against existing company programs. In fact, some went directly to the colleges and professional schools and established their own relationships. I was personally involved in college recruiting at this time, and I often competed more aggressively for recruits against other GE components than against other companies.

A CONFEDERATION, NOT A COMPANY

Borch's decentralization, as well as his endorsement of fee-based corporate services, contributed to making GE more like a confederation of independent, often competing businesses than like a single, coherent company.

Employees started to identify more with their individual businesses than with the company as a whole. Often there was competition among the departments, which added to the lack of company spirit. In my estimation, at least, this has continued to be an issue in the company.

TAKEAWAYS

Borch's Growth Opportunity Ventures taught GE many lessons, which GE later incorporated into its strategic thinking and management systems and into the GE Code as well. Let's review some of the reasons that only a few of the ventures survived and succeeded.

Leadership

Unrealistic view of how long ventures take to succeed. Most of the ideas that the Growth Council proposed have become real and profitable businesses. But it has taken decades for them to materialize, and it has required a sustained, long-term commitment and the investment of leadership, people, and money. This is evident with the ultimate success of jet engines and financial services, and—I would argue—the likely resurgence of nuclear power.

- *Recommendation*. Realistically assess the time it will take for your new ventures to grow and become profitable. Make sure that you err on the side of being conservative—and don't overpromise.

Too many ventures at one time. GE's biggest error was to believe that it could pursue all of these ventures at the same time and that it had the financial and human resources to make them all successful. Each of the opportunities required more cash and capital than anticipated, and the total requirements were enormous—beyond any one company's ability to fund them. In fact, it is amazing that the company didn't go broke during this period.

Without a doubt, Borch grew the company: Revenues increased more than $3 billion in three years. But it was a profitless growth, which clearly demonstrated that the company needed a new way of planning and setting priorities.

- *Recommendation*. Be selective. Don't bite off more than you can chew. Focus on the most attractive opportunities where you can most easily succeed and be sure that you have a clear understanding of what it will take to win before you embark.

Adaptability

Didn't understand the businesses. Though the council identified growth opportunities, it did a poor job of figuring out what it would take to sell the products or services. It lacked an appreciation of the competitive environment and the response of the incumbents, and—most important—it didn't take into consideration the power and influence of governments and labor unions.

- *Recommendation*. If you are planning to move into a new market, either by internal ventures or acquisitions, be sure you really understand what is critical to being successful.

Talent

Believed they could do anything. GE leaders believed that they could do anything and that the company's managers had been equipped to manage any business regardless of size, technologies, markets, and so on. Clearly, the outcomes of the ventures demonstrated that this conviction, which dates back to Cordiner and Smiddy, was simply wrong.

- *Recommendation*. Never assume that just because you have been successful in your current businesses that you have the skills and abilities to succeed in others. Recognize that *all* businesses have some distinct aspects that will separate the winners from the losers.

Networks

Made staff earn a living. Although Borch's assumption that he could reduce staff by requiring them to earn their keep turned out to be dead wrong, the idea of having a discretionary, fee-based staff is worth considering.

This approach has several advantages. First, it is Darwinian: Only the fit will survive. Second, it forces the staff to make a contribution to keep clients, and therefore it forces them to keep current. The major dangers are that some will survive just because they have friends inside the company and that the staff may become too myopic.

- *Recommendation*. Separate your staff organization into two groups: essential and discretionary. Determine if you need your own discretionary resource, or if you should outsource it. If you think there is an advantage to having your own staff, then make them earn their keep.

Admitted mistakes and changed. To Borch's credit, he too recognized these errors, and in the second half of his tenure, he changed the company's management system to ensure that these types of mistakes would not be repeated. The ability to admit mistakes and make major changes is clearly one of the major contributions that Borch made to the GE heritage.

- *Recommendation*. Everyone makes mistakes. Sometimes the mistakes are large, and sometimes they are small, but they are all a part of leading and taking risks. The key is to follow Borch's example and be willing to admit your mistakes, take corrective actions, and try not to hide or make excuses.

Now let's move to the second stage of Fred Borch's reign: the period of selectivity and the birth of strategic thinking and decision making.

Portfolio Leadership

GE's Third Stage, 1971 to 2001
Borch/Welch

HIGHLIGHTS

- *Admitting mistakes.* Borch's ventures proved to be overly ambitious and clearly demonstrated that the assumption that "good managers could manage anything" was incorrect. Only four of the ventures were successful, and even the successes took longer to be profitable than expected.
- *Strategic portfolio management.* In 1968, Borch instituted a highly innovative strategic portfolio management system. His successor, Reg Jones, refined and enhanced the system. Consistent with the company's tradition of providing in-depth training, all of the key managers and professionals were required to attend seminars and workshops to ensure that they could successfully apply the new thinking and decision-making processes. Both internal and external consultants were used extensively.
- *Fixation on succession planning.* Jones was committed to selecting the right person to replace him, and he instituted a very extensive suc-

cession planning system. It yielded a very successful individual, but it may also have caused GE to miss several major growth opportunities.

- *"Nothing and no one is sacred."* Jack Welch (1981 to 2001) aggressively challenged all of the business units, embarked on a major pruning and divestiture of unattractive GE businesses, and focused the company on using its financial strengths to become a global leader in financial services.
- *RCA returns to GE ownership.* Welch was able to acquire and merge RCA back into the company. This acquisition enabled GE to become a major player in the broadcast industry and permitted Welch to package RCA and GE businesses together and sell them at attractive prices. This made the strategic portfolio concept a reality.
- *A cultural revolution.* Welch made Crotonville his bully pulpit and used a series of initiatives to change the culture of the company and make himself a "celebrity CEO."
- *"Go home, Mr. Welch!"* The GE team miscalculated the power of the Common Market's administration, and it was refused permission to acquire Honeywell. Welch retired.

CHAPTER

Admitting Mistakes

PROFITLESS GROWTH

Borch's new ventures added more than $3 billion to GE's revenues in three years. But—as noted in Chapter 9—very little of that new revenue dropped to the bottom line. The company's cash position suffered, and investors and GE management alike became concerned. It was clear that the company had overextended itself, that only a few of the ventures were going to be successful, and that even those winners were going to take a longer time to become profitable than was assumed. Borch installed a new strategic management system and initiated a change in how the company evaluated its businesses (see Exhibit 10-1).

THE ORIGINS OF PORTFOLIO MANAGEMENT

The computer venture was the most frustrating and embarrassing of GE's ventures. Although GE was a genuine leader in using computers to streamline its own financial and management systems, that wasn't enough to make the company a real contender against the far stronger

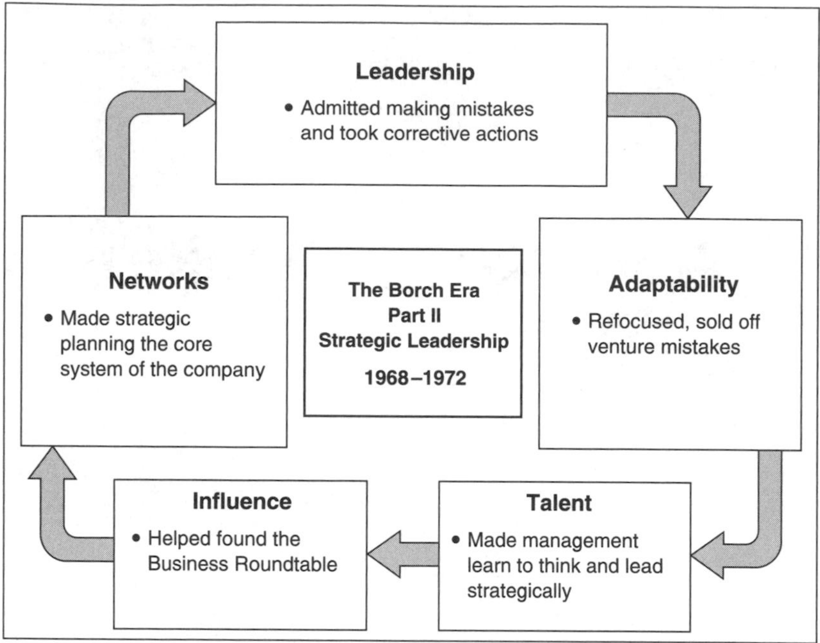

Exhibit 10-1 LATIN and the Borch II era from 1968 to 1972.

and entrenched IBM. The acquisition of the French computer maker Machine Bull improved GE's European market share, but it didn't help much in the United States. To compound these difficulties, GE experienced major problems integrating the American and French cultures.

GE's leaders believed that the answer was to acquire one of the other "dwarfs" to become a strong No. 2 in the market and then use this position to gain ground on IBM. Honeywell was selected as the best candidate, since it was also a strong player in the industrial computer markets.

Reginald Jones, a financial executive and strong negotiator, was assigned to acquire Honeywell. During the early stages of the discussions, it became apparent that Honeywell's management was more interested in acquiring than selling. It came as a pleasant surprise to Jones and Borch that they might be able to sell off the computer business and cut their losses. They assessed the situation, and ultimately they decided that selling was a better option than continuing to invest in a venture that might well keep losing money indefinitely.

GE sold Honeywell its mainframe business, but it held on to its emerging time-sharing services business. Time-sharing was a method of selling computer time to users on a subscription basis. The user had access to large computing power and storage via the telephone. This business appeared to hold considerable potential—and indeed, it turned out to be the forerunner to today's Internet and wireless systems.

Historically, GE had been a buyer rather than a seller. In fact, over the many decades of the company's history, there had been only a few examples of GE selling businesses. The computer sale departed from this tradition. The divestiture made it acceptable for GE to sell unattractive or nonstrategic businesses, and it was the first step toward the adoption of the company's strategic portfolio management systems. Henceforth, GE's many divisions would be viewed as a portfolio of companies—analogous to an individual's stock portfolio—which would be reviewed periodically for their strategic fit. If there was a perception that a particular unit was no longer a good fit, that division might well be divested.

One of the negatives of the computer sale was that GE agreed to continue to use GE/Honeywell computers in its operations rather than selecting the best computers to fit its needs. This was the same mistake that GE made when it entered the computer business, and it negatively impacted the company's operations for years to come.

WHAT ARE WE DOING WRONG?

When five of the nine ventures and the European consumer acquisitions failed, it was obvious that something needed to be changed in the way that GE evaluated its business opportunities.

In the GE tradition, Borch created another task force to determine what should be changed to make GE more successful in the future. The task force was headed by Dave Dance, the consumer business executive vice president. Dance's team sought the advice of academic and consulting leaders and eventually came up with an understanding of what had gone wrong.

Reason 1: Size and Span-of-Control Theories

When Cordiner established the product departments as the company's building blocks, he mandated that if a department exceeded $50 million in annual revenues, it had to be split into small units. This "span-of-control" theory held that a manager could manage only a specific number of direct reports and could handle revenues only up to a certain scale. Inevitably, this resulted in a proliferation of product departments, and—even worse—the product departments lost contact with their market and competitive environments. And finally, many departments were internal suppliers and not "businesses" at all.

Solution 1: Create Strategic Business Units

The study team recommended that product departments be dissolved and replaced with "strategic business units" (SBUs). All of the product departments were assessed to determine if they met three specific criteria:

1. They had to serve real external markets and not just be internal suppliers.
2. They had to have clearly identifiable customers and competitors.
3. They had to be able to control their own destinies and initiate actions without having to rely on other GE organizations.

Using these criteria, the number of SBUs was reduced from 125 to 43. This was a step in the right direction, but it was still not enough. Even though the number of company business units was reduced, there were still too many for the company to evaluate and manage properly. Further, the span-of-control mentality was maintained. This meant that the traditional hierarchical organization of groups, divisions, and departments was preserved. Even worse, the new organization permitted business units to range in size from $23 million in revenues all the way up to $1 billion.

Thus there were group-level strategic business units, such as major appliances, with revenues of $1 billion. Concurrently, there were numerous department-level units, such as wire and cable, with revenues in the tens of millions. Since the major appliances group reported to the chairman's office directly, it was reviewed only by the corporate management and staff organizations, while the wire and cable department reported to a divisional manager, who in turn reported to a group executive.

The result? The small, marginally profitable, and strategically irrelevant wire and cable unit was reviewed three times, while the more strategic larger businesses were reviewed only once. This forced senior management to waste time on units that were not important, and it took time away from assessing the strategies of the most important and most complex businesses.

Reason 2: No Formal Strategic Reviews

Cordiner and Borch's decentralized management system was based on management by objectives (MBO). The corporate leaders determined the overall objectives and goals and then expected the managers to achieve them. The business strategies were not reviewed and were left up to the operating managers to decide on their own. The only senior management reviews were financial.

In many cases, the operating businesses didn't do an adequate job of evaluating their markets, customers, and competitors, and they often failed to identify technological and sociopolitical trends and forces that could negatively impact their businesses. The result was that there were too many omissions, miscalculations, and surprises.

Solution 2: Institute Annual Review Systems

The task force recommended that a new management and strategic planning system be instituted. This would force the newly created SBUs to clearly understand what was happening in their markets and to begin to anticipate external, competitive, and resource changes that could impact their business. The objective was to reduce the number and severity of surprises and to be prepared if and when changes did occur.

As shown in Exhibit 10-2, the new management system was calendar based. It started in December and January with a thorough corporate review of the Big Picture. These findings were presented to the business units by internal and external experts. The result was that specific key outside-world assumptions—economic, political, and social—were given to the business units' management in Session A for their use in developing and assessing their own business strategies.

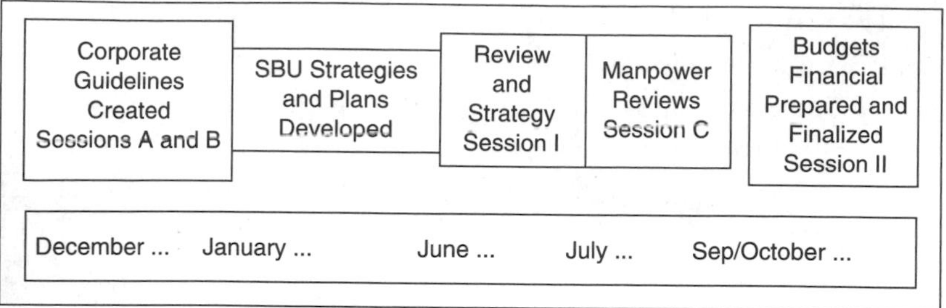

Exhibit 10-2 The calendar of the GE strategic planning system during the Borch era.

Next, in Session B, senior management provided the business units with a list of specific corporate financial goals and objectives. This was *not* the same as the traditional MBO process of the past, however, since the company realized that the final corporate goals and objectives had to be realistic, and this couldn't happen until the business units finished their strategies and the overall results could be assessed.

Using the insights and recommendations of both Sessions A and B, the strategic business units were required to develop their strategies and preliminary financials. Though there was no prescribed format in these presentations, there were three key requirements:

- First, the SBU leader had to personally make the presentation. He or she could invite some key people to be present in the meeting, but he or she alone had to explain and defend the strategy and financials.
- Second, all of the presentations had to be sent to the senior management and staff officers prior to the sessions in sufficient detail and time for them to be evaluated.
- Third, the presentations had to be graphic, clear, and concise. These requirements put the burden on the SBU leader to be the architect and defender of the strategies and financials.

In keeping with the tradition of GE, manpower was considered to be a vital part of the planning process, and a special session (Session C) was included in the process to help ensure that the right people would be available to implement and lead the company. This process will be discussed in more detail in the next chapter, since it was a key part of the Jones era.

Following Session I, each of the business units was given feedback and specific recommendations on what to change or keep in its strategies and financials. In addition, Corporate Finance finalized the company numbers and made sure that the SBU financials would help the company meet its investor and shareholder expectations.

This was a negotiation process. Typically, the business units' proposed financials were always lower than the company's requirements, so there was a series of meetings to negotiate the final numbers. The key was that the results be realistic and doable. Again, this will be discussed in the next chapter because it was Jones who perfected this process.

The overriding objective was to ensure that the business units had realistic expectations and weren't kidding themselves or senior management. Management had been surprised by *all* of the ventures, in one way or another, and this had negatively impacted its credibility on Wall Street. The new process was designed to ensure that these surprises were minimized and that promises were met. Once this process was in place, the worst thing that business unit managers could do was surprise senior management. If they did, they were often demoted or even fired.

Reason 3: Planners, Not Strategists

The Crotonville Advanced Management Program and Professional Business Management taught GE managers how to manage. They focused on planning, organizing, integrating, and measuring, but the program didn't cover strategic thinking, decision making, and planning. There were several reasons for this.

One was that GE truly believed that it could do anything. It had been convinced—by its successful war responses and other achievements—that if it wanted to enter a new business, it could do so without changing its way of managing.

Second, the company believed it had unlimited financial, human, and physical resources, and its managers could manage anything. Given this mindset, the company felt it didn't need to develop the strategic skills of its managers. All it had to do was tell them what needed to be done, and they would do it.

The failures of the ventures and acquisitions clearly demonstrated that these premises were wrong and that leaders lacked these key strategic skills.

Solution 3: Develop Strategic Planning Skills

Borch recognized that the new system required new skills. It was clear that the SBU leaders had to learn to think and act like general managers and not just functional experts. They needed to start with a sound understanding of the external world, customers, and competition and then objectively assess their resources and match what was needed with what was available. They could no longer assume that they already had the skills or that they could easily get them.

With this new and more humble way of looking at the world, Fred Borch asked Dave Dance how he planned to teach these new disciplines and skills. Dave said he planned to have his staff visit all of the business units and present the key concepts. Borch's response: "This is not sufficient . . . . I want to use Crotonville to teach strategic planning to all of the key officers, staff members, and business unit leaders . . . and I want it QUICKLY."

Recall that Crotonville had become a discretionary and/or fee-based service when Borch split the staff into two types. This meant that Crotonville had to justify its existence by providing programs that the business operations would be willing to pay for.

It was succeeding in this new challenge, in part by drawing on the skills and energies of managers in my age group. In fact, I was one of those managers, and one of the new programs that I had designed was a strategic thinking and decision-making course, which I had tentatively named "Planning for the Future." In fact, I was just about to offer a pilot run of this program when Borch announced the new strategic planning management systems.

When I heard about the new systems, I recommended to Lindy Saline, to whom I reported, that we should make a presentation to Dance and his associates to tell them about the course and how it could help to teach GE managers the art and science of strategic thinking. Dance accepted our offer, and a Crotonville team was put together to formalize the thinking process and develop a five-day course. The team included management scientist Cliff Springer, sales and marketing expert Ken Michel, computer expert Dave Sims, and me.

Although there certainly was a lot of literature available on the concept of strategy, there was no useful logic and thinking process that could do the job we needed done. So the team evaluated a number of complementary works, including the Kepner-Tregoe problem-solving and decision analysis process (which I taught), other academic works, as well as publications from the Boston Consulting Group (BCG), McKinsey & Associates, Arthur D. Little (ADL), and other sources.

The result was a unique *thinking* approach—one that started externally, systematically evaluating the competition, and then developing priorities and making decisions on where to allocate scarce resources. The process stressed logic and objective thinking, and it clearly stated that this was a means to help develop strategies rather than some sort of magic formula.

Though the Crotonville team was convinced the process would enable GE management to develop sound strategies and financial plans, GE senior managers were not really sure, and they wanted to test the concepts and educational process before they rolled out all of the programs. So they selected 20 of the most critical, aggressive executives they could find to become the test audience.

A one-week prototype course was developed and offered to this group. The five days were built around a modified, innovative in-basket simulation called Basic/Universal, and it focused on a typical utility business. Two teams competed against each other, and they had to develop a winning strategy. Since Borch and his management team wanted to avoid the perception that this program was like the old "Blue Books" used in the early days of decentralization, they didn't permit the teaching staff to give out books, manuals, or worksheets.

Over the five days, each step in the process was discussed, and then the team would apply this step. At the end of the five days, each team had to present its strategies to a group of "senior corporate executives." The participants were evaluated on the quality of both their strategies and their presentations.

At the end of the five days, Dance and his staff held a public critique of the course to determine whether the participants felt that the course, the concepts being taught, and the teaching staff should get companywide exposure. The Crotonville management, the teaching team, and I sat in the back, anxiously awaiting the verdict.

As it turned out, the evaluation of the course was very positive. The participants believed that the approach was highly professional and effective and that it should be taught companywide. They *did* agree, however, that they wanted more information, including a guide and worksheets that they could use to teach their business teams, as well as advice about how to get help from consultants, academics, and other companies.

The program was next presented in a four-hour overview form to Borch and the chairman's office. Borch was pleased, but he made it clear that he wanted to have all of the senior, corporate, business, and staff executives educated in the process as soon as possible. As a result, 13 three-and-a-half-day sessions of the Strategic Planning Executive Program were held at Crotonville in a 14-week period.

A modified version of the GE Basic/Universal computer business simulation was used to enable these senior executives—many of whom believed that they already were strategic thinkers and planners—to learn the process and to be exposed to several key academics and consultants.

Sessions were scheduled back to back over three and a half months, and there was little time to unwind. I led all of these sessions, and it was both exhausting and stimulating. I learned a lot from this experience, which helped prepare me to become a consultant and teacher in this dynamic area.

FURTHER STEPS

Since all of the business units were required to have their own strategic planners, it was critical that they be taught the process in more depth. For that reason and others, a two-week program was developed and offered. The first week of this program was applications oriented, and a more comprehensive version of the GE-based simulation was used. The second week enabled the planners to learn more about consulting help and other processes that would complement their planning efforts.

To avoid the appearance of creating another Cordiner/Smiddy type of indoctrinational approach, Borch's team decided that there would be no manuals or books issued. Each SBU leader, however, was given a highly professional audiovisual package that he or she could use to explain the concepts and describe how to apply the process to the participant's own business. This package introduced to GE the "bubble diagram," as shown in Exhibit 10-3, which was a logic flowchart that described the key steps of the process and their outputs.

The company wanted to be sure that the SBU strategic plans were not long, tedious academic dissertations, so it was stressed that the doc-

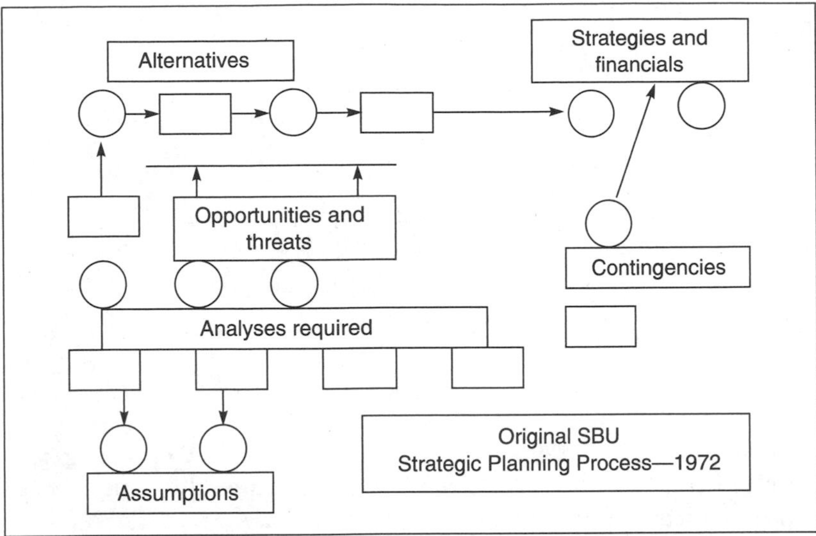

Exhibit 10-3 A bubble diagram of the strategic thinking and decision-making process used in the Borch and Jones eras.

uments had to be "short and understandable." Portfolio matrices were encouraged as a means of showing where the business and its key components were now and where they would be in the future.

In these workshops, both the Boston Consulting Group and A. D. Little consultants presented their versions of the matrices they recommended.

As shown in Exhibit 10-4, the BCG grid plotted businesses and segments on a four-cell matrix, depicting the market growth and the organization's relative market share. (Relative share was calculated by taking the organization's share and comparing with the market leader. If the market leader had 50 percent share and the company only had 10 percent, the company's relative share was 0.2. If, however, the company was the leader with a 50 percent share and the nearest competitor had only 10 percent, the company's relative share was 5.) BCG encouraged companies to harvest the cash cows and use the funds for the stars.

In contrast, ADL's grid, as shown in Exhibit 10-5, depicted return on investment and return on sales, and it asserted that companies should focus on those markets that had a high yield on both.

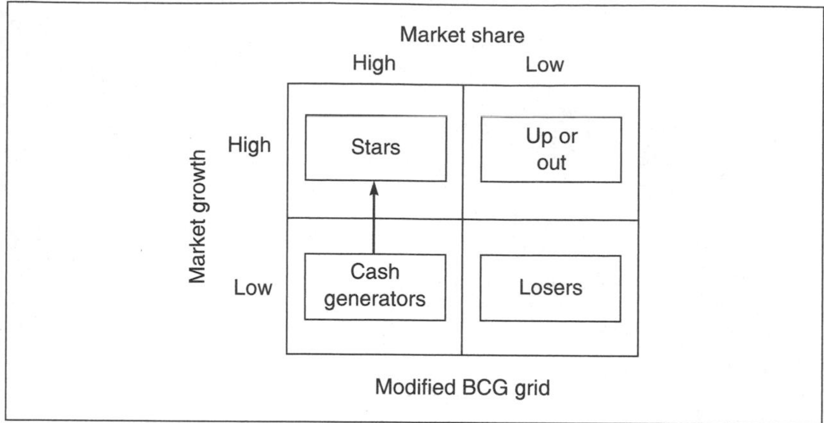

Exhibit 10-4 A modified version of the Boston Consulting grid used in the 1970s. It emphasized the need to use the cash cows to fund the future stars and get rid of the losers.

GE leaders liked the matrix as a means of showing the relative attractiveness and position of the business unit's portfolio, so—with the help of McKinsey—they created a new matrix that became known as the "nine-block matrix" (see Exhibit 10-6). Over time, this matrix was refined, and it became a requirement for all of the strategic planning

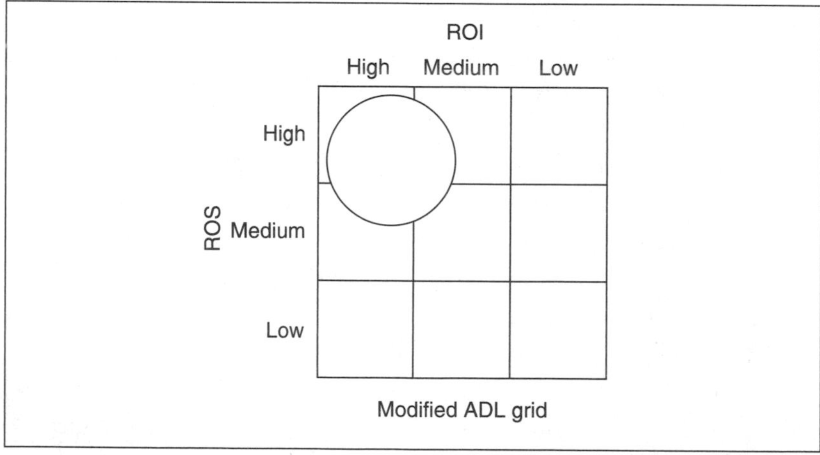

Exhibit 10-5 A modified version of the ADL portfolio grid taught in the GE workshops. It focused on investing in those businesses and products that optimize both return on investment and return on sales.

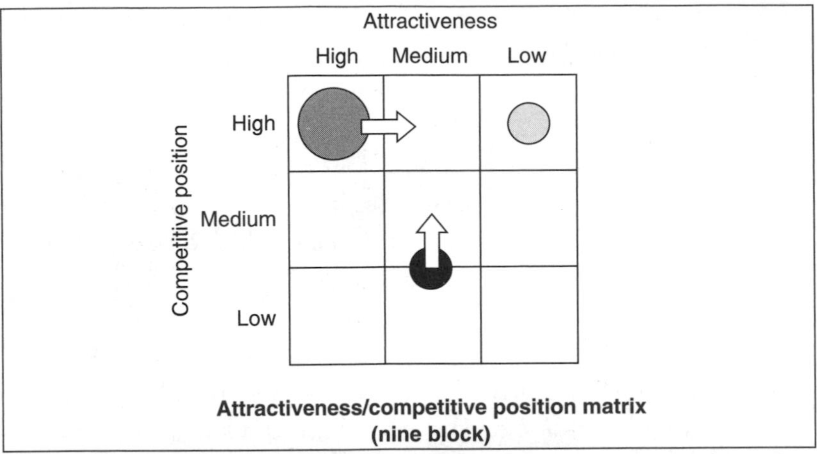

Exhibit 10-6 The nine-block matrix that GE used during the Borch and Jones eras. It emphasized the need to evaluate products and business units on both their attractiveness and competitive position. It included both quantitative and qualitative factors.

documents and was used to summarize the company's entire business portfolio.

GE encouraged its business unit managers to imagine that they were making a presentation to an investment banker to get funds for their businesses. It emphasized that the company had limited financial, physical, and human resources and that it was critical that these resources be allocated to the best businesses—and that other businesses would be either harvested, or even eliminated, to provide the right resources to the most attractive business units. This was the beginning of the emphasis on strategic portfolio management.

The company realized that this system would require the best data and intelligence possible. Therefore, the company encouraged the SBU managers to seek help:

- *Outside consultants.* In the workshops, several key consulting firms were spotlighted. GE encouraged the business units and staff organizations to use these consultants if they believed that they could help. Lists of consultants and market research firms were supplied to the business units. Many of the business units recruited these consultants to guide their planning organizations.

- *Inside consultants.* Meanwhile, Corporate Consulting Services provided a wide variety of consulting services and special workshops to help the operations. A new strategic planning and marketing consulting organization was created to support the strategy development and review efforts. (I was senior executive in this organization, which created many special offerings). Of course, these services had to be paid for by the business units, and fees had to be competitive.
- *Special workshops.* CCS and Crotonville offered special seminars and workshops. In addition, special modules were added to all of the key management courses, including the General Management and Management Development programs. In addition to teaching the art and science of strategic thinking, these modules and workshops improved the participants' awareness of what was going on in the world, as well as how to improve their competitive assessments and strategies.

One interesting subtext was provided by the larger society. This was the late 1960s: a period of considerable social unrest. Students were taking over their campuses, and there were riots and civil disobedience in major cities. These disturbances were having significant impacts on businesses and their workforces. Crotonville provided both sides of these issues, not only hiring the predictable pro-business presenters but also hiring individuals who were antibusiness and proponents of major social and political changes. Management gave them a free hand, and it even actively encouraged them as a way of improving the participants' understanding of key issues.

In short, it can fairly be said that Crotonville benefited from a high degree of intellectual freedom and energy.

This reflected a larger pattern at GE. Borch was committed to having an impact—and having GE have an impact—on a changing society and world. He therefore decided to form an alliance of business executives to play an active role in influencing public and government policies. The result was the creation of the Business Roundtable in 1972.

This alliance had two major goals.

1. To enable chief executives from different corporations to work together to analyze specific issues affecting the economy and business

2. To present the government and the public with both timely information and practical, positive proposals for action

Reg Jones continued to be a leader of this group and helped it remain a major force in political and economic policy areas. The Business Roundtable certainly continued the Cordiner/Boulware tradition of making sure that GE could control its own destiny with minimum governmental interference.

TAKEAWAYS
Leadership

Admitting mistakes. Borch was unique in that he was willing to recognize that he had tried to do too much and—as a result—was willing to change. In fact, he instituted a radical change in GE, enabling it for the first time to exit or prune products or even entire businesses.

- *Recommendation.* You need to periodically step back and review what you have done and see if your results are moving in the right direction. If you have made a mistake and the results are poor or even negative, then be willing to make corrections, and be forthright and timely in admitting you made a mistake.

Market-based business units. Cordiner's departments and divisions were internally determined. He was concerned about the span of control, so he cut up departments when they reached a predetermined revenue level. This caused the departments to compete internally and to lose sight of the external world. Borch employed several external criteria to determine the size of a strategic business unit; unfortunately, he permitted so many business units to evolve that they had difficulty retaining the traditional organizational structure.

- *Recommendation.* Review your organizational structure. Determine if your business units are really able to control their own destinies and make the right decisions or whether they are really parts of other businesses. If the business units are not based on real markets, don't have real competitors, and don't control their own destinies, either regroup them or just make them components of real business units. Keep the number of business units to a minimum and favor a flat organizational structure.

Strategic thinking, not just planning. The GE system focused on helping the business units learn to think and plan strategically and not just satisfy a company ritual. This was achieved through a combination of education, consulting, and reviews. Each unit was asked to present its story in any way it wanted, provided its leaders could answer key questions. The communications upward and downward were focused on helping all levels of management understand what it would take to be a winner. The system tended toward overkill, to be sure, but it was needed for a company of GE's size and complexity.

- *Recommendation.* Review the GE type of system to determine if it could be useful as a model to improve your own system. Be selective; it is unlikely that everything can be used, but some of the key pieces might be helpful.

Academic freedom. Crotonville has been used as a change agent since it was founded. Cordiner used it to sell decentralization and professional management. His system and approach were highly rigid, and they verged on brainwashing in their teaching techniques. Borch permitted Crotonville to take on a life of its own and to include "a variety of views." He and his team were not very involved. The key, in my view, is to blend both approaches.

- *Recommendation.* If you have your own management development and training programs or use the services of other organizations, be sure that they are not just propaganda and brainwashing mills. Permit conflicting perspectives to be addressed and understood. If you don't, you will turn off your people and—even worse—become myopic, which can lead to unpleasant surprises.

Minimize surprises and their impact. Borch recognized that he had been surprised too often. He took steps to create a system that would surface all aspects of the business, even the unpleasant ones.

- *Recommendation.* It is impossible to avoid all surprises, but it is important to have a management system that looks both inside and outside and tries to identify changes. If you believe a change can have a major impact on your business, then set up a monitoring system so that you can act rapidly and effectively. The key is to avoid being surprised—by either inside or outside developments.

CHAPTER

Pruning and Divesting

As BORCH LEFT office, the world was in turmoil. The Vietnam War was raging, and the Great Society was failing. There were riots, protests, and civil disobedience, and most of society's central institutions were under attack.

Borch had initiated changes in GE, but he recognized that his new system was just getting started and that Wall Street was still not convinced the company was on the right track. Borch wanted a successor, therefore, who could strengthen the company's ability to generate consistent, predictable earnings.

After much study, Borch selected his CFO, Reginald Jones, to be his successor.

Jones had enrolled in the Business Training Course in 1939, upon graduation from University of Pennsylvania's Wharton School. Following the Business Training Course, he became a member of the prestigious Traveling Audit Staff for eight years. He held general management positions in the consumer, utility, industrial, construction, and distribution businesses, and he was appointed CFO in 1968. He had led the team that successfully sold the ailing computer business to Honeywell.

Among his many other talents, Jones had the ability of a diplomat to lead by persuasion and not edict. He was considered a business leader both inside and outside the company, and he was widely respected for his honesty and integrity. He was a strong advocate of the new strategic management system (see Exhibit 11-1).

NEW CHAIRMAN'S OFFICE

Since Jones's mentor "Flip" Phillippe had died prematurely at age 59, Jones didn't have a coleader. Accordingly, he decided to create a new "chairman's office." He assumed the titles of chairman and CEO, and he eliminated the president's office, which had historically been the top management position.

Because Jones was adept at dealing with diverse personalities and leadership styles, he was able to install a group of colleagues with very different styles and personalities.

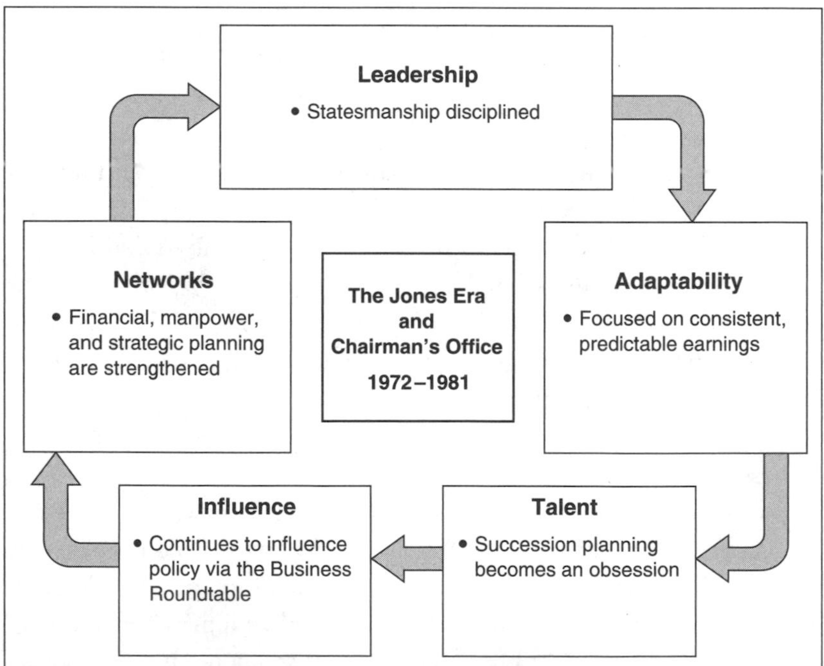

Exhibit 11-1 LATIN and the Jones era.

One of the team, for example, was a Teddy Roosevelt–like executive named Jack Parker. Parker was an individualist, and—like the legendary Rough Rider—he went on African safaris. He had headed the aerospace group, and he had been the successor to Lem Boulware as the head of employee relations. In that role, he continued to execute the theory and practice of being a tough negotiator and defending the company against Big Government and Big Labor.

Two other members of the newly formed chairman's office were Dave Dance—head of strategic planning and former consumer group executive—and Al Way, his CFO. Note that the CFO has always been, and continues to be, a key member of the company's leadership team.

The expanded leadership team was needed in part because the company's size and complexity continued to increase, and it was important to have skilled and senior managers to track, monitor, review, and help lead the new SBU structure.

BUYING AN ANNUITY: UTAH INTERNATIONAL

Jones believed that it was important to add a stable, predictable earnings and cash-flow generator to the GE portfolio. The then CEO of Utah International, Edmund Littlefield, was a member of the GE board of directors, and—knowing firsthand of Jones's interest in having a steady-income generator—suggested a merger of the companies.

Utah International (UI) was a dominant player in the metallurgical coal business, and it was the major supplier of this type of high-value coal to Japan. In addition, it was major supplier of uranium to electric utilities, and thus it was a potential complement to GE's electric utility business units. With the help of a few key associates, Jones evaluated UI and concluded that—because of its consistently high ROI and consistently positive cash flows—it was a good match for GE. Jones decided to plunge, making what was, up to that time, the largest acquisition by any company, anywhere, ever.

ANOTHER MISCALCULATION

Unfortunately, Jones guessed wrong. UI's coal business started to decline, so the sector was not the cash cow envisioned. In addition, unfortunately, it was far from a good fit with the rest of the company.

I was a senior executive in Corporate Planning at the time. Like most of my associates, I was shocked when Jones made the acquisition. It seemed to me that the UI analysis—performed by a select few within our company—was unduly optimistic about the ability of UI to continue to generate high returns.

In addition, the cultures of the two companies were different to the point of conflict. UI's headquarters was in San Francisco, and its major operations were in Australia and South Africa. GE managers really didn't understand the business, and UI managers were not willing to educate them. So from the beginning, the merger wasn't sound either strategically or operationally.

This was an excellent example of an acquisition based on wishful thinking and past results rather than on strategic planning. Jones never admitted this mistake, so it was left to Welch to make the decision to divest Utah International.

INSTITUTIONALIZING STRATEGIC MANAGEMENT AND PLANNING

Despite the UI strategic error, Jones generally supported Borch's strategic planning and management system. He recognized that it enabled the company to get a better grasp on what was happening in operations and avoid some of the mistakes that had occurred during the ventures period. He used corporate staff and Corporate Consulting Services to review all of the strategies and provide briefing documents on each of the SBU strategies. But, significantly, Jones did his own reviews, personally evaluating all of the strategies himself.

The strategy sessions described in the last chapter (Sessions I and II) were tough, but gentlemanly, and even if Jones didn't agree with the strategies, he would wait until the meetings were over to provide his feedback. Since his background was financial and he had extensive experience as a traveling auditor, he was a strong analyst and was able to identify major gaps or discontinuities in the strategies. He relied on the company's technical, marketing, and competitive specialists to provide other insights.

His approach was straightforward. The SBU managers had to make the presentations themselves and had to answer questions about the strategies and their underlying assumptions. If they couldn't answer them, then they had to provide answers quickly after the sessions. Business unit management received feedback from both Jones and the other vice chairmen. Staff members were not permitted to make direct recommendations.

Jones insisted that all of the business units have professional full-time strategic planners. All planners and general managers had to take the strategic planning programs offered at Crotonville. On the other hand, there were no required formats. Business units determined how they wished to present their strategies and plans. SBUs were told to think of the process as though they were independent companies that had to make presentations to their investors. The key, therefore, was to communicate as effectively as they could.

STRATEGIC PLANNING BECOMES BUREAUCRATIZED

Like most new processes, this one evolved in predictable directions. For the first few years, it clearly was very beneficial to the company. Strategies improved, and the financials became more predictable. Major surprises were avoided. As time passed, however, the system started to take on a life of its own. Meetings and paperwork proliferated. For example:

- *Annual planning meetings.* There were annual strategic planning meetings, which Welch later described as "planners talking to planners about planning."
- *Best-practices books.* These publications were developed and issued to focus on presentation and not necessarily strategic issues. I thought of them as nice but superficial—the GE equivalent of the Good Housekeeping Seal of Approval.
- *Meetings for reviewing and defending plans.* Too much time was spent defending plans. Each of the functional staff organizations (engineering, marketing, manufacturing, and finance) spent an inordinate amount of time and effort reviewing plans and forcing the business units to allocate time defending the plans rather than running the business. This habit got so bad that I was appointed head of strategy integration organization, specifically to prevent the functional organizations from destroying the intent and results of the business strategies.

It became even worse after the sectors were established, because all of the sectors had large planning staffs, and in some cases they infringed upon the power of the business unit leaders.

CREATING AND MEETING INVESTOR EXPECTATIONS

General Electric has had a consistent and predictable policy of providing a cash dividend each year. This goal was maintained and met even during the Great Depression. At the same time, GE's management has always had a goal of increasing the value of the stock so that its stockholders would benefit from both capital gains *and* dividend streams.

Never overpromise, and minimize surprises. This has been one of the hallmarks of the GE management team's governing philosophy over the years. In the 1950s, Cordiner initiated Investor Relations as one of the new corporate functional services. This organization's job was to help create realistic expectations among the investment analysts and then communicate the expectations internally so that the operating and executive officers understood the right level of profitability to achieve. This is now called "meeting Wall Street's expectations," and it's an almost universal corporate practice, but it was truly unique in the 1950s.

Jones was one of the most skilled executives in this regard. He established a team consisting of staff members from investor relations, finance, and strategic planning as well as his own vice chairmen to determine the expectations that could be set and achieved consistently.

This is the approach Jones and his staff used:

1. Interview key Wall Street analysts and determine what they were expecting.
2. Review all of the business strategies and their financial forecasts to determine if these would yield the results that were expected by Wall Street.
3. If not, strategically fill the gap.

STRATEGICALLY FILLING THE GAP

At GE, as at almost every other company in the world, it was common for the business units that were doing well to understate what they could achieve and then negotiate their way up to the lowest possible targets. (This way, they were most likely to succeed and be rewarded.) In sharp contrast, the businesses that were in trouble—and at risk of being restructured or even killed outright—always overpromised and rarely made their lofty targets.

The result, not surprisingly, was that the numbers from the operations were always lower than those desired at the corporate level.

Prior to Jones, the gap between what the operations said they could provide and what Wall Street expected was filled by raising everyone's budgets by the same percentage. But Jones recognized that if he compelled all of the businesses to increase their profit levels, he might negatively impact the ability of at least some divisions to execute their approved strategies. Further, he was concerned that many of the businesses might overpromise and not be able to deliver their promises—thus making it impossible for him to meet his own promises to Wall Street.

A Matrix to Spotlight Deviations

To address this conundrum, Corporate Planning and Finance created a review system that examined the business units' strategies and financial promises to determine if they were consistent. In keeping with the goal of using practices that were simple and easy to visualize, another matrix was developed. Exhibit 11-2 shows what it looked like.

SBUs were grouped into one of four investment categories: Category (or "Priority") I were the highest, and IV were the lowest. The strategies were evaluated to determine if they were consistent with their investment priority. A special matrix was used to plot the investment priority of the business and how aggressive its strategy was.

In the illustration you can see that the investment priorities and aggressiveness of Business A and Business B were consistent, while Business D—although a Priority II business—was not being aggressive enough and, in essence, was being harvested prematurely. On the other hand, Business C was too aggressive for its priority category.

Using these evaluations, Jones and the vice chairmen focused on business units that deviated from what was expected of them, and they probed to determine why. In some cases, the business strategies were changed. In other cases, the budgets were changed to ensure consistency and to make sure that the unit's resources were being allocated correctly so that expectations could be met.

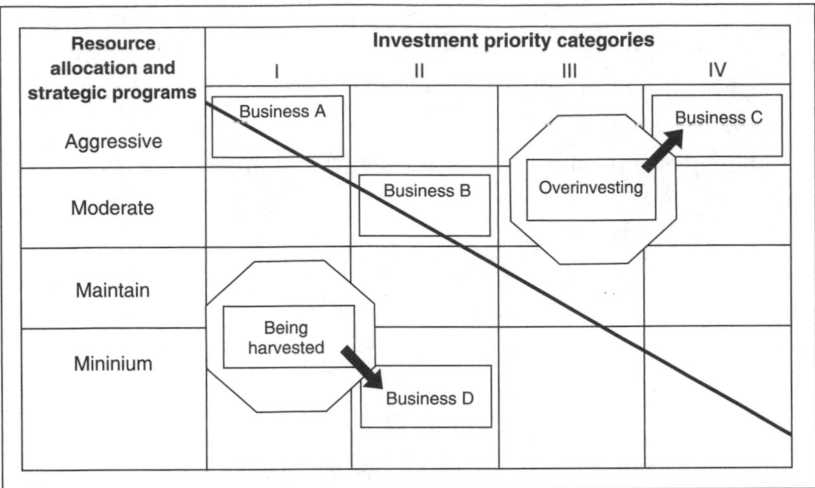

Exhibit 11-2 The grid used in the Jones era to determine if a business unit's strategy and resource allocation were consistent. If a business was not allocating sufficient resources, it was below the line; if a business was above the line, it was investing too much. Those along the line were doing what was required.

Economic Intelligence and Evaluations

Another input into the review and resource allocation process was economic forecasts. GE developed its own economic model to supplement what was available from outside vendors. Collectively, these analyses enabled the company to better identify potential opportunities and threats.

In addition, a unique program called the "Profit Optimization Model"—developed by Dr. Sidney Schoeffler—was used to determine the potential returns of different strategies. This model was derived from GE's historical performance.

Internal Venturing

Jones recognized the need to continue to find new business ventures and grow new businesses. Even though he acquired Utah International, he was still interested in creating new businesses based on internal skills and abilities.

He used four approaches:

1. The first was the planning system itself. As part of the process, he asked all of the business units to nominate new ventures.
2. Next, he created a venture organization in the Corporate Research and Development Center to identify ways of using GE's technological skills and abilities.
3. Then, he instituted a venture-capital-styled operation in Corporate Planning to help fund new ventures that were nominated by the business units.
4. Finally, he initiated a market-based corporate strategic plan. Jones decided he wanted a plan that would look at the company in a different way. He appointed Dan Fink, a vice president in the aerospace group, to the planning position. Dan, an MIT grad, had a reputation of being a very innovative leader. Shortly after Dan was appointed, he selected me to be his corporate strategist.

> One of the problems of any organizational structure is that dividing a company into business units, regardless of how they are structured, makes the units very parochial and myopic. This prevents opportunities that transcend the business units from being exploited—or even recognized.

Dan and I developed an innovative top-down, external view of the company, which intentionally pervaded sectors and SBUs and provided a means of seeing opportunities and threats *across the entire company*. The 1981 corporate plan grouped GE into six arenas:

1. Energy
2. Energy applications and productivity
3. Communications, information, and sensing
4. Materials and resources
5. Transportation and propulsion
6. Pervasive services

We decided that the plan would not be like any of its predecessors and would be concise, highly visual, and action oriented. There were four steps in the process:

1. *Determine the importance to GE.* First the arena's importance to GE now and in the future was evaluated. This included the revenues, earnings, and cash flows the arena contributed to the overall company, as well as what percentage of the company's investments and expense funds were being allocated.

   For instance, the energy arena, which included energy fuels, conversion equipment, and electric utility systems and services, over a five-year period contributed 20 percent of the company's revenues but only 10 percent of its earnings. Twenty-one percent of the company's investments and 17 percent of its expenses were allocated to this arena. This assessment raised an issue as to why energy was underperforming from an earnings perspective and whether the investments should continue to be made at the same rate.
2. *Specify GE's current and planned arena strategies and direction.* A unique graphic was created to visualize GE's participation and planned changes. It was called a "strategic battlefield map." On one page, all of the current and emerging products, systems, and services were displayed. The current and planned strategies were also described next to the map.

   For instance, GE had two different organizations that participated in the energy arena, Utah International and power systems. Utah focused on coal, uranium, and some petroleum exploration, while power systems provided turbines, generators, nuclear equipment, and systems and services.
3. *Identify strategic alternatives.* Using the strategic battlefield map, other energy arena companies were strategically evaluated and plotted to identify additional ways that GE might consider playing in the arena.

   In the energy arena, Exxon, Westinghouse, Siemens, Combustion Engineering, as well as specialists such as Parsons, Foster Wheeler, and McDermott were plotted and evaluated to determine if GE might learn from their vision and strategies.

4. *Make recommendations and issue challenges.* After completing a thorough evaluation of potential rewards and risks—including whether GE had the ability to change its strategies and become a major, successful participant—specific recommendations were made. These took the form of issuing challenges to the key business units and sectors involved in their respective arenas and requiring them to do more work and report their findings to the chairman's office as part of their next annual strategic planning session.

1981 Corporate Plan Strategic Recommendations

All six arenas were evaluated in this way, and the following recommendations were made in the 1981 corporate plan.

Energy

This arena included Utah International and power systems. Collectively, it represented 19.6 percent of the company. The recommended strategy was to transform GE into an energy systems company and focus on opportunities in coal conversion, expanding energy services, and developing new energy sources such as wind and solar energy.

Energy Applications and Productivity

This arena's strategy recommended shifting emphasis away from being a supplier of selective discrete products and services in favor of enabling customers to become more productive and reduce their energy usage. This included creating the "factory of the future" by integrating a variety of GE products and services and GE's own internal manufacturing expertise.

Communications, Information, and Sensing

This arena contributed 15.9 percent of the company's revenues. It was subdivided into information and communications software and services, information and communications systems, and equipment and communications networks. The recommendation was to focus on integrating GE's products, systems, and services to provide high-value information and solutions to the commercial, industrial, medical, and military markets. In short, GE would become a solutions provider rather than simply a hardware and equipment producer.

Materials and Resources

The recommendation was to continue the existing specialty materials applications extension game by such means as increasing the use of plastics, increasing the focus on electronics-related materials, and moving Utah International away from commodity metals into specialty metals such as ferroalloy ores and precious metals.

Transportation and Propulsion

This strategy recommended the continuing development of propulsion systems and focusing on new ways to make GE's airline customers more efficient (and, it was hoped, more solvent). A closely related key issue was finding out how to provide financing to the airline industry to prevent bankruptcies.

Pervasive Services

The major recommendation in this arena focused on how to make GE Credit a more pervasive and global financial services company and how to increase both its consumer and commercial offerings.

GOOD START, SHORT LIFE

Overall, the arena approach was designed to force more integration across the company and to identify selective, profitable ways of combining the talents of businesses to create and capitalize on new emerging opportunities. In effect, this was the same objective that Welch later called the "boundaryless company," and it has been one of the major challenges that all GE leaders since World War II have faced—namely, to demonstrate synergy in the context of a company that might appear to be just another conglomerate.

Jones was enthusiastic about the arena approach, but he retired shortly after the new strategic concept was developed. Many of the concepts and recommendations ultimately were adopted by the business units and were included in their strategies, but, as it turned out, Welch was not enthusiastic about the approach. There were several reasons:

- First of all, it was not *his* idea. Welch was very committed to using what he had invented rather than what already existed.
- Second, the concept was in too early a stage of its evolution, and Welch had other problems he wanted to address first.
- Third, Welch was very unhappy with the size of the planning organizations, and this became his first target of reducing corporate overhead costs. He used this organization to initiate his energetic (some would say vindictive) attack on the GE bureaucracy.

INITIATIVE MANAGEMENT IS BORN

During the early stages of the Jones regime, hyperinflation was rampant. Foreign competitors were aggressively attacking and winning in U.S. markets. New microprocessing technologies were getting off the laboratory bench and making their way into the workplace. Jones recognized that these challenges needed to be addressed by all of the business units and that they also needed to be supported by corporate programs and actions. So he created three key initiatives.

The first dealt with the major challenge of managing in a period of hyperinflation. Jones formed a team to determine what the business units—and the corporation overall—had to do to stay ahead of inflationary impacts.

The second initiative responded to the increasing aggressiveness and success of foreign competitors. Jones required that all of the business units' plans include assessments of their major competitors and summaries of the actions that they were taking to ensure that those competitors wouldn't gain a strong beachhead. In addition, he urged Corporate Planning to establish several companywide competitive teams to review some of the business competitors—both to determine the overall impact they were having on GE and to identify the required strategic responses.

These teams included all of the major business units and corporate staff. In a novel and audacious move, they developed a comprehensive corporate plan for each of these key competitors, along the lines of the real GE corporate plan. Detailed plans for Siemens, Hitachi, Westinghouse, Toshiba, and Philips were developed and given to Jones for his review, as well as being distributed to the business units who competed against these global, multi-industry competitors.

Although Jones's background was primarily financial, he became concerned about the impact of microprocessors on GE and the continuing competitiveness of GE's products. In the well-established GE tradition, Jones insisted that Crotonville take the lead in educating all of the business units about how these technologies should be addressed—both from a positive, business-creation perspective and from the negative side (that is, the possibility of major disruption to an existing business).

All of the SBUs had to participate. I can clearly recall the resistance we received from the lighting business, whose collective attitude was that microelectronics were irrelevant to that business. On the surface, the lighting people appeared to have a point—but while taking a seminar on lighting systems, GM Bob Corning quickly recognized that electronics would, indeed, change the nature and type of lighting systems. He left the session committed to requiring a more comprehensive review. He was right, of course: Today, lighting systems are significantly impacted by electronics, and many lighting systems are greatly dependent on high technology.

A HUMAN RESOURCE PORTFOLIO APPROACH

As described above and in the previous chapter, the GE strategic planning system was based on the reality that resources were limited and had to be allocated to those business units that had the highest potential.

It didn't take the company's leaders long to realize that *people* were one of the most critical and scarcest resources, so the planning system soon included a special session, called "Session C," to focus on the evaluation and development of key people and weed out those who didn't fit (see Exhibit 11-3).

Like the strategic planning sessions, this part of the system was time based. Prior to the April/May Session C meetings described in Chap-

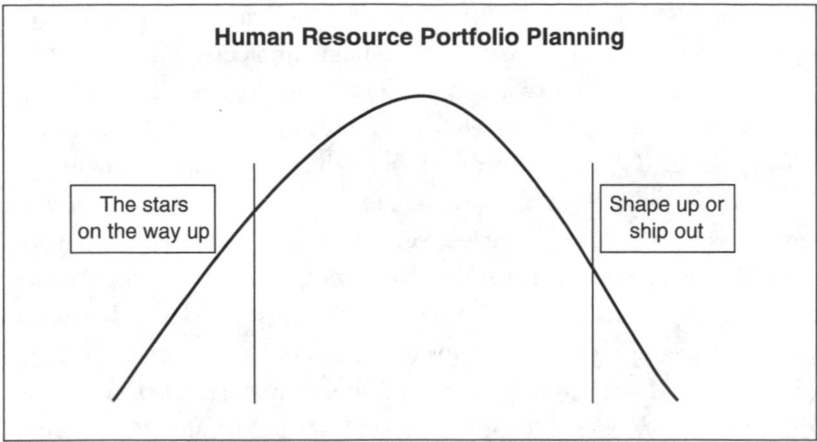

Exhibit 11-3 The diagram depicts the way GE professionals and managers were grouped based on appraisals of their performance.

ter 10, all of the business units' key management and professionals had to be appraised and given feedback about their performance. Then all of the key management and professional team members were put in one of three categories:

- Category I included the top 20 percent—that is, the "high-potential people." For each individual in this category, a career and succession plan had to be developed and shared with the individual. These were the individuals who would be selected to attend the executive management program at Crotonville and otherwise given special assignments and mentoring.
- Category II included the next 70 percent of the overall population—that is, people who were considered to be meeting their job standards but were probably not going to be promoted to senior management positions.
- Category III included the bottom 10 percent—those who were given the opportunity to improve their skills and performance or be fired.

Senior management evaluated all reviews and career plans of the top 20 percent and bottom 10 percent during the spring Session C. These reviews and career plans were either accepted or modified. In October, the second Session C was held to review what had happened since the spring and to ensure that the plans were being implemented. It was at this time that decisions were made about the bottom "ten-percenters." Many of these individuals were pruned from the organization, just as a business unit was pruned if it was not considered to be performing adequately.

In short, the process was designed to ensure that business strategies, financials, and human resources were internally consistent and would yield the desired long-term and short-term expectations and promises.

This system was a modification of the process developed in the aircraft engine and aerospace groups in the 1970s. The original work was initiated by Marion Kellogg, whom I mentioned earlier. Kellogg was the first GE female vice president and an expert in the personnel appraisal and evaluation systems area. She authored one of the first books on performance appraisals, *What to Do About Performance Appraisal*.

Again, a personal note: I spent my early career in human resources, mainly in the management development area, and I agreed that the manpower reviews described above were vital to the success of the company. Eventually, though, this practice too became a negative. Why? For one thing, I found that many individuals spent more of their time building their résumés than making real contributions.

One of the major problems of all of the reviews—and even the entry-level training and rotational programs—was that these programs implicitly taught people how to focus on the short range—that is, how to make a big splash, get recognition, and then move on, leaving it to the next trainee to do the job.

The same was true of many general managers and staff executives. They often became the equivalent of what we now call the "turnaround artist"—that is, the white knight who comes in when things are bad and "turns the business around." It is easy to show immediate results if you just focus on the cost side of the business and ignore the longer-term strategic time period. It's harder if you have to take responsibility for the kinds of long-term investments that will make the company prosper.

Unfortunately, the turnaround mentality is still widespread in Corporate America. We continue to witness CEOs who milk or suboptimize their businesses and get paid tens of millions of dollars while they cripple, or even destroy, their organizations.

STILL TAKING PUBLIC STANDS

While effecting major changes inside the company, Jones also continued the GE tradition of speaking out on major sociopolitical and economic issues.

He led the Business Roundtable, and he served on numerous government panels and studies. Jones was a very strong-minded individual, but he was not a self-important person, and he came to be applauded as a "statesman of business." He was appointed chairman of the President's Export Council, and he became an eloquent advocate for both the expansion of world trade and the restoration of U.S. competitiveness.

Jones is best known to the public for his role in improving the relationship between business and government. Three U.S. presidents and their cabinets called upon him frequently for counsel on economic policy. His most significant contribution in the policy arena came through his success in getting Washington to recognize the nation's capital-formation problem. He also played an important role as spokesman on issues such as tax policy, trade, monetary reform, unemployment, and human rights.

SUCCESSION PLANNING BECOMES AN OBSESSION

With the help of his manpower organization, Jones also developed one of the most elaborate and expensive succession systems anywhere.

It started in 1973, when GE's board considered a list of 12 potential candidates to succeed then CEO Jones. Jones made it 13 by penciling in Welch's name on the list—and thus began a fierce free-for-all.

By 1976, the list was reduced to six. That year, the sectors were created, mainly to enable Jones to select one of the six. The sector organization was overlaid on the already multitiered groups, divisions, and departments, some of which were designated as SBUs.

Each of the candidates was assigned to a sector in which he had *no experience or background.* Thus, Welch—who had spent his entire career in plastics—was assigned the consumer sector. Gault, a consumer veteran, was given the industrial sector. All of the candidates had to move to the Fairfield, Connecticut, corporate headquarters.

Each sector was given a challenge to grow profitably. All were encouraged to hire their own strategic planning, human resources, manpower development, financial, and functional staffs so that they could manage and review the SBUs assigned to them. In many cases, these staff organizations were as large as most corporate staff organizations.

Jones, his vice chairmen, and his manpower experts evaluated the performance of all the candidates and judged their executive and leadership abilities. Toward the end of the selection process—which took four years—the candidates were asked individually whom they would select to succeed them if they were killed in an airplane accident.

During this selection process, I taught a four-hour strategic history session in all of the major management development programs. It evaluated the strategies of all of the GE leaders. At the end of the session, I was always asked my opinion on who would win the election. Obviously, I didn't know, however I made one observation that I thought was amusing but that also proved to be a predictor of sorts.

I pointed out that all of the previous CEOs with the exception of Cordiner had either five or six letters in their names. Therefore, only two of the six candidates (Welch and Gault) qualified; the others either had too many letters or too few. I note that "Immelt" meets this profound criterion as well.

In any case, the result was the selection of what most considered the deep long-shot candidate: Jack Welch.

In the wake of Welch's anointment, three of the losing candidates left the company. Ed Hood and John Burlingame remained. Stan Gault took over Rubbermaid, in which his family had a stake. He did a great job of growing this company, and he was one of the most respected CEOs. After Rubbermaid, he ran Goodyear for a period of time. Tom Vanderslice became COO of GTE and was the heir apparent to the CEO there. Unfortunately, he ran into political problems and was forced out. He then took over Apollo Computer. Bob Frederick became the COO of RCA.

A VERY EXPENSIVE PROCESS

Admittedly, this elaborate, time-consuming, and expensive succession process led to the selection of one of the most successful GE CEOs. I submit, however, that it also produced several negative results:

1. The sectors became competitors, which split rather than united the company. This was one of the reasons that Welch saw the

need to initiate his "boundaryless" company initiative, which will be discussed in the next chapter.

2. The sectors added a great deal of overhead and staff that complicated the strategic planning process and made planning a competitive game rather than just a development of the most appropriate strategies. This led to the Work-Out process and Welch's seemingly vengeful attitude toward staff.
3. Sectors added another layer of management and reviews, which slowed down and complicated the strategic review process.
4. Even though the Borch ventures had demonstrated convincingly that managers couldn't manage just anything, the sector executives were assigned to areas in which they lacked experience and abilities.

In other words, Jones's succession process reinforced some of the negative patterns that he and others had been trying to expunge from GE. In a personal letter I received from Jones in 1993, he summarized his beliefs in discussing my book on strategic leadership: "You have made a fine contribution to the literature on management by the careful delineation of types of management and their applicability or usefulness at different stages of the enterprise. You certainly justified the time I devoted for the environment I envisioned for the future of the company. But let us never forget that it was thorough grounding of GE management in strategic planning, in which you played a significant role, that enabled us to see the challenges that lay ahead of us."

Clearly Jones strongly believed that he had made a great contribution to the company with both his strategic and succession planning systems.

WHAT IF WELCH HADN'T BEEN SELECTED?

I personally didn't think Welch would be selected—both because of his style and his age—and I think other people shared my view. It raises an intriguing question: How would GE have fared under the leadership of one of the other, more predictable candidates?

There is no question that Welch did a remarkable job. I'm personally convinced, however, that several of the other candidates would have also been successful. Stan Gault was more of a sales and marketing executive and probably would have emphasized the consumer businesses more. Vanderslice was more interested in technology and probably would have focused more on the communications and information arena, which Welch ignored. Hood and Frederick were very traditional GE executives and probably would have continued the status quo.

I think *all* of them would have emphasized financial and product services because these were already well recognized to be major profitable opportunities under Jones. In some cases the services were the only game in town, because the manufacturing of many of the core products and the markets they were sold in were either stagnant or even in decline.

Most likely, all the candidates would have sold off Utah International, and they probably would have made many of the other divestitures that first made Welch famous, or notorious, depending on your point of view. I'm less certain about what would have happened with RCA, which I believe ignited Welch's strategic climb. It is likely that Thornton Bradshaw might not have offered the other candidates the opportunity to acquire RCA at a bargain price—and even if he had, many of them may not have been as successful in liquidating the rest of the portfolio.

Finally, I don't think the other candidates would have stayed on the job for 20 years. This turnover might have negatively impacted the company's remarkable capital appreciation, because Wall Street is sometimes rattled by change at the top.

TAKEAWAYS

Do your own homework. One of the lessons I learned from Jones was his willingness to take the time to study the strategies and initiative responses himself and then use staff to supply another view. He did a thorough analysis, asked good questions, and listened. He made his own decisions, and he communicated the good and bad news personally.

- *Recommendation.* Take the time to personally review and study the strategies and programs that are key to your company's success. Use staff, but don't rely on them entirely.

Set realistic expectations. Jones was an expert in setting realistic expectations in terms of all of the key stakeholders. Most of the time he did what he said he would do—and when he didn't, he explained why.

- *Recommendation.* Use the commonsense approach to reviews. Ask, "Does this make sense?" As time progresses, see if the business units are doing what they said they would do. If not, find out why and make the appropriate changes.

Make succession planning the means to an end, not an obsession. I firmly believe that Jones's succession planning process became an obsession and that a good succession could have been achieved without creating sectors and a new level of bureaucracy.

- *Recommendation.* Review the GE approach and then simplify it to meet your needs. Be sure that you don't create more layers of management or add more people just for the purpose of selecting your successor. Remember: Succession planning is important, but it need not be a major distraction or cause good people to leave.

CHAPTER

Nothing Is Sacred

THE SELECTION of Jack Welch came as a surprise to many both inside and outside the company. He was young, brash, and probably the least "traditional" of the GE executives in the race. But Reg Jones recognized that the company needed new ideas and a different leadership style, and he concluded that Welch was the best person to move the company in a new direction.

Welch became the CEO the same year that GE's "great communicator," Ronald Reagan, became president of the United States. Inflation continued to pose a major challenge. Even though it was starting to decline, it still hovered at a 7 percent annual rate. Internationalism became a key requirement for the country and for its major companies.

Foreign competitors, led by the Japanese automakers, were successfully penetrating the traditional domestic markets. As Jones predicted, microelectronics was changing products, office procedures, and manufacturing systems. Persistent energy shortages and dislocations continued to increase costs, forcing companies either to seek substitute materials, outsource production, or even to exit businesses entirely.

In short, dynamic changes—pervasive and profound—required new thinking and priorities.

THE JONES LEGACY

Fortunately, Jones's leadership was paying off. The company, now financially strong, had regained the confidence of Wall Street. Jones had demonstrated that GE could consistently meet expectations and avoid major surprises. Revenues had doubled from $10 billion to $22 billion, and earnings grew even faster: from $575 million to $1.4 billion.

GE's strategic planning system had permitted the company to systematically evaluate its portfolio and determine which businesses it wanted to invest in and which it should harvest or divest. Resources were allocated to the highest-potential opportunities. A deep "people bench" was in place, and the company was able to institute changes to ensure that its most promising executives, managers, and professionals were being rewarded and motivated to remain with the company.

GE was now considered one of the best-managed companies in the world, and Jones—who had gained the respect of both the business and government communities—was considered an industrial leader.

On the other hand, there were still many problems to be solved. It was becoming very clear that Utah International would not provide the consistent and predictable earnings that Jones had believed it would. Further, its management was not really happy being part of GE. The sectors were no longer needed, and they had to be dismantled. The staff organization had become too large and increasingly bureaucratic, and it was often an inhibitor to change.

And even though the GE portfolio had been analyzed and priorities set, the company was having a very difficult time getting out of undesirable businesses. Jones had tried to sell the unattractive television business to Hitachi, but GE was denied permission by the U.S. government. Other dispositions were tried, but these too failed.

A DIFFERENT TYPE OF LEADER

Unlike the cookie-cutter succession planning of many major organizations, which often results in successors who are mirror images of their predecessors, GE has been willing to select individuals who have had different types of personalities, leadership styles, and priorities (see Exhibit 12-1).

Certainly, there were significant differences between Jones and Welch. Jones was a very gentlemanly, diplomatic person, both inside and outside the company. He listened carefully, reserving his comments and criticisms until an appropriate later moment.

Welch was the opposite. He would openly challenge, criticize, and even embarrass people if he believed that doing so would motivate them. "Welch takes pleasure in giving and receiving a challenge," one observer wrote, "whether grilling a subordinate or presenting his views in public. He once engaged a senior vice president in a prolonged, emotional shouting match embarrassing the room full of managers—but then congratulated the vice president for standing up to him."[1]

I can attest to the accuracy of this write-up, having had several experiences of my own like this with Welch.

The differences between Jones and Welch went far deeper than simply personal styles, however. For example: The *concept* of the portfolio

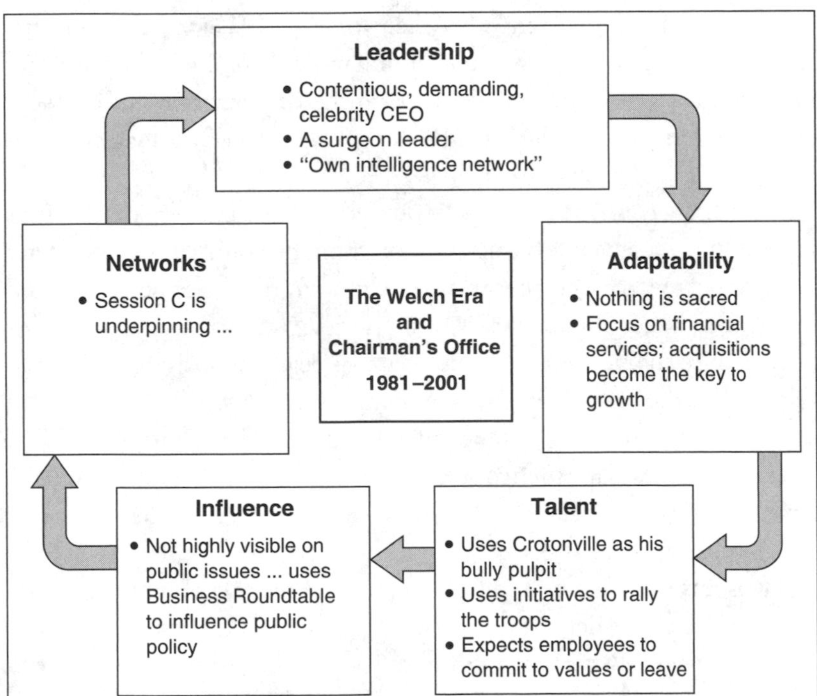

Exhibit 12-1 LATIN and the Welch era.

management system appealed to Jones and his senior management team. But they were traditional GE managers, and they had personal connections to many of the GE components. Thus, even though the GE evaluations clearly identified businesses to exit or restructure, Jones's team had trouble making it happen. In addition, they were unwilling to sell the GE monogram with the businesses, so many businesses were not that attractive to purchase.

Welch was *not* part of this culture. He prided himself as being an "outsider," even though GE was the only company he had ever worked for. As a result, Welch was willing to challenge almost everything, and he made it clear that nothing was sacrosanct. This enabled him to take actions that the Jones team had been reluctant to take.

The Jones culture also discouraged people from making promises that they could not keep—a guideline that had good intentions and some good outcomes but also intensified the already conservative culture. Welch, by contrast, "encouraged people to stretch. He proclaimed he would prefer managers to overpromise, if in the stretching, they could achieve more than expected."[2]

Another major difference between Jones and Welch was their attitude toward using the chain of command to communicate and get information. Jones worked *only* through the organization's official layers; he would not go below his direct reports to get information about the business and its major issues.

Welch, by contrast, used his Crotonville and management meetings to identify people in key business units whom he could call—both to get another perspective on what was happening in these business units and to identify issues for his strategy or human resources sessions. This enabled him to know more about what was really happening and to not rely on just the formal channels of communications. Welch reinforced these informal channels with personal handwritten notes to individuals, often to congratulate them for their professional accomplishments. I have a collection of these handwritten notes that Welch wrote to me. They were very effective.

This raises the issue of self-promotion versus corporate promotion. Prior to Welch, leaders were focused on building GE rather than their personal images. Beginning in the late 1980s, there was a torrent of articles and books featuring Welch and his leadership of GE—a sharp contrast to most of his predecessors, who didn't seek out the limelight.

One could make the case that the "cult of personality" that surrounded Welch made it more likely for Welch's personal tastes to have an impact on the company. No doubt Reg Jones liked some businesses more than others, but he never publicly communicated those preferences. Welch showed no such restraint.

Overall, Welch exhibited the talents and skills of a highly intuitive and perceptive portfolio manager who knew what he liked and who was willing to prune and exit businesses—and people—that didn't appear to contribute to his strategic objectives and vision.

KEEP IT SIMPLE: WELCH'S THREE RINGS

Welch liked to keep things very simple, so he invented words and visuals to communicate what he liked and disliked and what he wanted done as a result. One of his first visuals was his "three-ring diagram" (see Exhibit 12-2). This replaced the classic nine-cell matrix that had been used to display business units' priorities and strategic directions.

The three rings divided the company into services, technology, and core businesses, and it then called out those businesses that Welch believed were question marks and that needed to either be restructured or eliminated. This simplified approach to making assessments and decisions was typical of Welch, and without a doubt, it clearly communicated his likes and dislikes and what he intended to do.

The three-ring diagram looked novel—even radical—but in fact it captured the essence of what Jones had already decided to do as a result of his own strategy evaluations.

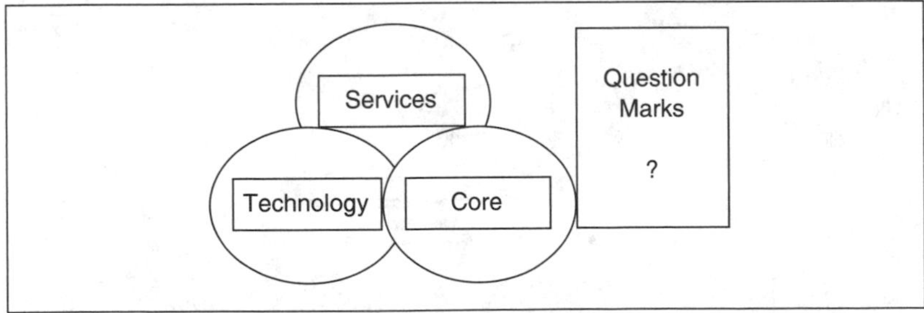

Exhibit 12-2 A simple graphic of Welch's three rings, which he used to depict his overall strategies and to identify the business units he had concerns about and that could therefore be eliminated.

Exhibit 12-3 shows the businesses that Welch placed within the three circles and those he left out. All of the business units in his circles were either Priority I or II. An exception was the aerospace business, which Welch included in his preferred businesses but which had been considered a Priority III during the Jones era. It is worth noting, however, that this is one of the business units that Welch combined with the RCA assets and later sold off.

Those not included in Welch's listing were either Priority III or IV, again with one exception—small appliances—that was rated a Priority II.

To reiterate: Although the Welch diagram was different from the traditional investment matrix, the results were very similar to Jones's evaluations. The company had determined its investment priorities under Jones, but the Jones administration had difficulty executing strategic decisions. This decision making emerged as a major Welch priority.

"JACK THE KNIFE"

In his first two years Welch sold 71 product lines and completed 118 deals, which he described as "peanuts":[3]

- *Central air-conditioners.* Welch never liked this business because it wasn't high tech and it lacked a strong market position. (Welch referred to it as a "plumbing business.") He sold it to Trane.

	Investment categories			
	Priorities I Invest/grow	**II** Select growth/ defend	**III** Harvest	**IV** Exit/divest
Services	Financial Information Construction and engineering Nuclear			
High technology	Materials Aircraft engine	Medical systems Industrial electronics	Aerospace	
Core	Lighting Turbines	Major appliances Transportation Motors Contract equipment		
Outside the circles		Small appliances	Central air-conditioning Large transformer	TV/audio Switchgear Wire/cable

Exhibit 12-3 Welch's three rings and question-mark businesses and how they compared to Jones's investment priorities.

- *Small electric appliances.* Called "GE Housewares," these were also on the Welch hit list. The business was low technology, had low margins, and was highly price competitive. When Bob Wright, currently a vice chairman, was repatriated from Cox Broadcasting, he was assigned to lead this division. Wright was unsuccessful in finding a way to turn the business around, so it was sold to Black & Decker.

SELLING THE GE MONOGRAM

One of the major reasons that Welch was able to make these divestitures is that he was willing to do something that none of his predecessors would do: *sell the GE monogram with the businesses.* Up to this point, the GE monogram had always been considered to be a highly valuable, almost sacred corporate asset. GE had always believed that its brand name was worth at least 5 points of market share in any market the company entered, and it possibly was worth more than the products themselves.

If the company allowed others to use it—so the theory went—the monogram would become tarnished, and that would negatively impact the rest of the company. When Jones cut a deal with Hitachi to dispose of the television business, accordingly, the monogram didn't go with it.

To sell the air-conditioning and small-appliance businesses, by contrast, Welch permitted Trane and Black & Decker to use the GE monogram for five years after the sale. He did it again when he sold off RCA and the consumer electronics business to Thomson but didn't include a time limit.

Utah International was another business Welch disliked. As noted earlier, UI was a metallurgical coal and uranium mining business whose major customers were Japanese and whose earnings were erratic and unpredictable. Welch had to be uncharacteristically delicate in UI's disposition, since it was one the major acquisitions of the Jones era and he didn't want to offend Jones.

The reason for selling the company, Welch later explained, was that "with inflation abating, it [Utah] didn't fit the objective of consistent earnings growth. Its lumpy earnings clashed with my goal to have everyone feel their individual contribution counted."[4]

Welch initially found few buyers for UI. Finally he was able to make a deal with Broken Hill Properties. The deal required splitting out and retaining Ladd Petroleum. GE received $2.4 billion for Utah, about

$100 million more than Jones had paid for it in 1977. Six years later, still in housecleaning mode, Welch sold off Ladd for $515 million.[5]

These dispositions helped to clean up the overall portfolio. But it was the RCA deal that really gave Welch an opportunity to package the RCA and GE assets and sell off several other parts of the company that didn't fit with his strategic portfolio.

WELCH'S PERSONAL DEAL

Thornton "Brad" Bradshaw had hired Bob Frederick, a career GE-er and one of Welch's competitors for the CEO position, and appointed him RCA's chief operating officer, thereby anointing him as the preferred candidate to become RCA's CEO when Bradshaw retired. But Bradshaw came to believe that RCA was no longer viable as a standalone business.

Bradshaw invited Jack Welch to an informal meeting in the apartment of legendary investment banker Felix Rohatyn, and—over cocktails—struck a deal whereby GE would purchase RCA.[6] It is inter-

RCA WAS A BIG WIN FOR BOTH GE AND JACK WELCH

1. It funded the Harris, Martin Marietta, and Thomson deals.
2. It enabled GE to move back into the television network business and to become a dominant player in this market.
3. It permitted GE to participate in the rapidly growing cable business, which Welch had previously failed to do because of the inability to purchase the Cox systems.
4. It strengthened and expanded the GE medical systems business globally.
5. It gave GE a strong position in the global satellite market.
6. It contributed tens of millions of positive cash flow that GE could use for other investments and growth opportunities.

Overall, GE got RCA for free and, by doing so, it enhanced its overall strategic portfolio.

esting to note that Frederick was not present at the meeting and therefore was not part of the initial deal.

One of the most visible assets gained through the RCA acquisition was the RCA—now the GE—building in Rockefeller Center. Recall that when Sarnoff forced GE and Westinghouse to divest RCA, General Electric wound up with the planned RCA corporate headquarters at 570 Lexington Avenue. RCA then built its highly prestigious corporate headquarters at the new Rockefeller Center, and GE was stuck with a very poorly designed building, which remained its headquarters until it moved to Fairfield, Connecticut. So when Bradshaw sold RCA to GE, GE gained control of the Rockefeller Center facility and renamed it the "GE Building," which it remains today.

CREATIVE BUNDLING AND PACKAGING

The deal was a significant coup for GE and Welch. Welch was able to bundle various GE and RCA businesses together to make them more attractive to divest. This enabled him to divest the consumer electronics businesses, the semiconductor business, and the aerospace divisions, none of which were favored by Welch.

Trading Consumer Electronics for Medical Systems

Welch integrated the GE and RCA consumer electronics brands, including television, made it No. 1, and then traded it with Thomson of France for the medical systems business, a business he had always loved. In addition, he received more than $1 billion in cash and a patent portfolio, worth $100 million, for 15 years. This is another example of how GE sold the monogram with the business. The GE and RCA consumer electronic brands are still used by Thomson.

Divesting Semiconductors

GE packaged the GE and RCA semiconductor businesses—another industry Welch really didn't like—and sold it to Harris. Harris got GE people and facilities; GE got $206 million in cash.

Divesting Aerospace

Welch combined the GE and RCA aerospace businesses and then sold them to Martin Marietta. In return, GE got 25 percent of Martin Marietta in the form of convertible preferred stock.

Though a cleaning-up of the GE portfolio was long overdue, these actions were not well received by many of its key stakeholders. The unions and the affected communities, not surprisingly, were very upset. The press, including the *New York Times* and many business magazines, took up their cause and christened Welch "Neutron Jack"—suggesting that like a neutron bomb, he saved the buildings but "killed" the workers inside.

On a personal note: I had left GE seven years earlier to start my own consulting firm, so I didn't have any personal stake in this debate. But I believed strongly that this sort of name-calling was *not* fair. Accordingly, I wrote a series of articles and a letter to the editor of the *New York Times* in which I stated that GE and Welch had "applied the principles of strategic thinking and management. Whether we like it or not, every organization has limited financial, human, and physical resources, so they must make trade-offs and focus on those pieces which can yield the best results."[7]

Of course, Welch rode out these criticisms, although the "Neutron Jack" nickname allegedly rankled him. GE had done its homework, knew what it wanted to do, and in Welch had a leader who was able to make it happen.

FINANCING BECOMES AN END, NOT JUST A MEANS

One of Welch's favorite businesses was GE Financial Services/GE Capital. Recall that this was originally a Borch venture, and it was highlighted in Jones's last corporate plan as a high-priority business.

When he was the consumer sector executive, Welch became highly enamored of GE Credit, which reported to him. With the insights and counsel of several GECC executives—including Dennis Dammerman and Larry Bossidy—and also of his own financial staff, Welch discovered the potential of the capital and financial services business. Welch later said he was struck by the potential of "melding the discipline and cash flows from manufacturing with financial ingenuity to build the business."[8]

When Welch took over GE Credit, it had $11 billion in assets and 10 businesses, and it operated only in North America. Ten years later, by then renamed "GE Capital," it had grown to $70 billion in assets, operated 21 businesses in three countries, and had $9 billion (12.8 percent of its total assets) outside the United States.

In its early stages, the favored division was far from perfect. For example, it experienced major write-offs: "From 1990 to 1992, GE Capital wrote off $1.1 billion in commercial real estate and loans on highly leveraged transactions. But it continued to take risks to improve their numbers."[9]

GECS emerged as a tough-minded, opportunistic deal maker, led by a character named Gary Wendt. Wendt, Welch later wrote, was "quirky, to say the least. You never knew where he was coming from or what kind of a mood he would be in. One thing he didn't like was supervision, and any boss drove him nuts."[10]

It was in the next 10 years that GECS really took off, dramatically changing its size, recasting its global mix, and adding new financial segments. By 2000, GECS had $370 assets, 24 businesses in 48 countries, and $140 billion in assets (37.8 percent) outside the United States. GECS became such a juggernaut, in fact, that many company and industry experts are today concerned about the size of GECS and how dependent GE has become on its earnings.[11]

KIDDER: A MAJOR PROBLEM

Welch explained his interest in acquiring investment banking firm Kidder this way:

> **Buying Kidder was simple. In the 1980s, leveraged buyouts were hot. GE Capital was already a big player in "LBOs." . . . We were getting tired of putting up all the money, taking all the risk, while watching the investment bankers walk away with huge upfront fees. We thought Kidder would give us first crack at more deals and access to new distribution without paying these big fees.[12]**

Unfortunately Kidder proved to be a problem and an embarrassment, in part because the once-proud firm had serious problems even before GE made the acquisition. Kidder was struggling to recover from an insider-trading scandal, and it had been forced by the SEC to shut down its successful risk arbitrage department. Meanwhile, according to *Fortune*, Kidder's retail business was "hobbled by high expenses and many unproductive brokers: half of the firm's retail offices produced no profit at all."[13]

In 1994, another major problem cropped up: a Kidder trader—who had recently been celebrated as a high performer—appeared to have absconded with $350 million. During the investigation that followed, it was discovered that five-year Kidder head Mike Carpenter—an old friend of Welch's—wasn't even a licensed securities broker.[14]

So Welch took draconian steps to clear up the mess. First, he told his old friend Michael Carpenter, "This isn't going away until you go," and removed him from the job.[15] Then he sold Kidder to Paine Webber in October 1994 for $670 million, plus a 24 percent stake in Paine Webber. Executed under pressure, the deal ensured that Welch and GE would land on their feet. It gave GE an after-tax return of 10 percent a year over the next 14 years.

Some might call this luck, but I don't believe it. I think the deal underscored Welch's remarkable ability to make the best of a bad situation and come out smelling like a rose.

GLOBALIZATION

"Welch sees the future," a 1993 *BusinessWeek* headline read. "It's China, India and Mexico."[16]

I know from personal experience that Welch didn't always feel this way. In 1983, I went to China to teach at a U.S. State Department–sponsored strategic program at Dalian Institute of Technology and to meet with several Chinese government officials. Upon my return, I wrote a short overview of the Chinese environment and included a proposal to Welch recommending that GE position itself to participate in the emerging Chinese infrastructure markets. His response: "This is the most unimportant priority I have." In retrospect, I agree that Welch had many more critical issues to address, because the Chinese markets were still in their embryonic stages, but his decision did delay GE's ability to gain a major share of this now enormous market.

A decade afterward, however, Welch had become convinced that GE was far too domestic in its orientation. The company's only truly global businesses were the two he had led: plastics and medical systems. Everything else was predominantly United States oriented. Welch credits GE executive Paolo Fresco—a true internationalist, whom Welch ultimately promoted to vice chairman—for helping to prompt this realization.

Later, Fresco left GE to become the Fiat chairman. But the revolution he had sparked at GE continued. As Welch later explained, "We focused most of our attention on areas of the world that were either in transition or out of favor. In the early to mid-1990s, when Europe was slumping, we saw many opportunities, particularly in financial services."[17]

Appliances created joint ventures in India and Mexico. Jet engines opened service centers in 17 Chinese cities and moved its marketing office to Beijing. Plastics purchased a Mexican resin. Medical systems created a joint venture to develop a low-cost imaging system in China. Power systems targeted Asian and Mexican orders.

GO HOME, MR. WELCH

The Honeywell deal was intended to be Welch's last major coup. GE looked at Honeywell in February 2000 and was impressed by its apparent fit with GE. At least on paper, Honeywell would enhance the GE aircraft engine, industrial systems, and plastics components businesses. Then, for internal reasons, Honeywell's stock price started to decline, and the potential deal looked even more attractive.

United Technologies (UTC) made a play for Honeywell, and Welch took immediate action to counter the UTC bid. He called the Honeywell CEO out of a board meeting and told him that GE would give Honeywell stockholders a better return. He promised that he would pay *8 percent* of GE's market value—a staggering sum.

In return, of course, he expected that GE would get a *16 percent* earnings bump.

Unfortunately for Welch, he and his team didn't do all the necessary homework. They miscalculated the power of the European Economic Community (EEC) in general and of Mario Monti in particular. Monti—an Italian economics professor and member of the EEC responsible for competition—demanded concessions that would have gutted the deal.

At one meeting, Monti told Welch that he could include a new chapter in his book: "Go Home, Mr. Welch!" Everyone laughed, but as Welch later admitted, "My heart sank." His last major deal was in peril—and in fact, it subsequently collapsed.[18]

Some media reports focused on the negatives for GE. For my part, I believe that Monti actually did GE a huge favor by scuttling the Honeywell deal. I say this for three reasons:

1. *Honeywell really was not an exciting company.* If the deal had been consummated, GE would have had to do a lot of pruning and packaging. Even though this was a proven strength of both GE and Welch, it would have come at a very difficult time, and the company would have suffered.
2. *The second reason is even more fundamental: I think that had the deal gone through, Welch would not have retired.* This would have broken the long GE tradition of executives retiring "at the top of their game."
3. *Finally, Welch's ultimate successor would have had limited options.* A deal of that size would have constrained even mighty GE, and it would have consumed a great deal of the CEO's attention.

TAKEAWAYS

Remember that nothing is sacred. This is the underpinning principle of a sound strategic portfolio system. All of the businesses must be evaluated with the same objectivity and criticality. None can be exempt or given a special status. Even though Jones and Borch both professed to be willing to evaluate all of the businesses equally, they clearly had biases. Welch was more challenging, and—even though he had favorites—he demanded that all of the businesses be evaluated with the same rigor.

- *Recommendations.* Be willing to challenge all of your businesses, even if they are very profitable. Don't give a pass to units that you managed or worked in and for which you may have fond memories. Recognize that things change, and the best may become the worst. Move systematically to make changes but don't hesitate when it is necessary to take action.

Avoid fire sales. Welch made money on all of his dispositions, even when they were problems (Kidder is an excellent example). He recognized that even if a business was not attractive to him and didn't fit his strategies, it most likely had value to someone else.

- *Recommendation.* Take the time to find someone who might be interested in a business or product line that you want to exit. Package the product or business so that it is very attractive to the potential buyer. Be reasonable and have patience.

Services and financing are an end, not a means. Beginning with Jones, it became very clear that GE could make more money by providing the after-sales services and parts and by financing products than it could by selling the products themselves. Welch clearly used this as the underpinning principle of his strategy.

- *Recommendation.* Know where and how you make money. Often, services and financing are more profitable than the products or systems you're selling.

CHAPTER

GE's Cultural Revolution

LEN SCHLESINGER, a Harvard Business School professor, was clearly impressed by the GE management programs—designed to transform the company—in which he had been invited to participate. "This is one of the biggest planned efforts to alter people's behavior," he told *Fortune*, "since the Cultural Revolution."[1]

Jack Welch made human resources planning, training, and development his highest priority, and he continued to use Crotonville as his major change agent. Welch made it clear that his most important job was the selection, evaluation, and motivation of people.

BUILDING A TEAM

One of the first things that Welch did in all his key assignments was to get his own team in place as soon as possible. He selected people whom he knew from past assignments, often from lower in the organization. The people he liked were like himself—loud and confrontational—but generally younger.

One of his discoveries was Larry Bossidy, whom he described as "brusque, smart, funny, quick talking."[2] Welch found him at a management meeting and played Ping-Pong with him. "We both played like our lives depended on it," Welch later recalled approvingly.[3] Bossidy was a GE Credit middle manager; Welch ultimately promoted him to vice chairman. Bossidy left GE to become the CEO of Allied Signal. Later Allied Signal acquired Honeywell and took the Honeywell name, thus making Bossidy the CEO at the new Honeywell.

When Welch was appointed head of the chemical and metallurgical division, the first thing he did was scrutinize his team. "With few exceptions," he wrote, "I found them wanting."[4] He replaced them with people with whom he had had past associations. Notably, he reached down to people in the organization who were not on the standard promotional list.

Selecting Strong Financial Advisors

Welch recognized his own limitations in finance. When he was promoted to consumer sector executive, therefore, he appointed Bob Nelson and Dennis Dammerman to be his tutors.

Both Dammerman and Nelson came from the appliance business. When Welch was appointed to this sector, he had no experience in the consumer business. Dave Dance—his new boss—had been the head of the appliance business. His major competitor for the CEO job was Stan Gault, who had been the appliance group's executive.

Dammerman and Nelson took the appliance business's financial statements apart, which gave Welch a competitive advantage. Welch remembered and rewarded them both. Dammerman became the CFO and later one of Welch's vice chairmen. Nelson—by all accounts a talented strategist and analyst—served for more than 20 years as Welch's personal strategic financial advisor.

FIXING LEGAL

Another key function that Welch was determined to strengthen was the legal staff. In this case, he looked inside the company for nontraditionalists, but he also looked outside. Welch recruited a Washington lawyer,

Ben Heineman, to do the external recruiting; he gave Heineman authority to spend top dollars to get the best people he could find.

ELIMINATING THE BUREAUCRACY

At the same time that he strengthened specific functions, Welch also moved to pare down what he perceived to be a bloated corporate bureaucracy. Finance was an obvious target. Historically, GE had taken pride in its large and powerful financial organization, but Welch set out to reduce both the size and power of this organization.

His first CFO was Tom Thorsen. Thorsen was very strong willed, and he was reluctant to make the cuts in the financial organization that Welch wanted, so Welch encouraged him to leave. Thorsen became the CFO of Travelers Insurance. Welch replaced him with Dennis Dammerman—mentioned above—who was a middle-level GECC financial manager and had no strong allegiance to the financial organization. Dammerman did the deed, and again Welch rewarded him.

Welch's attack on the oversized bureaucracy was a way to make a statement that he wanted his business units in command. In some areas, such as strategic planning and finance, there was a large number of people, but this was more a result of the sector organization than of runaway corporate bloat.

The corporate strategic planning organizations—objects of Welch's scorn—really weren't that large. As the corporate strategist, I had about 20 people in my organization, but this number included a corporate business library organization staff and several senior economists; both of these organizations were there to serve the CEO.

Corporate Planning itself was very small and, in fact, got larger after I left GE to start my own consulting and development business. The other part of the so-called bureaucracy was the CCS organization, which—as I have described—had been placed on a self-sustaining basis and provided services that internal customers and vendors perceived to be valuable.

Again, it was the sector staff organizations that had grown enormously. The sector staffs were the hideouts of all those people who slowed down the decision-making and implementation processes. I think that Welch wanted to make a point, so he laid waste to the sector bureaucracy to demonstrate that he was determined to be lean and mean—a posture that the outside world bought and applauded.

But it's clear that Welch picked an easy target. No one likes bureaucrats, and anyone who gets rid of bureaucrats must be on the right path.

JACK WELCH'S SIX RULES

1. Face reality as it is, not as it was or as you wish it were.
2. Be candid with everyone.
3. Don't manage; lead.
4. Change before you have to.
5. If you don't have a competitive advantage, don't compete.
6. Control your own destiny, or someone else will.[5]

MAINSTREAMERS AND "VALUES"

Welch used GE mainstreamers when it was necessary.

For instance, when GE nuclear was in trouble, he picked Roy Beaton, a career GE manager, to lead the turnaround. Beaton was not a Welch type; he was a good soldier and a very competent manager who was able to get rid of what Welch called the "bureaucrats" in the nuclear business.

Welch asserted that these types of appointments made it clear to the rest of the people in the organization that they didn't have to fit a certain stereotype—that is, be like Welch himself—to be successful in the new GE. All you had to do, Welch said repeatedly, was face reality and perform. "Self-delusion can grip an entire organization," Welch once wrote, "and lead the people into to ridiculous conclusion."[6]

But it wasn't quite as simple as "face reality and perform." Since the Borch days, Session C had been a vital part of the selection of key executives. Traditionally performance was the key measure, but Welch added a new dimension to the process: a commitment to "shared values." His team created a new classification scheme (see Exhibit 13-1).

Meets commitments	Accepts and practices company values: Yes	Accepts and practices company values: No
Yes	Type 1 Reward and promote	Type 4 Consider as candidates for liquidation
No	Type 3 Give a second chance	Type 2 Remove immediately

Exhibit 13-1 Welch's four types of managers and professionals.

- Type 1 are those who deliver results and share company values. These are the winners and should be promoted and rewarded.
- Type 2 are those who haven't delivered and don't appear to share the company's values. These employees should be removed.
- Type 3 are those who miss short-term commitments but share all the values. These employees should be given a chance to improve.
- Type 4 are those who deliver on commitments, make the numbers, but don't share the values. These employees are also candidates for removal from the organization.[7]

Note that there is nothing magic or even particularly unusual about the GE human resources system. The classifications are logical, and they make sense even though there are certainly many other ways to group and evaluate people. The major reason that the system has been successful for GE is that Welch and his predecessors were personally involved and made it happen. They believed in it, and they committed the time to make sure it was being executed.

At the same time, it's important to recognize that the system was not universally implemented "as advertised." Some managers did a great job and were very honest and helpful; others simply went through the motions and in some cases were not candid and honest. And of course, this is true of all systems.

DISCOVERING AND UPGRADING THE TEMPLE OF CHANGE

Recall that Crotonville was originally opened in 1953 to indoctrinate management on the art and science of professional business management. It became a fee-based institute during the Borch era, and although Jones used the center to teach strategic planning and several initiatives, it was still self-funding.

Crotonville leader Lindy Saline was able to generate enough money to add a smaller version of the Pit, called the "Cave," and several other classrooms, as well as an addition to the living quarters. Overall, though, the facility remained a very stark and almost monastic setting.

Welch had not been a strong proponent of the institute; in fact, he took a somewhat perverse pride in the fact that he had attended only one Crotonville course in his long GE career. The Welch-led division and group tended to view the center as a place that employees were sent when they were in between jobs or were on their way out of the company; they definitely did not see it as a resource for the best and brightest.

But when Welch became the CEO, he lectured at a few course sessions, and he gradually came to realize that Crotonville could become a strong ally in his efforts to change the company. His enthusiasm increased for the facility that he had once scorned.

Simultaneously, Tom Vanderslice—COO of General Telephone and Electronics—hired Ken Michel from Crotonville, and together they constructed a state-of-the-art, upscale facility: the Learning Center in Norwalk, Connecticut. Welch visited the new GTE center, and he was so impressed he decided to invest in Crotonville and make it a "five-star" facility. By this time, he had already built a small, five-star, European-style hotel to receive guests at the Fairfield corporate headquarters.

Making Crotonville the Bully Pulpit

Jones and his predecessors played a very small role in Crotonville courses. In fact, when I was leading the Manager Development Course,

I intentionally limited the number of senior management presentations.

There were two reasons. First, the senior-level managers often just read speeches rather than conducting interactive sessions. Second, they often had views that were in conflict with the topics being covered, so they were not positive reinforcements.

Welch was different. His style was perfect for the Crotonville interactive sessions. In fact, he rarely if ever presented anything; he just showed up and was willing to create an impromptu dialog or even challenge the participants and the faculty. He enjoyed the interactions.

"In 1984," he later recorded, "I started going to Crotonville for every one of our top three management classes. We overhauled all of them. They had been based on case studies at other companies. We changed that to tackle real GE issues."[8]

One of the major changes, however, was the personal involvement and commitment of time by Welch to teach in the management programs. Welch became the center of the programs, and he used these sessions to spread his message, identify high-potential individuals, and glean the insights and concerns of the participants.

This might be an appropriate juncture to take a little detour into Welch's public image, which became equally as aggressive as his inside-the-company image. It wasn't always so: Welch was relatively quiet during the first six years of his tenure.

At first, stung by negative press and the "Neutron Jack" nickname, he was standoffish with the press. Once the pruning was largely over and the coverage became more favorable, however, Welch agreed to have many books written about the company, several of which highlighted his entrepreneurial leadership style. When he retired, he added to the growing torrent of positive coverage about his tenure by writing his first book: *Jack: Straight from the Gut.*

All of this was very, very new for GE. Welch's predecessors generally received highly positive press coverage, and yet, they didn't encourage books and articles that highlighted themselves. They tried to keep the focus on the *company* rather than on the company's leader. Not so with Welch.

RE-CREATING THE PIT EVERYWHERE

As the following excerpts from Welch's first autobiographical work indicate, Welch's thinking about Crotonville—and executive development in general—continued to evolve:

> **One afternoon in September 1988, I left Crotonville frustrated as hell. I had just about had it. That day had produced a particularly good session. The people in class poured out their frustrations about trying to change their businesses. I knew we had to get the candor and passion out of the classroom and back into the workplace. We had to re-create the Crotonville Pit all over the company. . . .**
>
> **This was the beginning of a GE game-changer called Work-Out. . . . We came up with the idea of bringing in trained facilitators from the outside, mainly university professors who had no ax to grind. . . .**
>
> **Work-Out was patterned after the traditional New England town meeting. Groups of 40 to 100 employees were invited to share their views on the business and the bureaucracy that got in way, particularly approvals, reports, meetings, and measurements.[9]**

Welch expected every business to hold hundreds of Work-Outs. A typical Work-Out lasted two to three days. "The boss was expected to give a yes-or-no decision on at least 75 percent of the ideas," Welch wrote. "If a decision couldn't be made on the spot, there was an agreed-upon date for the decision. . . . It became a bureaucracy buster."[10]

RALLYING THE TROOPS THROUGH KEY INITIATIVES

The use of initiatives is very common in most U.S. companies. These are launched to rally the troops around a common cause. The cause may be increasing sales, reducing costs, restructuring, or otherwise dealing with a compelling opportunity or threat. During his eight years in office, Reg Jones used three initiatives to focus the company on what he considered to be key issues.

Welch, too, was a firm believer in this approach, and he instituted six major initiatives during his 20 years in power. Let's review some of the key initiatives he used.

The Boundaryless Company

When it was clear that he had achieved as much as he could from the Work-Outs, Welch launched what he called the "boundaryless company" initiative.

"The 'boundaryless' company I saw would remove all the barriers among functions," Welch explained. "It would recognize no distinction between domestic and foreign operations. 'Boundaryless' behavior allows ideas to come from anywhere."[11]

Many scholars and pundits consider corporate scale and scope to be a major disadvantage when the size of a company has passed a certain point. Therefore, many are critical of GE because of its size. But all of the company's CEOs, including the incumbent, have argued that the combination of scale and scope is one of GE's great strengths and that it goes far beyond simple portfolio balancing.

On the other hand, scale and scope naturally lead to a proliferation of procedures, which in turn lead to boundaries between units. Welch decided that there was a need to increase the integration of the separate parts of the company and to motivate people to exchange ideas across the business units. Consistent with his style, he created a new word: *boundaryless*.

He used this word to communicate his desire get ideas exchanged and plans implemented. In addition, he made it part of the Session C and the measurement and reward systems. This was typical of Welch, reflecting his conviction that things didn't change without using both the carrot and stick.

Six Sigma Becomes Welch's PBM Program

Recall how Cordiner invested heavily in making professional business management (PBM) a vital element of GE's management process and a form of religion. Welch did the same with Six Sigma, a statistical quality control program.

One of Welch's most famous initiatives involved GE's embrace of the "Six-Sigma quality program." Six Sigma was not homegrown; in fact, it was imported from Motorola via Honeywell, based on the recommendation of Welch's former vice chairman and personal friend, Larry Bossidy. But Welch bought into the program in a big way, and he instituted an adapted Six-Sigma program of the same magnitude—and possibly at a higher cost—at GE.

Among other things, Welch took the following steps in implementing Six Sigma at GE:

1. He appointed a senior-level executive to become the program czar, similar to Cordiner's appointment of management scientist Harold Smiddy.
2. He assigned the "best and brightest" employees to become the program's missionaries and reviewers. "We told the business CEOs," Welch explained, "to make their best people six sigma leaders. That meant taking our people off their existing jobs and giving them two-year project assignments to qualify them for what were called 'black belts' in six sigma terminology. Black-belt projects sprang up in every business, improving call center response rates, increasing factory capacity, and reducing billing errors and inventories."
3. He made sure that the program trained key people. GE trained thousands of people as "green belts" (the next level down from black belts).
4. He tied Six Sigma to the reward and measurement systems. Again, Welch brought together the carrot and stick. Sixty percent of an executive's incentive was based on financials and 40 percent on Six Sigma.

Welch clearly saw the huge bottom-line impact from pursuing Six Sigma, which is why he thumped this tub so hard. As he later wrote: "Bob Nelson, my longtime financial analyst, ran a cost-benefit analysis to study the approach and determine its potential payouts. They showed that if GE was running at three to four sigma, the cost-saving opportunity of raising this quality to six sigma was somewhere between \$7 and \$10 billion. This amounted to a huge number, 10 to 15 percent of sales."[12]

E-business

Welch was very late in recognizing the power of the Internet. As I explained earlier, Welch was a high-touch, handwritten-notes type of communicator. But once Welch became convinced of the power of the Internet, he invested heavily in new technologies, and he insisted that all GE businesses use the Internet to interact more effectively with their key stakeholders—and especially their customers.

In short, Welch followed the tradition of his predecessors by launching initiatives that were needed. The major difference between Welch and his predecessors was the degree of his personal involvement and his use of the carrot-and-stick approach to get response. True, all GE leaders used the measurement and reward system to make their point and enforce their dictates, but Welch made it even more obvious and even personal. He would use a "nonconformist" or "poor responder" as a public example and even criticize that hapless individual in a public forum.

WHY THE WELCH INITIATIVES WERE SUCCESSFUL

- Welch was the creator and leader of each initiative.
- He rewarded cooperators and punished nonconformists.
- He invested in people to make them successful.

FIXING SUCCESSION PLANNING

As we've seen, Reg Jones became obsessed with selecting the right successor—so much so that he got in his own way and made life difficult for the finalists.

Jack Welch was dedicated not to repeat this ritual. He started the process to select his heir in 1994, working with the following specs:

1. Integrity and values
2. Experience
3. Vision

4. Leadership
5. Edge
6. Stature
7. Fairness
8. Energy, balance, and courage

He later added additional characteristics, including an insatiable appetite for increasing knowledge, demonstrating "courageous advocacy," being comfortable operating under a microscope, and having the stomach to play for high stakes.

A total of 23 people were on Welch's original succession list. Of these, we should note at the outset, only 9 are with GE today.

There were three finalists with the following characteristics:

- Youth (young enough to serve 10 years)
- Homegrown
- GE heritage
- Strong track record
- Ability to integrate acquisitions and make the business prosper

Let's look briefly at each.

Young Enough to Lead for 10 Years

Welch wanted to be sure that his successor had the same opportunity that he had—that is, to serve 10 years. He believed that a CEO needed this long to develop his own strategy and see it to its conclusion. All of the three finalists were young enough to lead the company for 10 years, but Immelt was the youngest of the group, 45, and could serve 20 years, as Welch had.

Homegrown

Though Jeff Immelt had spent a few years at P&G, he was really a typical "from-trainee-to-leader" candidate. Jim McNerney had come from McKinsey, but he was also a true homegrown and developed product, as was Bob Nardelli.

It is also interesting that all of these candidates had a GE "heritage." Immelt's father had worked for the aircraft engine business, Nardelli had come from Schenectady, and Jim McNerney was a Cincinnati product. In short, the candidates met the "GE-grown-and-developed" status.

Strong Track Record

- Immelt (age 45) had worked in plastics, one of Welch's first loves, and he had then been given one of Welch's real favorites—the medical systems business—to run. This was a business that Welch had fallen in love with when he was the group executive responsible for it. He had a vision for this business, and he committed the resources to make it a star. Welch removed another favorite, John Trani, from this job and gave it to Immelt. Trani was disappointed and left the company to become the CEO for Stanley Works.
- McNerney (age 52) was assigned to the lighting business in the Asia Pacific and then finally to the aircraft engine business. All of these, with the possible exception of Asia Pacific, were Welch favorites, and McNerney performed well.
- Nardelli (age 53) led the power systems business, the generation piece of the "Benign Cycle," and the part that GE kept after it spun off the transmission and distribution businesses. He, too, was highly successful.

Another common characteristic of these three was that they had all demonstrated the ability to integrate acquisitions and make the business prosper. This is a requirement of GE's CEOs now because acquisition has become the major growth engine. This is not surprising: When you are a $130 billion company and want to grow at a 10 percent compounded growth rate, you must include some acquisitions and deal making.

Up or Out

Another major difference from the Jones approach was that Welch insisted that if the candidates didn't win, they had to leave. Of course, they were all marketable, and it is likely that GE even helped the unsuccessful candidates to find jobs.

Nardelli went to Home Depot, and as of the time this book is being written, he is under pressure to explain his huge compensation package while the stock is declining.

McNerney went on to 3M where he followed the Welch tradition of doing aggressive surgery, and he was rewarded by a higher stock price. In August 2005 he became the Boeing CEO. Boeing stock increased and 3M stock dropped when McNerney announced he was leaving 3M. At the time of this writing, McNerney is praised for his success in addressing Boeing's past scandals, and the business and its stock are thriving.

TAKEAWAYS

Celebrity CEO. Welch used his own image as an entrepreneurial leader to sell GE, and it appears to have continued to increase shareholder value. This option is not available to all leaders, and it must be used carefully, but it is an option you may wish to consider.

- *Recommendation.* Consider how you can personally enhance the business and its reputation. If you have a unique personality or ability to motivate, use it. But also don't get carried away with your own press releases, because, ultimately, you're not on an ego trip. Know when to stop.

Total system, not just slogans. From the beginning, GE was willing to make a full commitment and heavy investments to change. Each of the CEOs, up to and including Welch, implemented a complete system when he wanted to make changes. This included missionaries, education, and rewards.

- *Recommendation.* Determine where and when you want to make a major change. Put together a complete package and make a personal commitment. Be sure to tie the change to the rewards and measurement systems. Avoid having the slogan of the week, month, or year. Be selective and do it right.

"Back to the Future"

GE's Fourth Stage, 2001 to the Present
Immelt

HIGHLIGHTS

- *Succeeding a legend and 9/11.* Jeff Immelt succeeded Welch four days before the horrific events of September 11, 2001. He had to demonstrate that he could lead the company as well as Welch and deal with the negative impacts of the terrorists' attacks on the World Trade Center.
- *Go BIG.* Immelt continues to assert that size is a GE asset and that he can continue to grow the company's organic revenues in the 8 percent range.
- *Back to technology.* Immelt has refocused the company on technology and has invested heavily in expanding the research and development centers globally while making significant acquisitions to enhance the company's ability to provide ecologically friendly systems and products.
- *Portfolio management continues.* GE continues to evaluate its portfolio and challenge both the winners and the losers. Adding and subtract-

ing businesses remains a cornerstone of the company strategy and management philosophy.

- *Ecomagination.* Immelt has established his own theme and programs to enhance the company's ability to develop innovative, ecologically friendly products and services for the global marketplace.

CHAPTER

Go BIG!

HINDSIGHT AND FORESIGHT

So far, this book has been about what we can learn from the past. Now, I would like to discuss the present and the future.

I worked at GE for almost 30 years, and I personally knew many of the leaders. In previous chapters, I have shared a few of my own experiences with some of those leaders and the company. But this part of the book is necessarily different because I have no first-hand knowledge of the current leadership team. Therefore, I will use four sources of intelligence to describe, analyze, and critique the current GE:

1. What the company and its leadership say
2. What the company is doing
3. What others say about the company, its strategies, and its leadership
4. My own professional insights and experiences

Let's begin with a snapshot of what Immelt inherited and the challenges it has presented.

A TOUGH ACT TO FOLLOW

Imagine that you have just been selected to be the CEO of one of the largest and most visible companies in the world. Imagine, further, that you're inheriting the following situation.

Fantastic Financials

Your predecessor was in office for over 20 years. During his tenure, revenues grew to more than $125 billion—up from $90 billion 5 years earlier—and net income increased $4.4 billion during this same period to $13.6 billion. In addition, all of the ratios are at all-time highs. Return on sales has moved from 9 to 11 percent, and return on stockholder equity has increased from 25 to 27.1 percent.

Under your predecessor's leadership, revenues grew at a 7.8 percent compounded annual rate, and earnings grew at almost twice this rate, at 13.4 percent compounded. The enterprise became one of the largest-capitalized companies in the world, and the press loved both the CEO and the company.

Succeeding a Legend

Dozens of books and articles were written about your predecessor, lauding him as one of the greatest leaders and entrepreneurs of all time. He personalized the company and convinced many that he had dramatically transformed the company from a bureaucratic, stodgy, and slow-growing company into a highly entrepreneurial, dynamic, and rapidly growing institution.

Maturing a Skewed Portfolio

Over the 20 years of your predecessor's reign, the company has moved from being an internally grown, technological innovator to a portfolio of relatively mature, financially driven business units. More than 46 percent of its revenues and 26 percent of its earnings are generated by its highly aggressive financial services company. Most of its growth has come from acquisitions and portfolio change. But the company was recently embarrassed when it was prohibited by the European Economic Community from completing a major acquisition that had been intended to enable the company to continue to grow and prosper.

September 11, 2001: A Day That Changed the World

Now let's complicate the picture even further. Let's imagine that four days after you take control of the company, the world is changed forever by the horrific events of September 11. You immediately have to deal with the impact of this great tragedy in which your company has lost two employees who worked in the World Trade Center, taken a $600 million hit to its insurance business, and lost one of the planes it owned.

Let's imagine that your company's stock drops 11 percent in the first six days after the attack.[1] This was what Jeff Immelt had to face when he became the CEO of GE on September 7, 2001.

IMMELT AND HIS CHALLENGES

I've previously described the process that Jack Welch used to select his successor. Jeff Immelt came out the winner and became GE's tenth chief executive officer (see Exhibit 14-1).

Immelt joined GE in 1982 as a member of Corporate Consulting Service's Marketing Training Program. He graduated from Dartmouth College in 1978 with a BS degree in applied mathematics, and he received his MBA from Harvard in 1982. Immelt was the first CEO in GE's history to have an MBA, which may explain some of his strategies and some of the changes he is making.

Over his 22-year GE career, he held marketing and general management positions in GE plastics—where he first met Jack Welch—and major appliances, and he then was given responsibility for one of Welch's favorite businesses: medical systems. Immelt did a good job of growing medical systems through a series of acquisitions, and it became a $12 billion business on his watch.

About a year an a half into that watch, the *Wall Street Journal* attempted a character sketch:

> **Mr. Immelt emphasizes the need for teamwork, regularly meets with employees, circulates earnest e-mails, and uses self-deprecating humor to deflate tension.**

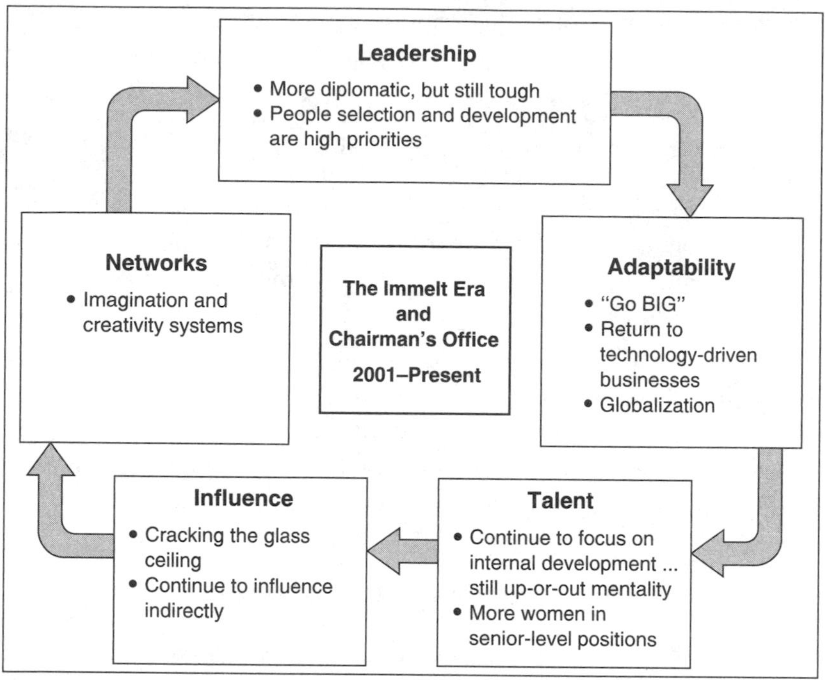

Exhibit 14-1 LATIN and the Immelt era.

> **Insiders, including manufacturing workers, insist that GE's demanding culture hasn't mellowed. Managers are still ranked, given high goals and expected to work long hours. Though not much of a table-pounding screamer, Mr. Immelt can be every bit as blunt as his predecessor, managers say. He often plays on the guilt of poor performers, telling them they are letting the team down. The technique "makes you feel terrible," says Larry Johnston, Chairman and CEO of Albertsons Inc., who worked for Mr. Immelt at GE Medical Systems. *"You don't want to let this guy down."*[2]**

Immelt had to respond quickly to the tragedy of 9/11 and minimize its impact on GE. He also had to determine whether the Welch strategies and portfolio could provide the revenues and earnings growth that the world had come to expect of GE. And finally, of course, he faced the challenge of becoming "his own man" and not a pale imitation of Welch.

This was made even more difficult because Welch, unlike his GE predecessors, wanted to remain in the limelight and continue to be a business guru. Welch published his first book, *Jack: Straight from the Gut,* in 2001 and another book, *Winning,* in 2004, and he became a frequent participant in lectures, seminars, and television shows. In 2006, Jack and his wife initiated a column in *BusinessWeek*.

Welch wasn't going to make it easy for the world to forget Welch.

Despite this background noise, Immelt methodically began assembling his own team. In his (relatively) quiet way, Immelt was as tough and thoroughgoing as his predecessor. As of October 2006, only Bob Wright remained from Jack's team.

Immelt's new team consists of GE grown and trained career executives in their late 40s. When Immelt appointed three of his new vice chairmen, he did so for several reasons. First, each of these individuals complemented Immelt's own skills. And, like other key GE executives, they were being aggressively recruited; if Immelt had not appointed them to senior positions, they would most likely have left the company.

Adding vice chairmen also opened up other positions in which to place high-potential people. And finally, expanding the executive corps enabled Immelt to change the face of that group. For example, more women are now in executive and senior management positions than ever before.

GO BIG

In the June 2006 issue of the *Harvard Business Review*, Immelt said: "Another decade of 4% growth, and GE will cease to be a great company."[3]

This was the theme of GE's 2005 annual report, and it captures the major issue that Immelt and his team must address: how to continue to grow a $150 billion company at an 8 percent compounded growth rate forever. This means that GE must add $14 billion plus revenues and $1.5 billion plus earnings, compounded every year.

Most observers, including me, don't believe that an 8 percent organic growth rate is a sustainable growth rate for a company of GE's size. Ultimately, it seems, the leadership must face the inexorable realities of big numbers and be willing to split the company.

Prior to Immelt's selection as CEO, I wrote a short article for *Chief Executive* magazine entitled "Succeeding a Legend" in which I outlined the challenges and strategic alternatives available for Welch's successor. One of the options I described was to divide the company into three parts: financial services, technology, and traditional GE. I ventured the opinion that this outcome may be inevitable regardless of the desires of the GE leadership.

So far, Immelt and his team have rejected the notion that the company is too big. They appear to truly believe that bigness is an asset rather than a liability and that GE has the proven ability to continue to grow profitably regardless of its size. As Immelt puts it:

> **There are pure "numerologists" in the world who say that a company like GE is too big to grow. Our job is to turn this around and prove that size will spur GE's growth. We have used our financial strength to build a fast-growth portfolio. Now we are using our breadth and depth to create unique GE solutions in technology, services, commercial excellence and globalization. We are using our process skills to make innovation more reliable. Our 11 businesses will grow one customer at a time.[4]**

REINVENTION STRATEGIES

So beyond the platitudes, *how* is Immelt trying to meet this objective? It appears that his strategy has the following parts:

1. Returning to GE's technology-based heritage on a global scale
2. Globalization
3. Betting on three big hits

Let's look at each of these building blocks for reinvention and for "going BIG."

Returning to GE's Technology-Based Heritage on a Global Scale

Prior to Borch and the introduction of strategic portfolio management, GE was considered by most to be a technology- and innovation-driven company. Up until the mid-1970s, in fact, GE was granted more patents annually than any other company. Its R&D center and product departments were encouraged to create new products that could be turned into new businesses and even industries.

But this changed when the company made the R&D center into a quasi-profit center, which required that it rely more on getting funding from the product divisions or external sources. By so doing, it shifted the R&D focus from long-term breakthroughs to short-term applications and results.

During the Welch tenure, as noted, most of the new businesses were acquired and not internally developed, and the company moved from being driven by advances in technology to being driven by its financial product services and applications.

This appears to be changing. "Technology and innovation are at the heart of our initiatives," Immelt wrote in the company's 2003 annual report. "Technology produces high-margin products, wins competitive battles, and creates new markets. Research and development of new products is a part of the overall strategy."[5]

GE has invested more than $400 million in upgrading its Schenectady R&D labs and building research facilities in India, China, and Germany. The total research budget was more than $3.1 billion in 2004. The amount the company spent on trying to develop new and cleaner forms of energy increased from $700 million to $1.3 billion. Further, the company is encouraging more long-term research, and it is putting less focus on short-term projects. Patents have been given more emphasis as well. In 2002, for example, the company filed 28 patents in the nanotechnology arena alone.

This is clearly a major change in resource allocation from the Welch era. Welch, despite his Ph.D. in chemical engineering, was really never a major proponent of technology. It's fair to say that on his watch, GE lost its edge in R&D—an edge that Immelt seems determined to regain.

Unfortunately, spending money on R&D doesn't guarantee that it will yield timely results—or *any* results, for that matter. A number of attempts have been made in the past to move ideas from the lab bench to the marketplace, and many more of those have failed than have succeeded. Why? First of all, even if the lab works on a real customer problem—which Immelt is emphasizing—the customer may not be willing or able to use or finance the new technology for a period of time.

Second, the implementation of new technologies is often delayed or hobbled by regulations and government interference.

Other potential problems with Immelt's multilab, global research and development initiative are getting people to share and managing personnel across cultures. I've had several clients with labs in different countries, and in most of these cases, the challenge has been to get the labs to work together rather than compete against each other.

Globalization

We live in a global society, and any major company must be global. Further, a globally ambitious company must be a player in developing nations. "It's not by choice but by necessity," wrote Immelt. "Developing countries are where the fastest growth is occurring and more sustainable growth."[6]

The company had global revenues of almost $78 billion in 2005, up 16 percent. Fifty-one percent of the 2005 global revenues came from Europe, 25 percent from the Pacific Basin, and 14 percent from the Americas. China and India were expected to provide the greatest future global growth.

> **We can take every growth idea and multiply its effectiveness through globalization. Globalization is a GE core competency. We have made and sold products outside the U.S. for 100 years, and one-third of our leadership team is global.[7]**

China is a major growth opportunity, and it contributed revenues of $2.6 billion (1.9 percent of the total company revenues) in 2004. The company is targeting major Chinese opportunities in energy, aviation, water, and health care—*within this decade*. GE sees the 2008 Olympics as a major opportunity and believes that it can complete a superior in-country technology infrastructure at a competitive cost. The company has built a Chinese laboratory, significantly increased the size of the sales force, and in effect is treating China like a developed nation.

India, long a disappointment for GE's industrial businesses, is now at the beginning stages of a major transformation, and GE expects to generate $1 billion in India in 2005. GE established a wholly owned affiliate to provide back-office, accounting, and call center services, and in 2004 it sold 60 percent of this captive firm to two private Indian equity firms.[8]

Other major targeted growth areas are consumer and commercial finance in Eastern Europe, the modernization of rail and power projects in Russia, and the rebuilding of Iraq's power network.

Obviously, globalization has its critics, especially when it appears to be benefiting other nations at the expense of GE's home base: the United States. But Immelt is not cowed by these critics. As he puts it:

> **I am proud to be an American CEO of an American company. But growing GE requires us to view the world as our market. GE has several responsibilities in the pursuit of global trade. We must continue to give our employees everywhere the investments in technology and management training that make them competitive.**
>
> **Will globalization result in the loss of jobs in developed economies? It probably will be in low-tech industries that lack differentiation in the eyes of their customers. But in industries that are technically based and innovative, globalization will unlock decades of growth and jobs that create wealth. At GE we plan to bridge this global transition by being competitive in all of our businesses—a leader in innovation—and compassionate to employees who are impacted by change.**[9]

There is no question that there are huge opportunities in China and other developing nations—and that a major company such as GE must be a player in those dynamic contexts. But it must also be recognized that making money in these countries will require a continuing effort and assessment.

As a student and stockholder of GE, I think that Immelt is making good moves, but I am also concerned about the stability of China. This is an enormous, sprawling, heterogeneous, and disorganized country, with many, many problems to solve. It may well have to endure civil strife—even revolutions—as the have-nots demand more from the privileged few in the ruling caste. The *Wall Street Journal* in August 2006 reported another problem for foreign companies operating in China: "Strong competition for experienced employees, the cultural complexities of working in a Western company and the sense that top positions will always be held by European and U.S. managers push many Chinese workers out after a few years."[10]

In addition, it must be noted that the Chinese have a long tradition of misappropriating other people's intellectual properties, violating patents, and infringing on copyrights. We have to recognize the possibility that GE may never make an acceptable return on its intellectual and financial investments in China.

Betting on Three Big Hits

Immelt soon made it clear that he was placing large bets in the following three areas:

1. Health care
2. Show biz
3. Infrastructure and the "greening of the world"

Let's take them in that order, which doesn't represent their current importance—infrastructure alone is bigger than the first two—but it may represent their perceived potential for the company.

Health Care

In 2005, this business generated $15.1 billion in revenues and $2.6 billion in net income.

- Diagnostic imaging
- Biosciences
- Clinical systems
- Information technology
- Services

Health care has been one focus of GE's efforts since the 1920s. Beginning with the invention of the X-ray tube in 1920, GE has had a love affair with the medical systems business.

Health care was included in the Borch new ventures, strongly supported in Jones's "arenas," and received extensive infusions of money and talent under Welch. In fact, Welch traded consumer electronics for the European Thomson medical systems businesses.

GE Healthcare plans to develop the next generation of equipment to detect diseases earlier and more accurately and to help tailor treatment for individual patients ("personalized" health care). The company has invested about $1 billion annually in health-related research and development, and it is focused on developing gene-based technologies that can identify the genetic "fingerprints" of certain diseases, to better predict how a disease will develop.[11]

A key part of this strategy is to establish partnerships with drug companies to measure the impact of new drugs on the brain. Another key thrust is digitalizing health records and thereby doing away with handwritten and paper files. This will make the health-care system both more cost-effective and less inclined toward errors.

To accommodate William Castell—the current vice chairman in charge of this business—the company moved its headquarters from Milwaukee, where it had been located since its inception—to the United Kingdom. Both the appointment of an outsider as a vice chairman and the relocation of the headquarters of one of the key business headquarters to accommodate an individual are counter to GE tradition, clearly demonstrating Immelt's intention to be flexible.

Immelt, as noted earlier, ran the business beginning in 1997, and he made many acquisitions to expand the business scope and geographic positions. This included making key acquisitions in electron beam topography, ultrasound, 3D imaging systems, information technology, diagnostic imaging agents, and life sciences. These acquisitions—which continued after Immelt was named CEO—created a $15 billion health-care business by 2005. Immelt also created key alliances with Glaxo Smith Kline and Amersham Health.

GE Medical Systems has a significant operating presence in Europe and Asia, including the operations of its affiliates, GE Medical Systems S.A. (France), GE Yokogawa Medical Systems (Japan), and WIPRO GE Medical Systems (India).

Immelt replicated the successful aircraft engine strategy by using GE Capital's financial services to enable the medical systems business to provide a comprehensive set of financial products and services to that market, including financing for equipment, information technology systems, real estate, acquisitions, "recapitalizations," turnarounds, and working capital. He also provided tax-exempt financing for nonprofit hospitals, vendor financing programs for medical equipment suppliers, and equity capital for medical real estate investments, including nursing homes.

Show Biz

In 2005 this business generated $14.8 billion in revenues and $3.1 billion in net income.

- Network
- Film
- Stations
- Entertainment
- Cable
- TVPD
- Sports and the Olympics
- Parks

Broadcasting and show biz have also been high on GE's venture list. Remember that the company was the first to put together a successful television transmission, that it created (and lost) the RCA venture, and that entertainment was one of Borch's nine major ventures.

Welch first became enamored of cable when he was the consumer sector executive, and he tried to purchase Cox. This acquisition failed, but the RCA windfall gave GE another opportunity to become a network leader. Welch appointed his close associate Bob Wright to lead NBC. As anticipated, the business generated excellent cash flows and earnings.

With Wright's encouragement, NBC purchased the Financial Network and renamed it "CNBC." It is now the leading business cable network in the world. In addition, a relatively short-lived partnership with Microsoft created "MSNBC."[12]

One of Immelt's first acquisitions as GE's new CEO came in October 2001: Telemundo, a Spanish-language network with 25 percent of the Hispanic audience. Next, NBC established a strategic alliance with Dow Jones and merged the European and Asian business news services of Dow Jones with those of CNBC to form CNBC Europe and CNBC

Asia. Among other things, this venture enables NBC to use Dow Jones's editorial resources in the United States.

In 2003, GE merged NBC and Vivendi Universal Entertainment. GE owned 80 percent of this new company called "NBCU." The 2003 GE annual report described the merger as follows:

> **The merger of NBC with Vivendi Universal Entertainment (VUE) creates a media company positioned for a digital future. Over the years, we have built a strong NBC franchise. However, broadcast television will be impacted by changes in entertainment technology and distribution, and we felt that NBC could not stand still.**
>
> **VUE adds tremendous assets to NBC, including great content, attractive cable services, a leading film studio, diversified revenue streams and an excellent management team.[13]**

The company believes that there are significant opportunities in creating original programming for cable, broadband, and cellular networks, as well as in marketing its vast movie libraries in DVD format.

SOME PROBLEMS WITH SHOW BIZ

- GE's fear of overpaying
- Losing share
- Aggressive competition for advertising dollars
- Equating "show biz" to the plastics business

In 2005, NBC began negotiating to acquire DreamWorks to purchase its assets and library. NBC assumed that the bid was high enough to discourage others from trying to out-bid it, but NBC was wrong. Viacom wanted DreamWorks more than GE wanted it, and so Viacom raised the ante. GE decided DreamWorks was too expensive and ultimately lost the deal.

Recall one of Jack Welch's key strategies, which dictated that any unit or company that was not No. 1 or 2 in its market would be fixed, closed, or sold.

It appears that this is not one of GE's current criteria, at least insofar as NBC is concerned. NBC has fallen from No. 1 to No. 4 in a four-horse race, and it appears to have lost the creative skills to move back up to its former leadership position. (Universal, too, flunks the No. 1/No. 2 test: It is now No. 6 among the studios, and it has also had problems in the creativity area.) Immelt has stated that he believes this is typical of all businesses—that is, that all of them decline at some point and must be resurrected.

Network advertising has been declining as advertisers continue to use more targeted cable and Internet advertising approaches. In 2005, prime time accounted for only 15 percent of GE's revenues from this business, while 60 percent of the revenues came from television and cable affiliates. It is not the cash cow that it once was, and paying top dollar for major events such as the Olympics and the Super Bowl has become far riskier.

One of the traditional GE strategies, after making an acquisition, has been to move in and cut costs. Wright did this in the early days of NBC, and he encountered significant resistance. The strategy appears to have worked, however, since NBC rebounded financially after a period of time. Wright has followed the same pattern at Universal, with the same predictable reactions: People are resisting the changes, and some of the creative talent is leaving.

But Wright and Immelt believe that traditional, proven GE management and marketing practices can be used to make this business more successful and profitable. Hollywood would have you believe that it is something unique and special; GE doesn't buy it. In a December 2004 *Wall Street Journal* interview, Wright commented: "In some ways, the television business is very much like the plastics business; . . . both require huge investments." He articulated a number of principles that he believed would work in show biz as they do in other types of businesses:

- Stick to areas of creative expertise.
- Don't be afraid to shut down a project that isn't working even if you've spent a chunk of money on it.
- Analyze what you can, such as a movie director's delivery against costs.
- Spread the financial risk by seeking out partners.

- "Don't get lost in the glitter. A creative business is still revenues and costs."[14]

Part of the Universal acquisition included theme parks—a business involvement that Bob Wright has defended as follows:

> **The parks turn out to be very well run. Long-term it's always going to be a business that's got a high cost. It takes a lot of people to run them. You also can't raise prices much more. But we don't have a park we need to renovate in the near term, and we don't need to build expensive new attractions. With the rebound in travel, they're stars right now.**

In October, 2006 NBCU announced it planned to alter its primetime programming and reduce its workforce by 700 (5 percent of the total workforce) in order to save $750 million by the end of 2007. This raises the issue as to whether this is the beginning of moving NBCU into a harvest or even a divest mode.[15]

Infrastructure and the "Greening of the World"

In 2005 the infrastructure business generated $41.8 billion in revenues and $7.7 billion in net income.

- Aircraft engines
- Energy
- Oil and gas
- Water
- Energy finance
- Aviation finance

The infrastructure business was configured in June 2005, and it was led by Dave Calhoun, former head of the locomotive business, to provide *one-stop infrastructure shopping* for developing nations. (Dave Calhoun left GE in September 2006 to become VNU CEO.) It includes jet engines, rail products, water, energy, oil and gas equipment, and financial units. The targeted nations are China, India, Vietnam, and Abu Dhabi. The objective is to increase sales to these developing nations, which now account for only 15 percent of the company's total revenues and represent only a third of the total international revenues.

To this category, I've chosen to add what I call the "greening" businesses, to which we'll return shortly. These are all the businesses—mostly small today, but possibly huge tomorrow—that take advantage of people's increasing inclination and need to consume fewer resources while still maintaining a high standard of living.

"Energy" includes all of the traditional electrical generation systems such as steam, gas, and nuclear. Welch divested the power and distribution transformer and switchgear businesses, but he kept the generation systems businesses.

There have been few nuclear and large steam plants built in the past three decades, both because of the impact of environmental regulations (and lobbying) and the deregulation and restructuring of the electric utility businesses. Even so, these businesses have been very profitable because of the utilities' need to upgrade, repair, and service these generators. Unique spare parts and know-how enable GE and others to obtain high margins.

One of GE's most audacious bets is on coal. The steam turbine business collapsed in the wake of the U.S. power bubble. Unit sales fell from 323 units in 2002 to 122 units in 2003: a dismal showing. But the company believes that there will be major constraints placed on coal-burning units by 2011 and that there is a need for a new low-polluting turbine. It is working on a unit that strips out most of the pollution associated with coal burning on the front end of the combustion cycle. GE forecasts that there is an $85 billion clean-up opportunity in China alone.

Recall that in the heyday of nuclear power, GE backed the boiling water reactors (BWRs), not the pressurized water reactors (PWRs). Over 75 percent of the installed nuclear units are PWRs, and in many emerging markets such as China, PWRs dominate. "China is a potentially very large nuclear opportunity, since it plans to build 32 nuclear reactors by 2020, in addition to 10 already in use or under construction."[16]

In January 2006, British Nuclear Fuels—the owner of what was left of Westinghouse, including its nuclear assets—decided to put it up for sale. GE allied with Hitachi to make a bid. The two other bidders were both Japanese companies: Mitsubishi Heavy Industries and Toshiba. Toshiba bid $5.4 billion and acquired Westinghouse. GE believed the bid was too high, but by failing to match Toshiba's price, it missed the opportunity to get access to the PWR technology and a large installed base, as well as possibly losing access to the Chinese market. However, it should be noted that GE has a relationship with Hitachi, which has been a PWR supplier. This may be one of the reasons that GE decided not to increase its bid for Westinghouse, and it plans to use the combination of its own BWR and Hitachi's PWR to capture a significant share of the Chinese opportunity. The *Wall Street Journal* reported: "In 2006, China planned to sign a contract to build 4 nuclear power plants and Westinghouse had the lead."[17] This may indicate that GE's unwillingness to pay top dollar for Westinghouse was a miscalculation. Only time will tell!

Immelt believes that there is a business in trying to help electric utility and industrial customers avoid painful regulations such as the CO_2 caps in Europe or the lawsuit launched last year in New York State. He therefore has embarked on a series of business ventures that will help these customers by providing new and more effective ways of reducing emissions or in some cases producing no emissions at all.

Here we begin to make the transition from "infrastructure" to "greening." Immelt recently began using a made-up word, "ecomagination," which is (as he puts it) about "greening and protecting the environment by combining ecology and imagination." Ecomagination, reports *Forbes*, was the result of "dreaming sessions" with heads of energy and heavy industry companies at Crotonville."[18]

Wind power is part of the ecomagination strategy, as well. GE acquired the technology and the ability to provide these systems, which are appealing because they are nonpolluting and don't require oil or gas.

But even wind power isn't free of critics. One of the problems is to get communities to be willing to allow wind parks in their areas. Often, desirable sites for windmills are also highly attractive and expensive areas, such as Cape Cod in Massachusetts. To begin to overcome this obstacle, GE recently purchased several wind parks in Europe not only to reap the wind power but also to learn more about operating them. (This is a good example of how GE's financial clout provides opportunities that aren't available to smaller and cash-starved companies.) Presumably, the knowledge GE gains in Europe can be brought to bear on places such as Cape Cod. At the time that this book was written, it was reported that the wind power business was very successful and there was a significant backlog of orders. (Note that wind power was one of the ventures recommended in Jones's arena strategies in 1981 and is an illustration of how long it takes for a technology-based business to become a reality.)

It is interesting to note that GE's equity ownership and operations of wind farms and a transmission system in Chile puts it back in the same position as the early Edison Company, when the company was an equity owner of U.S. utilities. Of course, the scale is tiny, but it does place GE back into the utility ownership and operation role, and it may be that due to continuing deregulation, the company might even move back into the ownership of major utilities.

Water is clearly a nontraditional GE business. But based on a recent pattern of acquisitions, Immelt clearly believes that this is another global opportunity for GE to pursue. One of the most significant of these acquisitions was Ionics, a water purification and desalination company purchased toward the end of 2004 for $1.1 billion.

It seemed like a pricey acquisition at the time, but it may well be paying off. In June 2005, GE created a partnership with an Algerian energy company to build a $270 million water desalination plant in Algeria. GE will invest $20 million in the project, and it will receive a 30 percent stake in the plant. It is now negotiating to build a plant in Kuwait in partnership with the Kuwait government, and it expects to build and operate three or four desalination plants per year in the $200 to $300 million range. It estimates the total market to be about $400 billion.[19]

NOT FOR EVERYONE, BUT GOOD FOR GE?

Are these attractive opportunities? It depends on your point of view, which in turn depends on your company's skills and asset base. What do these opportunities have in common? I can point to seven attributes:

1. Big and global
2. Capital intensive
3. Require financing the customer or taking an equity position
4. Long decision cycle
5. A winner-take-all game

6. Strong adversaries
7. Strong continuing service and upgrade revenues

Clearly, these attributes would be negatives—even strong negatives—for most companies. But of course, they are highly consistent with GE's past successes. GE has always done best in large markets, with customers who need extraordinary kinds of assistance—especially financing—and where there is an opportunity to make continuing high-margin revenues on services, parts, and upgrades.

CHAPTER

More Cultural Changes

We have to change the company—to become more innovation driven—in order to deal with this new environment.[1]
—Jeff Immelt, 2006

Since taking over as CEO, Jeff Immelt has continued the traditional GE leadership approach—that is, adapting the company culture to fit his style and priorities. This has included making major organizational changes, such as breaking up GE Capital; it has also involved developing companywide initiatives and clearly communicating what is expected.

These are just a few of the key actions he has taken in his first five years in office, and they are the subject of this chapter.

NEUTRALIZING GE CAPITAL'S POWER

GE Capital was, by all accounts, an astounding success. It had become so big, in fact, that to many outside observers, it seemed that GE was primarily a financial services company with some vestigial manufacturing arms.

Insiders felt the clout of GE Capital as well. In fact, the organization had become so powerful that it appeared to be able to do more or less whatever it wanted to do. When Gary Wendt left, things started to change. But Immelt was bound and determined to rein in the power of GE Capital and make it part of the company again.

Several actions demonstrate this. First, he sold off the reinsurance business to Swiss Re and took a $3 billion write-off. Clearly, there was a nonfinancial agenda at work here—although GE did wind up with a 12 percent stake in Swiss Re, and GE likely will get some of its money back, just as Welch did in the Kidder deal.

Second, Immelt decided that GE Capital's insurance business's 9 percent return on equity was unacceptable, so—beginning in May 2004 and ending in March 2005—he spun off the shares of a newly formed company, Genworth. It is interesting to note that Genworth performed better as an independent company than it did under GE, and its stock rose 74 percent over this period, mainly because Genworth practiced the art of portfolio management and focused on its most profitable lines: long-term care and mortgage insurance.[2]

Third, GE Capital was split up into two parts: Commercial Financial Services (2005 revenues of $20.6 billion) and Consumer Finance, now called GE Money ($19.6 billion). These are considered to be selective growth opportunities, and although they continue to make acquisitions and move globally, it appears that they are far less free to do whatever they want.

And finally, two GE Capital components—health care and finance—were assigned to other business units to enhance their marketing efforts.

All in all, it was a convincing "assault" by Immelt, conducted on multiple fronts against a business unit that was starting to resist central control. I view the Immelt attack on GE Capital's power as very similar to what Cordiner did to assert his control over the electrical utility and industrial warlords in the 1950s.

THE REBIRTH OF INTERNAL VENTURING

Prior to the Welch era, GE took pride in its being able to create new businesses from within and not relying on major acquisitions. This was the underpinning principle of the Borch nine ventures, which were 95 percent internal.

Jones's acquisition of Utah International was the largest such purchase ever recorded for an industrial company, and it started GE on the acquisition track. But Jones was also committed to organic growth and internal ventures. He initiated two different venture organizations to create new businesses, and he used his arena concept to stimulate new ventures that required multibusiness integration.

But acquisitions and mergers became the major growth vehicle under Welch, and that has continued to be true under Immelt. (As noted in the previous chapter, a company as large as GE *has* to acquire, and acquire big, to keep growing.) But Immelt is trying to focus more on organic growth, as well as on acquisitions.

To identify and develop organic growth opportunities, Immelt initiated a process for innovation that he called "imagination breakthroughs." Imagination breakthroughs are designed to identify new opportunities that have the potential to generate $100 million of incremental growth. There are four categories:

- Technological innovations
- Ideas that create value for customers and GE
- Opportunities to expand markets
- Projects that make great ideas commercial products[3]

Over a four-year period, Immelt reported in 2004, he planned to invest $5 billion in these projects, and he expected to increase revenues by $25 billion.[4] And the 2005 GE annual report proudly declares that "our *organic growth* has expanded to 8 percent versus the historical 5 percent."

I believe this is a very ambitious undertaking, and it will be interesting to see if these lofty goals can be achieved. I personally have guided many internal venture projects, both inside and outside of GE, and I have found that the key is senior management support and encouragement, along with the selection of teams that are willing to bet their careers on making the projects successful.

It is very hard to conceive that this can yield $25 billion in new revenues in four years. However, at the risk of sounding biased, I'd say that if anyone can do it, GE can.

A PROCESS OF HIS OWN

Immelt, like his predecessors, has developed his own process to help the company become more creative. In the June 2006 *Harvard Business Review*, he outlines what he calls "Execute for Growth: A Six Part Process."

The article uses six circles to depict the key parts of the process (reminiscent of Welch's first attempt to explain his portfolio priorities):

1. Circle 1 focuses on *customers* and the need to use the process to satisfy customers and drive growth.
2. Next is *innovation*, generating new ideas and developing the capabilities to make them a reality.
3. *Great technology* is No. 3, stressing the need to have best products, content, and services.
4. No. 4 is *commercial excellence*, developing world-class sales and marketing talent while demonstrating the value of one GE.
5. *Globalization* is No. 5, creating opportunities everywhere and expanding in developing global markets.
6. The final element is to develop *growth leaders* who can inspire and develop people who know how to help customers and GE grow.

I am sure that this process will be integrated into all of the key management and professional development and training programs and will become an integral part of the Immelt culture, just as Cordiner used professional business management, Jones strategic thinking, and Welch Six Sigma.

CONTINUING SUCCESSFUL STRATEGIES AND INITIATIVES

Thus far, I've focused on how Immelt's strategies and initiatives have differed from Welch's, but in fact, the continuities far outweigh the departures. Let's look at a few areas of continuity.

MORE OF THE SAME

- Nothing is still sacred: portfolio management of businesses
- Portfolio management and development of people
- Unifying themes and initiatives

Nothing Is Still Sacred: Portfolio Management of Businesses

Immelt clearly is a portfolio manager. Initially, he described the company as having two types of businesses: growth businesses and cash generators that would enable the growth businesses to grow. The growth engines were energy, health care, infrastructure, transportation, NBC, commercial finance, and consumer finance. The cash generators included consumer and industrial, advanced materials, and insurance.

Jeff Immelt continues the Jones/Welch tradition of evaluating the entire business portfolio annually. The management team appears to be focused on investing in only those businesses that will provide high returns and growth.

Between 2001 and 2005, GE divested the insurance business, appliance motors, industrial diamonds, and its India-based outsourcing operation. In mid-2006 General Electric Supply, which was established in the 1920s to distribute the full line of GE consumer and industrial products, was sold to a French distribution company.

In September 2006 the company signed an agreement with an investment banking organization, Apollo, to divest the advanced materials business (producer and marketer of silicon-based materials).

It is clear that Immelt will continue to evaluate all of the businesses and weed out those who don't contribute to growth and profitability (see Exhibit 15-1).

The "People Portfolio" and Developing a New Culture

Immelt has regularly emphasized his commitment to continuing the development and evaluation of people. In 2005, he put it this way:

Health Care $15.1 billion $2.6 billion	NBCU* $14.7 billion $3.1 billion	Infrastructure $41.7 billion $7.8 billion	Industrial $32.6 billion $2.6 billion	Commercial Financial $20.6 billion $4.3 billion	Consumer Finance $19.6 billion $3.1 billion
• Diagnostic imaging • Biosciences • Clinical systems • Info tech • Services	• Network • Film • Stations • Entertainment • Cable • TVPD • Sports/ Olympics • Parks *NBC Universal	• Aircraft engine • Energy • Oil and gas • Water • Energy finance • Aviation finance	• Consumer and industrial • Plastics • Silicones/ quartz • Security • Sensing • Fanuc • Inspect tech • Equipment services	• Leasing • Real estate • Corp. financial services • Healthcare financial services • Insurance	• Europe • Asia • Americas • Australia

Exhibit 15-1 Immelt's six key business units in 2006.

> **Developing and motivating people are the most important part of my job. I spend one third of my time on people. I spend the entire month of April in our talent development process called Session C. I spend most of my time on the top 600 leaders in the company. We don't run it like a big company. We run it like a big partnership, where every leader can make a contribution not just to their job, but to the entire company.[5]**

Session C continues to be one of the key management processes, beginning in January and ending in December. Its purpose is the same as it has been in the past: to identify and focus resources on the "winners," and discard the "losers."

Under Immelt, however, the tone of the sessions seems to be a little less threatening. There appears to be more emphasis on helping employees develop themselves, perhaps reflecting Immelt's personality and style. There seems to be an increased focus on helping women crack GE's "glass ceiling," and many more women have been promoted to senior corporate and business unit executive and professional positions. Again, this may reflect Immelt's own convictions. He has taken a leading national position on helping women, and he has received several awards from Catalyst, a women's organization on whose board he sits.

The John F. Welch Learning Center

One of the first official steps that Immelt took was to rename Crotonville to honor Welch. Again, this is a departure from tradition; in the past, GE refrained from naming things after their retired CEOs. But after a late start, Welch made the center his own personal pulpit and a major resource for change. And finally, of course, Welch is Welch, and most likely he didn't object to this very visible form of acknowledgment.

The Crotonville programs continue to be a vital element in the company's management development activities. GE spends a reported $1 billion a year on the Welch Learning Center and other in-house leadership development programs.[6] The overall approach appears to be consistent with the past. Participants are selected based on their Session C ratings and evaluations. Both external and internal faculty are used to teach the GE way and to focus on current initiatives.

Immelt is clearly continuing the tradition of developing a strong and deep bench and filling key professional and management positions from within.

In a 2005 letter to shareholders, Immelt outlined what it takes for a company to be successful and how he is using these characteristics to train and measure his key people:

> **We studied the attributes of companies that had long-term success with organic growth. We found they had five common traits:**
>
> 1. **They had external focus that defined success in market terms;**
> 2. **They were clear thinkers who simplified strategy into specific actions, made decisions and communicated priorities;**
> 3. **They had imagination and courage to take risks on both people and ideas;**
> 4. **They were energized by inclusiveness and connection with people, which builds loyalty and commitment;**
> 5. **They develop expertise in a function or domain, using depth as a source of confidence to drive change.**
>
> **In 2005, we developed training to teach these skills. In 2006, we will assess our leaders on these traits.**

Thus it is clear that Immelt is continuing to replicate the Welch success of using Crotonville, training programs, and Session C to convert the troops and ensure that they clearly understand what it will take to succeed in GE. The fundamental principles of "making management a religion" remain in place.

Entry-Level Training: Still a Strong Component

It's always tempting to focus on management and professional training when talking about GE's "people development" programs. But the fact is, a myriad of functional programs aimed at people further down the ladder—entry-level technical, sales, financial, marketing, and human relations training programs—continue as they have since Coffin's day. The major differences today, of course, are that all of the programs are global and the trainees are encouraged to pursue advanced degrees at local colleges.

In addition, several new programs have been added:

- There is now an Information Management Leadership Program (IMLP) to develop skilled information technology talents.
- Given Immelt's strong interest in strengthening the marketing and sales functions, there are two marketing programs. There is a bachelor's level Commercial Leadership Program, and there is a master's level Experienced Commercial Leadership Program.

And finally, there are several business-specific programs. GE Capital, industrial systems, power systems, and GE supply all have their own training programs, and there are still internships and co-op programs.

Unifying Themes and Initiatives

Since the Swope/Young era, GE has used an overall, simple corporate theme to help communicate what the company is and wants to be. Let's review those themes briefly:

- In the 1930s through the early 1950s, GE urged its customers to "Live Better Electrically."
- Cordiner, using Ronald Reagan as the corporate spokesman, then created "Progress Is Our Most Important Product" to communicate the diversity and innovations of the company.
- Jones initiated and Welch maintained the "We Bring Good Things to Life" theme for more than a quarter century.

- Immelt has tried out two themes—"Imagination at Work" and "Ecomagination"—to communicate that GE intends to become more innovative.

PERSPECTIVES AND INSIGHTS

Jeff Immelt has been reinventing GE and moving it in a direction different from his predecessor's. I believe this was necessary. When he assumed control, the company had a mature portfolio, and it had moved from a technology- and products-oriented company to one more dependent on financial services. It had generated huge cash flows, and its earnings growth was almost double its revenue growth, most likely due to a combination of its successful services businesses and the systematic harvesting of some of its lower-priority businesses.

Immelt has built his new strategy on his strong belief that all successful businesses must start with the customers, and they must develop innovative products and services that meet and anticipate the customers' needs. This is clear from his emphasis on increasing the creativity of the company and developing systems and solutions to solve some major customer problems. Immelt has also invested heavily in the Corporate Research and Development Labs, and he has opened new R&D centers in strategic locations worldwide.

Impressive Results but Poor Stock Performance

Since Immelt took command, GE's revenues have increased from $108 billion to $150 billion, and its net income has increased from $13.8 billion to $16.3 billion. Both revenues are expected to increase in 2006, with revenues reaching a $160 billion and earnings to $19 billion. Global revenues are expected to reach $80 billion in 2006, almost double the 2001 level.

In 2005, cash flows increased 42 percent to $21.6 billion, and return on total capital increased 16.4 percent. GE continues to maintain its AAA credit rating.

In short, Immelt and the team have done a remarkable job to grow the company's revenues and earnings and simultaneously overcome the problems that faced them during the period.

Unfortunately, the stock price and investors have not responded favorably. At the time I was writing this book, the price had dropped 13 percent since Immelt assumed control. The market still expects the higher returns of the past.

This decline has been extremely frustrating for Immelt and his team, and it is clear he is trying to move the stock price upward. But it is all about creating and meeting the expectations!

Meeting High Expectations

Welch created very high levels of expectations, and Immelt, as we just said, has achieved excellent results. The issue is whether Immelt has created such high expectations that many don't believe they are realistic and can be achieved.

Listed below are four major areas of concern I have about Immelt's ability to meet the expectations he has articulated to the world.

Ability to "Go BIG"

It is clear that Immelt continues to assert that GE can grow at an 8 percent compounded organic growth. He has even created a new process that he believes will enable the company to achieve these unprecedented results.

In the *Harvard Business Review* June 2006 article cited earlier in the chapter, Immelt said that he recognizes the challenge, and he points out that the company achieved this growth in 2005 and will do so again in 2006.

He is clearly convinced and has the missionary zeal to make it happen. However, based on my experience and study, I am not convinced that he can do it and am concerned that he has created an unrealistic expectation. It is possible that in the long term he will have doubled the revenues every nine years, but is it really possible to add $14 billion plus revenues year after year?

What happens if he doesn't make it, even for one year? Will this have a negative impact on the stock price and put his reputation in jeopardy? I think it will!

Selling Solutions Globally

Because GE wants to continue to Go BIG, it is forced to move more aggressively and become more dependent on selling major systems, solutions, and one-stop packages in major developing nations in Asia and the Middle East. Unfortunately, I have found few companies that have been able to pull this off effectively and make money.

It is easy enough to "buy share" and get a foothold in these countries. The leaders of these developing countries welcome anyone who will give them access to high technology—and in some cases will even finance it—but they have always been reluctant to allow these companies to make large profits and repatriate those earnings. Often, if the company is successful, they will nationalize it or even take it over and find a new partner.

In addition, these governments tend to be unstable, so the foreign countries may have to deal with new leaders who have gained power because they are anticapitalist. In such situations, social unrest is very likely, and business does not flourish.

It Always Takes Longer Than You Think

While I was at GE, there were three embryonic ventures that in retrospect can be seen as noteworthy because they have since become major new markets and even industries. One of these ventures involved positioning GE as a major player in the emerging cellular radio market by acquiring licenses. Another was moving GE's unique projection television receiver into the mass market. The third was the development of a hybrid electric automobile in partnership with Volkswagen.

All were viable, and all are now major businesses. But it took decades for them to become real businesses—and several are still struggling to achieve their full potential.

My point is that even if Immelt is successful in identifying new products and systems, it will likely take longer than he thinks to turn powerful technologies into real businesses with real customers. Meanwhile, to sustain growth, major acquisitions will still be required. It's not clear how many of these will be available at a price that GE is willing to pay.

Maintaining a Strong and Deep Bench

It is clear that one of GE's great strengths has been its deep and talented professional and management team. It has been able to attract, grow, and retain leaders at all levels. The real issue is whether this can be continued and whether it will be able to have sufficient numbers of leaders to continually grow, especially internationally.

Today many companies have adopted what I call a "just-in-time human resources approach." These companies don't invest in developing their own leaders, managers, and professionals. Instead, they rely on the ability of executive search firms to get them the right people when they are needed. These search firms find people by targeting companies, such as GE, that have a strong and deep bench and a reputation for excellent people.

Thus GE is and will continue to be a major source of talented professionals, which will make it very difficult for GE to keep its talented people and not have them pirated away.

An excellent example is the pirating of Dave Calhoun. The January 2006 issue of *Fortune* had a feature article entitled "Leading headhunters agree: The No. 1 draft pick in the game of grabbing top executive talent—the most lusted-after managerial star who isn't already a CEO—is Dave Calhoun of General Electric." Calhoun had been just promoted to vice chairman at GE and said, "My heart and soul are in GE. This opportunity is very appealing to me."[7]

Six months later, on August 23, 2006, Calhoun was enticed by a very attractive financial package and became the CEO of VNU. It is clear that the GE stars are on the list of all of the key headhunters and can be enticed to move on to bigger and more financially attractive opportunities, thus depleting the GE talent pool.

In short, I am not convinced that Immelt and his team will be able to grow GE organically at unprecedented rates by innovation and globalization or that they will continue to have the strong, deep, talented bench that they have had in the past. However, I continue to be a strong fan of this remarkable company, and I hope that my concerns will be unfounded and that Immelt and his team will continue to grow the company and adapt to both external and internal changes, as his predecessors were so successful in doing.

CHAPTER

Success Factors

NOW THAT we have journeyed all the way through the 126 years of General Electric's history and we have discussed the company's strategies, policies, successes, and failures, I would like to conclude by highlighting what I believe are the insights that grow out of that history.

GE's ability to grow and prosper over this long period can be summarized in five themes. As in earlier chapters, each still ties to the acronym LATIN: leadership, adaptability, talent, influence, and networks.

As we review these five categories, I encourage you to think about how their inherent lessons may apply to your own organization.

1. *Leadership: No cookie cutters.* GE has had many diverse types of leaders, who were clearly the right leaders for the right time—in part because they recognized that the world changes continually and therefore requires different types of leadership.
2. *Adaptability: Nothing is sacred or indispensable.* The second factor was the ability to challenge every business and policy—*even when*

they were working. This has enabled the company to make changes before it was too late.

3. *Talent: Cultural evolutions.* GE's culture has evolved, which has permitted it to continue to attract, retain, and motivate a strong and deep talent pool.
4. *Influence: Being politically incorrect when necessary.* GE has long recognized that there are multiple stakeholders that must be considered, some of whom are friends and others of whom are adversaries, at least at the moment.
5. *Networks: It's all about expectations.* Setting viable expectations that it has met consistently has been a hallmark of the company, and it has helped minimize the number of major surprises.

Let's examine how these were achieved and explore how you can apply them to your own situation (see Exhibit 16-1).

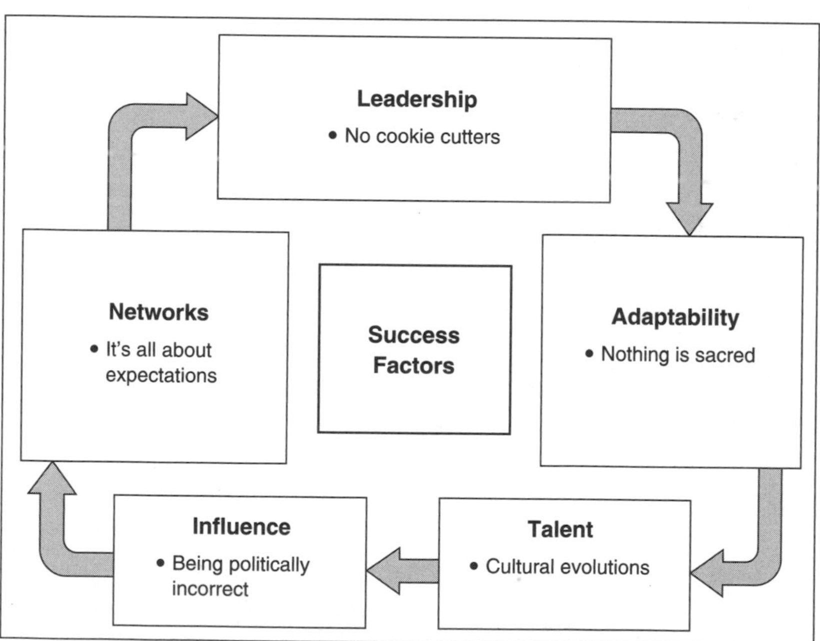

Exhibit 16-1 The LATIN success factors.

THE RIGHT LEADER FOR THE RIGHT TIME: NO COOKIE CUTTERS

One of the most important things to recognize is that the future is likely to be different from the past or present. GE installed a system that allowed the CEOs to select successors who were very different from them (see Exhibit 16-2). The company recognized that leaders had to fit the requirements of the changing markets, competition, technologies, and sociopolitical philosophies.

Some things to consider. Take a look at where your company is in its life cycle and recognize that the right leader for the embryonic stage of the cycle is not likely to be successful when the company matures. Review the strategic changes that may be needed and recognize that if a new strategy is required, it will necessitate different skills. For instance, a technology-driven strategy requires different skills than does a marketing-differentiated strategy. Global systems markets will require leaders different from domestic, product-driven markets.

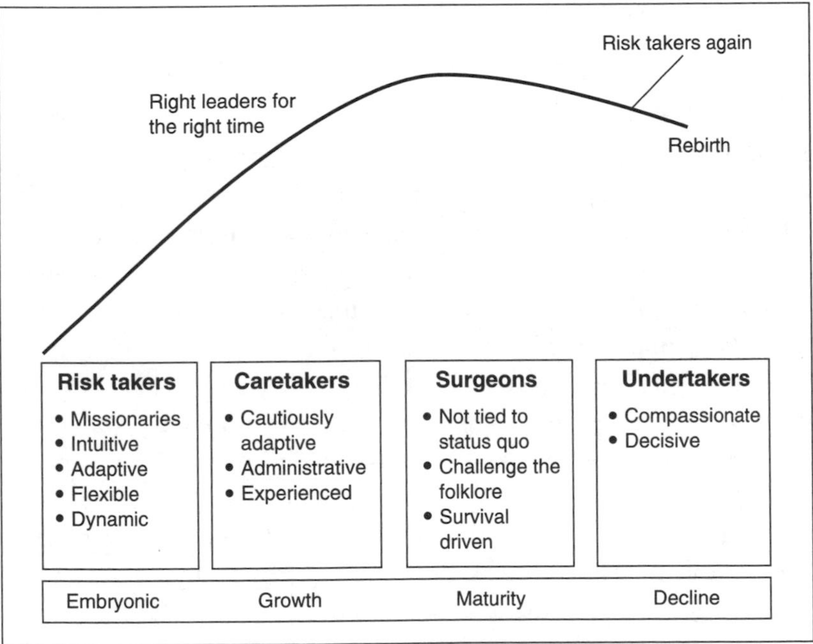

Exhibit 16-2 Different leaders are required for each stage of the life cycle. GE has been fortunate to have such leaders at all levels of the company.

Sharing Power

From the beginning, GE's CEOs have shared their power with others. From Coffin to Borch, there was a two-man team leading the company. Beginning with Borch and continuing today, there has been a "chairman's office." The teams have consisted of different types of individuals. Coffin was a marketing and relationship leader teamed with Rice, a manufacturing-oriented leader. Swope was an engineer partnered with Young, a lawyer. Borch decided to introduce the chairman's office, and he selected a highly diverse group of executives to share his leadership role. This approach enabled the company to get different perspectives and insights in making its strategic decisions.

Some things to consider. Sharing leadership and power is not appropriate for every organization. Even though the current preference in the United States is to have consensus and power-sharing leaders, this practice may not be consistent with the needs of the organization or fit its leadership style and personality. Consider how you can share power and authority and get the best input from your team, but be sure that you can live with it and make it work.

A Personal Commitment

Jones, Welch, and Immelt clearly demonstrated that they believed that management development was their most important responsibility. Though they had a staff organization to help, they were personally involved in the evaluation and decision making regarding key people. Immelt has said that he focuses on the top 600 people—which sounds like a huge number except in the context of a company that employs several hundred thousand people worldwide. It is undoubtedly true that if Immelt had more hours in the day, he'd spend more hours on people.

Some things to consider. GE's succession planning system is one of the underpinnings of its entire management system, and it is very successful at identifying and promoting the "best of the best." But remember that this is a *very* time consuming and demanding process. Immelt reports that he spends the entire month of April on it. This is a major commitment, and most CEOs don't have this amount of time to commit to a single element of their job.

Making It a Partnership

Immelt described GE as a "partnership," rather than a large company. Professional partnerships—such as law, consulting, and accounting firms—have an up-or-out philosophy. Professionals and managers either make partner within a specified period of time, or they are asked to leave.

This has been the essence of the GE Session C process. It is based on the willingness and ability of management to objectively and systematically evaluate the key people—and to make the decision as to whether an individual is a high-potential person (top 20 percent), a middle-of-the-road person (70 percent), or a nonperformer (10 percent), and then taking required actions. Welch asserted that the key to making the system work was candor and honesty.

Some things to consider. All organizations need to focus on the best people and weed out those who don't fit. But this is rarely easy to do. The GE system took several decades to evolve, and it is still only as good as the ability of the individual manager to make objective assessments and then decide who moves up and who moves out. Further, it assumes that appropriate actions will be taken in a timely manner.

Don't Wait Too Long

Selecting a successor takes time. Beginning with Jones, GE has taken several years to identify, evaluate, and select successors at all levels. The candidates all came from within, in part so that they could be given challenging assignments and evaluated on their performance.

Some things to consider. I recommend that you allow yourself a *minimum of three years* to select the next CEO or senior managers. This should be sufficient time to evaluate the candidates. But also avoid creating a "crown prince" situation, because this will discourage others, and your best people may leave prematurely. Be honest but not foolish!

Leaders Need Enough Time to Do the Job and Be Measured

In today's world, many organizations treat their CEOs the way the professional sports leagues treat their coaches and athletes. (Note that a 2006 survey indicated that the average American CEO is on the job only 4.7 years.) Companies sign their CEOs to 5-year contracts and guarantee that the CEOs will get large payouts even if they fail. GE has not done this. GE has had only 10 CEOs in its 126 years. Some of the CEOs—such as Welch and Swope—were on the job for more than 20 years. This relatively long tenure permitted them to develop and implement their own strategies and be measured on the results. Having a long-term CEO is beneficial to the company—assuming, of course, that he or she is a good CEO.

Some things to consider. Having a CEO on the job for 20 years may not be a great idea in all cases. It may make the incumbent so dominant that he or she can rule the company with little effective opposition. For many of the same reasons that we limit the term of U.S. presidents, I think term limits need to be established for company leaders. Determine what you think is sufficient time to enable the CEO to do the job and prevent that person from being able to rest on his or her laurels or—even worse—starting to believe his or her own press releases.

Consider More Than One Candidate

GE has grown its own team since its inception. This has allowed the company to select from within and to have a sufficient number of good or even excellent candidates for most of its leadership positions. Jones had six finalist candidates for the CEO position; Welch had three. In both cases, all the candidates were homegrown and well known. Their performances had been carefully evaluated, and all could do the job well.

Some things to consider. I believe that the Welch approach was about right. All three of the candidates were young and proven executives. I prefer insiders to outsiders, provided that they are not just carbon copies of the incumbent and are adaptable and smart enough to deal with the future.

Relying on external candidates, conversely, bothers me because it is impossible to really know whether they can do the job until they are appointed. Résumés and references are no substitute for personal observations and evaluations. Be sure the candidates fit the needs of the organization.

An Outsider Board of Directors

GE has had a predominantly outsider board of directors since its beginning. In his book *New Frontiers for Professional Management* Cordiner emphasized the value of having a strong outsider board. GE's board members have been required to do more than just show up for meetings, and they are now required to visit business units. Like the CEO, GE's board members have had long tenures, some longer than 10 years. As a rule, they appear to be dedicated and major contributors to the company's governance, and not just rubber stamps.

Some things to consider. I endorse the concept of having a predominantly outsider board of directors, provided that the members are committed and participate in the governance. Unfortunately, this is not the case in many companies. Some boards are populated by "professional board members" who serve on multiple company boards and may not even show up for the meetings. Other boards are populated by the CEO's friends and neighbors and therefore are merely rubber stamps for the CEO's decisions.

As I advocated doing for CEOs, for board members I would set term limits. Board members should not serve more than 10 years. The longer they are on the board, the more power they accumulate, which may be detrimental to the company. However, based on the 2006 HP fiasco, it is important that the board members be trustworthy and willing to respect the confidential nature of the information they have.

Leave and Get Out of the Way

This is another critical piece of GE leadership's success. GE leaders have been *required* to leave when they retired and not permitted to hang around either as members of the board of directors or as advisors. This practice has enabled the new leader to take command without being second-guessed by his or her predecessor.

Some things to consider. I believe that this has been a key element in GE's success. Having the former CEO lurking in the hallways, and especially in the board room, inhibits change. I recommend that you have a rule such as GE's: "Thanks for your service, but now it is time for you to move on and get a new life."

Overall, GE's succession planning system is a good model. But it is only a model and not something that can be replicated by others without adaptation. The elements are very worthwhile, but the execution must be selective.

ADAPTABILITY: NOTHING IS SACRED OR INDISPENSABLE

For more than 30 years, GE's leaders have had a systematic way of evaluating not only the company's people but its businesses. They have challenged all of the businesses, even those that were "making the numbers" and winning. They have instituted a sound and effective portfolio management system, which they've used to rank all of the key businesses. During the Jones and Welch eras, the company pruned, exited, sold off, and refocused its businesses; as a result, the company today is very different from the one that Jones took over. Immelt has christened this activity "reinventing" the company, and he has taken steps to continue this tradition.

Some things to consider. It is critical that all businesses are evaluated using the same criteria. Take the time to clearly understand the financial results, and don't get lulled into thinking that just because a business has been successful, it will continue to be successful in the future. Do the pruning and exiting when the business has value and when it is in the intensive care unit.

Avoid Trying to Be All Things to All People

Up until the late 1960s, GE believed that it could do everything and be all things to all people. The company believed that it had infinite resources and that its managers could manage anything. The failure of the Borch ventures proved these assumptions wrong and led to the introduction of the strategic portfolio management system that is still being used by GE today. Portfolio management forced GE's leaders to be *selective* and recognize that they could not continue to add without subtracting something.

Some things to consider. I believe that this is one of the major reasons that GE has been successful where others have failed. Most companies still continue to add and not subtract; even worse, they wait too long to do the subtraction, and the entire business founders. The key to being a strong portfolio manager is that you must *know where you are strong* and enable the people who are most effective—namely, those in the business units—to be involved in the process. You must recognize that there will be both successes and failures, and you must be willing to admit your mistakes and move on.

Know What Makes Your Company Profitable

GE's strategic planning system started with identifying the key factors that made it successful and then using these factors to rank the attractiveness of the business. GE developed a listing of the key factors that made some business units profitable and compared those businesses to those that were not profitable. These criteria were applied systematically across the company to rank the relative attractiveness of all businesses in the past and the present and—within reason—to project future profitability.

Some things to consider. It is important to note that this list may vary from one company to another. For instance, some companies do well in small, rapidly growing regional businesses, while others do well when the market is large, diverse, moderately growing, and global. The key is to spend the time to determine the factors that make your company successful and profitable and to not use just a generic listing.

All Winners Are Different in Some Real Way

This principle has been the foundation of GE's business strategies. The company has used its unique abilities to create a sustainable competitive advantage. Swope and Young used total systems and solving customer problems to create a leadership position. During the Wilson-to-Borch era, GE took advantage of its ability to create new and sophisticated products and systems. Welch capitalized on GE's Triple A credit rating and strong financial services capabilities to lead in selective markets. Immelt's approach is to integrate problem solving, systems, technologies, and financial strengths to assure that GE remains a leader and can continue to "be big."

Some things to consider. The combination of sound market analyses, customer interactions, and competitive assessments is required to identify real strengths. This includes the recognition that markets, competition, and technology changes necessarily affect your ability to remain the leader. This requires selectivity and a commitment. It is not just an annual empty ritual but a continuing process of making evaluations and decisions.

Keep It Simple

GE recognized early that strategic planning could generate huge volumes of information that collectively could make the process unwieldy. The company has therefore continually tried to simplify output in the form of matrices, diagrams, executive summaries, and so on. This has added clarity and utility to the system.

Some things to consider. I strongly recommend that all of the strategies be simplified by using these different types of visuals. One of my rules is that if you can't get the main ideas summarized on one or two pages, you probably don't understand your business, and it is likely to fail.

Establish a Bottom-Up, Not Top-Down, Organization

No one will want to work for a divested or harvested business: This was one of the early reactions to the portfolio management approach. Most managers believed that if employees found out they were in a harvested organization, they would quickly jump ship. They were wrong! GE found that people could accept reality and not panic provided that the evaluations were done honestly and the people most affected by the changes were included in the process. This is one of the reasons that the strategies were developed within the business and not from the top down or from the outside in.

Some things to consider. Business units must do their own analyses and buy into the results. This may take several iterations because during the first pass, it is very likely that the business unit may be overly enamored of its business attractiveness and competitive position, and it may be unwilling to be objective. But based on my personal experience, after several iterations, reality will sink in, after which the businesses will be ready and able to make realistic recommendations, even nominating themselves as candidates for pruning and liquidation. I also found something even more interesting: After a few years, many GE managers appeared to be more willing to harvest a business than take the risk of growing it. This is one of the reasons that Jones initiated his new venture program.

Admit Mistakes and Move On

No system or organization does everything right. Mistakes will be made, especially if the organization is moving into a different direction or industry. *The key is to be willing to recognize when you have made a mistake and correct it before it is too late. You must be willing to admit the mistake and then move on.* GE's track record is mixed in this regard. In some cases, it admitted the mistake, while in other cases—such as the "Great Electrical Conspiracy"—it tried unsuccessfully to cover it up.

TALENT: CULTURAL EVOLUTIONS

Over the course of its history, GE has embarked on several culture-changing projects. Most of them were evolutionary rather than revolutionary, but they had the same elements. Cordiner created the "professional manager" concept; Borch moved to make the company more venturesome; and Jones instilled the need to be selective and instituted the practice of having initiatives to unite the company in a common cause. Welch and Immelt have both worked to "reinvent" the company.

Let's examine what it takes to develop a culture.

Start Early

GE has always recognized the need to recruit early, be selective and demanding, and teach the GE Way. Coffin created three key programs that still exist. Over time, these programs have been amended, and new ones have been added to the mix, but all of them are focused on recruiting or retaining young men and women who fit the GE culture and will commit to the company. This has provided a very strong bench and the ability to have multiple candidates for all key managerial and professional positions.

Some things to consider. This approach seems to be the antithesis of what is happening today. Most companies have adopted what I call the "just-in-time" staffing strategy. They wait to the last minute to hire, and so they are stuck with whoever is available. The word *selective* is worth emphasizing again. You may not be able to grow your own for all positions, and it may not even be worthwhile to do so, but for *vital positions*, having several homegrown candidates is critically important.

The GE Way

Teaching the GE Way has been one of the key elements in creating the GE culture. It has permitted the diverse, often competitive business units to communicate and interact, and it has allowed for the movement of key people across businesses. Having your own unique "way" may not be possible across the board, but it may be very important in selective areas.

One of the areas that I have recommended to my clients is having a customized company strategic thinking and development system. This may be built on the procedures other companies use, but it should also comprise unique elements.

Continuing Education

Having its own "executive development center" enabled GE to teach the GE Way with customized programs. The interaction among the faculty, consultants, and management helped the company identify and select key initiatives.

Selective, Periodic Initiatives

Innovation was introduced to the company by all of the leaders in different ways. Swope and Young wanted a participative organization, so they created the Elfun Society. Cordiner believed that management needed to become more professional, so he established his own "temple" at Crotonville. Borch recognized the need to change the way the company set priorities, so he set up education and training programs to convert the management team to this new way of thinking. Jones focused the company on dealing with hyperinflation and the microprocessing revolution. Welch emphasized the need to reduce bureaucracy and improve quality. Immelt has already focused the company on trying to *start with the customer* to create new business opportunities and being more imaginative.

In each case, these leaders made sure that the conversion process was complete and based on sound processes. Let's examine what they did:

- First, they were *selective* and made sure that the issues and initiatives were pervasive throughout the company and had a clear impact on the company's bottom line.
- Second, they hired the best academics and consultants to help develop the processes required to deal with the issues. This is different than just creating a slogan, putting up a banner, and failing to help execute.
- Third, in each case, they established educational and indoctrination programs to teach the theory and the key actions required and to ensure that the participants were equipped and motivated to act.
- Fourth, they selected missionaries to spread the word to all of the business units. These missionaries reinforced what was taught in the courses.
- Finally, they *measured*, *rewarded*, and *punished*. The initiatives were included in the performance and salary reviews. Those who demonstrated conviction and successful execution received salary increases and promotions; those who did not were either given another chance or were encouraged to find other employment.

Some things to consider. There is a major difference between the GE initiative programs and the run-of-the-mill, slogan-of-the-year approach used by most companies. The difference is *commitment* and *completeness*. You must be willing to do what is necessary to ignite the changes required and not think that you can make a few speeches, put up a few banners, and get real results. It is important to select only issues that require major changes.

Sharing the Wealth

Even though GE received some bad press when Jack Welch's retirement perks were challenged in 2002, GE management has had—and continues to have—a balanced view of sharing the company's wealth.

The motto "do right voluntarily" was the essence of the Boulware labor philosophy, but I believe it has been an underpinning principle of all of the company's human resources programs. GE employees at all levels and all disciplines have been paid competitively (although not excessively). The benefit programs have been in advance of demand.

The pension trust still provides the benefits it promised (although the fact that it is recorded as contributing more than $1 billion to GE's annual profits can be challenged). The result is that most GE employees and alumni have a positive feeling about the company and leave only if and when it is necessary for their own career development or because it is obvious that their path upward is limited. There is a very strong GE alumni group, and the company often taps it to fill open positions when internal candidates are not available.

Some things to consider. The amounts given in executive compensation packages and special perks have become major issues, and the resolutions of these issues may have profound and negative impacts on many companies. Many people, especially hourly workers, believe that they are being penalized because senior management employees are getting huge salaries, incentives, pensions, and special benefits. In many situations, this isn't true—but it's *perceived* to be true, and perception is often reality. I strongly recommend that all leaders and boards of directors take a close look at what they are doing in this area and be sure that the wealth is shared.

People Are an Investment, Not an Expense

Many organizations today have the attitude that people are just an expense item rather than an asset. Accordingly, they don't invest in people, believing that they can get the talent if and when it is needed.

Starting with Coffin, more than 100 years ago, GE instituted programs to hire key people, indoctrinate and train them, reward and motivate the best of them, and discard those who didn't make the cut. With the exception of the Borch period when training programs became discretionary, GE consistently has made the investment needed to have a strong and deep bench. In fact, in my experience as a consultant working with many good companies, there is a clear difference in the depth of skills at GE and most other companies.

I believe that Immelt's comment—that people development and selection are the most important parts of his job—is correct. The leader must recognize and commit to developing people. Of course, this goes along with a sound strategy and a vision of where the company is going in the future. But the best strategy and the most compelling vision don't add up to much without great *people* behind them.

INFLUENCE: BEING POLITICALLY INCORRECT WHEN NECESSARY

The fourth key element to GE's success has been its willingness to take a stand on major external issues, even when the stands were not popular.

Stakeholders, Not Just Stockholders

Immelt opens his annual report with a letter to "stakeholders," not just to "shareholders." This is clearly in the tradition of GE. Beginning with Swope and Young, GE's leaders have recognized that the company has many key groups that have a stake in the company. This has always included the obvious ones—shareholders, investors, management, and employees—and has gradually expanded to include society, government, unions, and local communities.

Stakeholders: Friends or Foes?

Swope and Young believed that unions and government were allies. Wilson viewed unions as foes rather than friends. Cordiner added Big Government to the list of foes. Beginning in the mid-1950s, GE took an anti-Big Government, anti-Big Labor stand because it believed that both of these institutions were trying to seize control of the company and limit its ability to determine its own fate.

This philosophy helped GE withstand the problems of "giveaways" that are haunting major companies like GM and Ford today. And in a lucky accident, GE contributed to the education of Ronald Reagan, who actually implemented many of the pro-business, small-business, antiunion recommendations that were part of the Boulware philosophy.

It is important to focus only on issues that impact the organization and not try to take a stand on all issues. GE took stands on many major issues over its history. Swope and Young took active and personal stands on helping workers survive the Depression, assuring health and pensions, and enabling American companies to defend their home turf. This was not just because they were trying to "do good" but because they recognized that if consumers were unable to pay their electric bills and purchase consumer products, it would have a negative impact on the company.

Cordiner played an active role in inhibiting the power of governments and unions because he knew that it would inhibit his ability to lead and increase the cost of doing business. Jones and Phillippe took active roles in helping minorities both because it was the *right* thing to do and because it would enhance GE.

Some things to consider. I am not an advocate of business leaders' becoming social scientists and seeking to make changes just because it is the "right thing to do." On the other hand, social and political changes can have more impact on business than changing markets and competition, and therefore leaders may *have* to be activists.

NETWORKS: INFLUENCING, MEETING EXPECTATIONS, AND DEALING WITH SURPRISES

Creating and meeting expectations is the most important element of leadership. The key is being able to set realistic expectations and not get in the trap of overpromising and then disappointing the key stakeholders. Most often, overpromising is a result of poor strategic thinking and decision making.

GE instituted its strategic thinking and decision-making process, as well as the Session C component of the process, because Borch and Jones recognized that it was critical to set the right expectations for all of the key stakeholders, starting with the employees and the investors.

Some things to consider. The key is doing your homework and getting input from both inside and outside the organization. This was covered earlier when we discussed leadership, but it is worth repeating. *Avoiding surprises* is the main objective. Obviously, there are some things that can't be anticipated, but in most cases, surprise is a result of not having a good system.

Let's review some GE surprises and what the company did in response:

1. Wilson didn't recognize the power of unions and expectations of his workforce. This resulted in a very violent strike that changed GE's relationships with the unions, hourly workforce, and local GE communities forever.
   - *"Boulwarism" and "doing right voluntarily."* The 1947 labor strike led to the company's strong labor relations strategies and practices, which included doing extensive research about issues and trends that could impact the workers' expectations.
2. Villard and Coffin were surprised and unprepared for the impact of the Panic of 1893, and it almost cost the company its life.
   - *Strong accounting systems and organization.* GE learned from these and many other surprises. The Panic of 1893 led to the establishment of a highly conservative and professionally staffed and trained accounting organization, including one of the best internal auditing staffs in the business world. This staff continued its operations until it was downsized by Welch—a downsizing that may have been one of the reasons for the Kidder fiasco.
3. Cordiner was surprised by the price-fixing scandal, and GE was not prepared for it. It resulted in GE's losing some very strong leaders, it slowed the company's growth, and it forced the high-risk Borch ventures.
   - *Strategic planning.* Borch was surprised that two-thirds of his ventures failed, and so he instituted strategic planning, which forced the company to clearly understand what was happening in its markets and anticipate competitive and technological changes. It led to a critical, in-depth evaluation of the entire portfolio, and it positioned the company to reallocate its resources to winners and away from losers.
4. Jones was surprised that the GE stock was not performing well, and he recognized that it was vital to clearly understand the expectations of investors and stockholders, especially the newly emerging mutual fund and portfolio managers.
   - *Influencing shareholder and investor expectations.* Jones established a way of working with the business units to help meet

the external expectations, while preserving the integrity of the priorities and the approved strategies.

Over the course of GE's history, the company has recognized that meeting customers' quality expectations was critical to continuing sales. In the 1950s, GE instituted "total quality" control, which arguably predated the Deming quality approaches. Six Sigma is the most recent manifestation of this same quality focus. In each case, the emphasis has been on *establishing realistic quality expectations* and then *consistently meeting them*.

GE: A GREAT MODEL

Although I've tried to be even-handed in my treatment of the company—reporting on its flaws as well as its strengths—I continue to think that GE is a remarkable company, blessed with remarkable leaders, and that many of its actions and policies are broadly applicable.

On the other hand, as I have said throughout this book, it is critical that you *adapt*, rather than adopt, the GE approach. The GE Way doesn't always work consistently for GE; it can't possibly work for any other company that attempts to embrace it indiscriminantly.

I hope that this book has given you insight into the reasons for GE's successful longevity and consistent prosperity and that you will select what makes sense for you.

The key word, again, is *selectivity*. Study the GE Way, figure out what makes sense for *you*, adapt those elements as necessary—and then go to market with pride and confidence.

Notes

Chapter 1

1. "Business History Resources in Edison National Historic Site Archives," cpmserv.cpm.ehime-u-ac.jp/ehnet/bhc/Exchange/Edison.html.
2. Thomas A. Edison Quotes, www.quotationspage.com/quotes.php3?author =Thomas+A.+Edison.
3. This is ironic since Edison subsequently made Schenectady GE's headquarters, and the city became known as a GE "company town." For its part, GE never acknowledged the Westinghouse connection.
4. This would make Westinghouse four years older than GE, not counting the Edison years.
5. George Westinghouse Reference Library, www.campusprogram.com/ reference/en/wikipedia/g/ge/george_westinghouse.html.

Chapter 2

1. www.tardis.union.edu.
2. Almost a century later, Jack Welch would become famous for his handwritten notes.
3. www.tardis.union.edu/community/project95/HOH/Biographcy/Coffin.
4. www.americanhistory.si.edu/lighting/history/blotters/blotbx2.htm.
5. Ibid.
6. www.ketupa.net/nbc2.htm.
7. Ibid.
8. www.bridgew.edu/HOBA/inductees/Latimer.htm.

Chapter 3

1. www.GE.com.
2. www.elfun.org/history.
3. Ibid.

4. www.ranknfile-ue.org/unity2003_barghist.html.
5. GE 2005 annual report, Note 7.
6. www.geworkersunited.org.
7. www.reformation.org/wall-st-fdr-ch9.htm.
8. Ibid.
9. www.reformation.org/wall-st-fdr-app-a.html.
10. www.chem..ch.huji.ac.il/eugeniik/history/steinmentz/htlm.

Chapter 4

1. General Electric Company, Gerard Swope, 1930s, www.scripophily.net. genelcom19.html.
2. www.americanhistory.si.edu/lighting/history/blotters/blotbx2.htm.

Chapter 6

1. Ralph J. Cordiner, *New Frontiers for Professional Managers* (New York: McGraw-Hill, 1956), page 15.
2. Ibid., pages 33–34.
3. GE 1955 annual report.
4. Cordiner, *New Frontiers*, pages 20–21.
5. cbi.um.edu/collections/inv/cbi00195.

Chapter 7

1. Ralph J. Cordiner, *New Frontiers*, page 17.
2. Ibid., pages 73–74.
3. Ibid., page 96.

Chapter 8

1. Ralph J. Cordiner, *New Frontiers*, pages 37–38.
2. www.GE.com.
3. Libertyhaven.com/politicsandcurrentevents/unionandotherorganizations/boulwarism.htm.

Chapter 12

1. *BusinessWeek*, June 30, 1986, page 66.
2. *Forbes*, October 10, 1994, page 92.
3. Jack Welch, *Jack: Straight from the Gut* (New York: Warner Business Books, 2001), page 111.
4. Ibid., page 114.
5. Ibid., page 117.

6. *Forbes*, March 23, 1987, page 80.
7. *New York Times*, May 27, 1990, page F7.
8. Welch, *Jack: Straight from the Gut*, page 233.
9. *Fortune*, February 21, 1994, page 84.
10. Welch, *Jack: Straight from the Gut*, page 247.
11. GE 2000 annual report.
12. Welch, *Jack: Straight from the Gut*, page 219.
13. *Fortune*, September 5, 1994, page 42.
14. Ibid.
15. Welch, *Jack: Straight from the Gut*, page 227.
16. *BusinessWeek*, November 8, 1993, page 64.
17. Welch, *Jack: Straight from the Gut*, page 311.
18. Ibid., page 371.

Chapter 13

1. *Fortune*, August 12, 1991, special reprint.
2. Jack Welch, *Jack: Straight from the Gut*, page 73.
3. Ibid.
4. Ibid., page 111.
5. *Fortune*, March 27, 1989, page 50.
6. Welch, *Jack: Straight from the Gut*, page 103.
7. Jeffrey A. Krames, *Jack Welch and the 4E's of Leadership* (New York: McGraw-Hill, 2005), page 10.
8. Welch, *Jack: Straight from the Gut*, page 173.
9. Ibid., pages 181–183.
10. Ibid., page 183.
11. Ibid., page 186.
12. Ibid., page 329.

Chapter 14

1. www.businessweek.com.
2. *Wall Street Journal*, February 6, 2003, page B1.
3. *Harvard Business Review*, June 2006, page 2.
4. GE 2004 annual report.
5. GE 2003 annual report.
6. *Wall Street Journal*, March 2, 2005, page A3.
7. GE 2003 annual report.
8. *Wall Street Journal*, March 2, 2005, page A3.
9. GE 2005 annual report.
10. *Wall Street Journal*, August 11, 2006, page A4.
11. Ibid., March 25, 2005, page A83.
12. In 2006, the Microsoft partnership was dissolved, and GE took 100 percent ownership.
13. GE 2003 annual report.

14. *Wall Street Journal*, December 27, 2004, page B1.
15. *New York Times*, October 20, 2006, page C1.
16. Ibid., September 16, 2006, page A4.
17. Ibid.
18. *Forbes*, August 2005, page 82.
19. *Wall Street Journal*, June 24, 2005, page A8.

Chapter 15

1. *Harvard Business Review*, June 2006.
2. *The Economist*, March 11, 2006, page 66.
3. GE 2004 annual report, page 9.
4. Ibid.
5. GE 2005 annual report, Letter to Stakeholders.
6. *Wall Street Journal*, January 16, 2006, page B1.
7. CNNMoney.com, January 24, 2006.

Index

An *f* next to a page number indicates a figure on that page.

J

X

Y

About the Author

Bill Rothschild has very fond memories of the wide range of challenging professional and managerial positions he held during his career of almost 30 years at GE. These varied experiences included his participation in helping to develop the company's strategic thinking and decision-making processes and skills and creating the company's first market-focused corporate strategy.

Since 1984, Bill and his consulting firm, Rothschild Strategies Unlimited, LLC, have helped company leaders and their management teams develop processes and skills to enable them to create innovative and successful strategies and implementation programs. His clients have ranged from small new ventures to major companies in a wide variety of industries located in the United States, Europe, and the Far East.

Bill's four previous books have enabled their readers not only to learn and apply the art and science of strategic thinking but also to learn how to develop creative strategies, how to make in-depth, people-oriented competitive evaluations, and how to link leadership and strategies together. Each book has been translated into several languages, and all are used in executive and MBA programs. He continues to consult selectively, participate in executive and MBA programs, and teach as an adjunct professor.